Secularism and Hermeneutics

INTELLECTUAL HISTORY OF THE MODERN AGE

Series Editors
Angus Burgin
Peter E. Gordon
Joel Isaac
Karuna Mantena
Samuel Moyn
Jennifer Ratner-Rosenhagen
Camille Robcis
Sophia Rosenfeld

Secularism and Hermeneutics

Yael Almog

PENN

UNIVERSITY OF PENNSYLVANIA PRESS

PHILADELPHIA

Published by
University of Pennsylvania Press
Philadelphia, Pennsylvania 19104-4112
www.upenn.edu/pennpress

Printed in the United States of America
on acid-free paper

10 9 8 7 6 5 4 3 2 1

Library of Congress Cataloging-in-Publication Data

Names: Almog, Yael, author.
  Title: Secularism and hermeneutics / Yael Almog.
  Other titles: Intellectual history of the modern age.
  Description: 1st edition. | Philadelphia : University of Pennsylvania Press,
    [2019] | Series: Intellectual history of the modern age | Includes bibliographical
    references and index.
  Identifiers: LCCN 2018050997| ISBN 9780812251258 (hardcover : alk. paper) |
    ISBN 0812251253 (hardcover : alk. paper)
  Subjects: LCSH: Bible—Criticism, interpretation, etc.—Germany—History—
    18th century. | Bible—Criticism, interpretation, etc.—Germany—19th century. |
    Bible—Hermeneutics. | Secularism—Germany—History—18th century. |
    Secularism—Germany—History—19th century.
  Classification: LCC BS511.3 .A45 2019 | DDC 220.60943—dc23
  LC record available at https://lccn.loc.gov/2018050997

Contents

Secularism and Hermeneutics:
The Rise of Modern Readership

In the late eighteenth century, a new imperative began to inform theories of interpretation: all texts should be read in the same way that we read the Bible. This premise, however, concealed an inherent problem: there was no coherent "we" who read the Bible in the same way. This book argues that a cohesive group of biblical readers did not exist before this modern attempt to model interpretation on a collective "we." Quite the reverse, I demonstrate that the use of this imaginary "we" in the establishment of a modern community of interpreters itself created a cohesive collective of biblical readers. Placing this dialectic at its center, *Secularism and Hermeneutics* describes textual interpretation between the years 1750 and 1850 as reliant on diverse—and at times contradictory—explanations of how to read the Bible as a universal asset of civilization.

Coming up with new approaches to texts was central to the enterprise of creating a Bible whose interpretation would pertain to all individuals. In the writings of Johann Gottfried Herder, Johann Georg Hamann, Moses Mendelssohn, Friedrich Daniel Ernst Schleiermacher, and Georg Wilhelm Friedrich Hegel, I trace attempts to create a universal Bible. Their theological writings not only established scriptural interpretation as a universal practice but also yielded norms of reading that became constitutive of modern interpretation. Their writings gave rise to major concepts within modern literary readership and aesthetics, such as world literature and historicist reading.

Addressing biblical readers as a cohesive group has continued to be a central source of tension within literary production and interpretation, as hermeneutics has become a widespread intellectual practice. Occurring in public places (such as schools and universities) and perceived as neutral with regard to religious belief, secular interpretation brings with it the presupposition that acts of interpretation depend upon human capacities honed through education. One's ability to interpret a text is seen to derive not from faith but from literacy and literary education. Literary interpretation, therefore, is intertwined with a main organizing principle of the modern political community: the assumption that confessional belonging is separate from the sphere of education.[1]

Importantly, this organization does not merely assume that hermeneutics occurs under the auspices of modern state institutions that relegate religious practices to the private sphere; it also dictates an array of norms regarding semiotics and interpretation.[2] *Secularism and Hermeneutics* argues that eighteenth-century hermeneutics bore a special significance to the emerging political surroundings in which it was performed. Its theorists conceptualized a structural similarity between the hermeneutic community and the political community of the emerging modern political collective. They took both communities to include members of different ideological groups and contended that universal human merits (such as autonomous judgment, interpersonal empathy, and the striving for self-education) enable polemics and productive coexistence of different members of society.[3]

Despite its cultural eminence, modern hermeneutics has constantly faced disruption from the starkly divergent reading cultures that confessional belonging sustains. The persistence of the Bible as an unchanging object of worship among some groups has posed a particular challenge to models of interpretation that insist upon the restoration of an original text as the foremost purpose of reading. As I will show in Chapters 4 and 5, literature makes apparent the disjunction between textual interpretation and confessional belonging in modernity and challenges the presupposition that textual interpretation is indifferent to religious conduct. My analysis focuses on the work of Heinrich Heine (in Chapter 4) and Annette von Droste-Hülshoff (in Chapter 5), in which they engage the impact of confessional affiliation on the reading of literature and, by extension, on the interpretation of their own texts.

From 1750 through the 1780s, a period that straddles the late German Enlightenment and early Romanticism, theologians, philosophers, and poets shifted the focus of scriptural interpretation from the theological imperative of the biblical text to reading itself as a revelatory process. Crucial to this shift were polemics that discussed the exact ways in which the Scriptures should be newly approached. Naming the object at the center of these debates the

"Enlightenment Bible," historian Jonathan Sheehan has shown how a large wave of biblical translations throughout the eighteenth century drove a new conception of the Scriptures.[4] The personalization of the Bible during this period parallels today's understanding of the Bible as a cultural and literary asset to which each and every member of Western society can relate. Sheehan's book is one in a series of publications that challenge the view that the European Enlightenment was antagonistic to faith. It does so not by presenting empirical evidence that demonstrates the endurance of religious practices but by demonstrating how the theological dynamics of the period shaped modern norms of social and civil conduct.[5]

Building upon Sheehan's work, *Secularism and Hermeneutics* demonstrates that as the Enlightenment Bible took on the status of a cultural artifact that transcends confessional specificity, it also came to serve as the privileged model for the interpretation of cultural artifacts, especially literary texts. This book presupposes that from the 1750s through the 1780s, theologians were primarily invested in readings of the Old Testament as they amalgamated biblical interpretation with general theories of textual comprehension.[6] *Secularism and Hermeneutics* centers on the contention that the making of the Hebrew Bible into a universal cultural artifact during the late Enlightenment was both instrumental to and emblematic of the construction of a global community of interpreters. *Secularism and Hermeneutics* does not provide a review of hermeneutics in each epoch where it appears. Rather, the book focuses on the conceptual roots of major principles of "literary hermeneutics" in the contemporary understanding of this term as a methodological approach to literature. I take Schleiermacher to be the agreed-upon major propagator of this method. As scholarship has shown, although Herder had already articulated Schleiermacher's overall methodological principles, Schleiermacher presented them paradigmatically.[7]

In contemplating political secularism, I distinguish between "Judeo" and "Christian" components. The notion of toleration toward religious minorities maintains that certain readers hold distinct presumptions that guide their approach to the Bible. It presumes that there is an initial difference between confessions. The examination of the new approachability of the Scriptures in the eighteenth century emphasized the Enlightenment's awareness of and dialectic with the presence of traditional believers in the emerging modern state. In Germany, the direct context was Jewish integration in German-speaking society. Because Protestant and Jewish exchange centered on the learning, interpretation, and circulation of Biblical Hebrew, the Old Testament became a constitutive object through which religious difference was to be negotiated.[8] Debates concerning the Jewish presence in the emerging citizen state show how religious toleration became formative for the conceptualization of certain norms of cultural production, sensibility, and textual comprehension as global human capacities.

In the late eighteenth century, Judaism became the emblem of religious toleration. Yet, for Enlightenment society to accept Jews as competent political agents and, in a second step, to characterize itself as tolerant through this acceptance, it had to rethink the toleration of traditional reading cultures. Taking the toleration of Jews as an accomplishment required as well that Jews be seen as inherently different from other political agents.

I focus on a salient aspect of this disparity: the standing of Jews as believers whose adherence to ritual jeopardized their entrance into the general community of readers and interpreters. Taken to be universal, interpretive practices were meant to overcome religious difference—with the model example being Christian and Jewish perspectives on the Old Testament. I contend that modern hermeneutics thus parallels the conception of a political realm of equal agents under conditions of secular and self-governing sovereignty. *Secularism and Hermeneutics* views Mendelssohn's exchange with the Romantics on aesthetics, exegesis, and politics as emblematic of this dynamic. Mendelssohn endorses aesthetics as grounded in universal human skills such as judgment, preference for mimesis, and support for literacy.[9] Mendelssohn's writings on aesthetics, as well as on biblical interpretation, form a universalistic stance that draws on the religious ethos of a religious minority—of practicing Jewish believers—in order to portray humankind as a collective. In so doing, Mendelssohn's stance on aesthetics prepares the way for his famous political manifesto, *Jerusalem, or On Religious Power and Judaism* (1783).

During these early years of German idealism, the fragmentary character of the Old Testament made it a paragon for experiments with theories that sought to explore the universal contours of human reason. Reading the Bible helped diverse thinkers, who were debating with one another, hone proto-Kantian theories of comprehension. Embedded in the imaginary childhood of humankind, the Hebrew Bible—particularly the Genesis stories—was taken up as a universal source that could be recuperated through communal effort. Prominent thinkers who applied theories of human reason to reading, such as Herder, identified the Old Testament with the deleterious influence of a religious minority but also maintained that such influence could be collectively overcome through textual interpretation. At the same time, because interpretive practices were taken to be universal, they were meant to overcome religious difference.

Debates on how to comprehend the Old Testament in the late eighteenth century thus set in motion new political deliberations during the development of the modern state. The notion of religious toleration, which was at the core of some seminal portrayals of humankind as collective, rendered the co-existence of different religious cultures acceptable.[10] This new political sphere thus had to accommodate traditional reading practices that understood the Bible to be a product of divine revelation and not an artifact that had been damaged with time. Following the tensions between acceptance and exclusion in the late Enlightenment, *Secularism and Hermeneutics* investigates the structural parallel between, on the one hand, the community of interpreters established with the presumption that textual comprehension is a universal human capacity and, on the other, the community of citizens in the emerging modern political community.

Organization

A main objective of the collective of readers has been the attempt to restore the original meaning of a text. Against the backdrop of Germany's fascination with Genesis in the 1760s, Chapter 1 follows the development of Herder's theory of textual interpretation, which pushes readers to grasp the cultural and historical circumstances behind the writing of a text. This theory breaks not only with his own early theological writings but also with those of his close friend Hamann. For Hamann, true engagement with the Bible disconnects textual interpretation from historical inquiries, whereas for Herder, the Hebrew Bible embodies the attempt to bridge the difference between fictional and historiographical texts. The examination of these approaches to the Old Testament demonstrates that inherently diverging dispositions—such as those for and against the historical understanding of the Scriptures—have shared a conceptualization of the Hebrew Bible as a universal object. Herder's mature interpretation theory makes restoration the collective task of modern readers, and it presents humanity's primordial origins as the emblematic object of this effort.

Chapter 2 investigates further Herder's interpretation theory. It shows how Herder's praise of the Bible's aesthetic merits in his *On the Spirit of Hebrew Poetry* (1782–83) advanced his interventions into aesthetic theory, in particular his challenges to Gotthold Ephraim Lessing's *Laocoön* (1766).

Herder's writings on the Old Testament in turn provoked the imagination of his influential interlocutor: the young Johann Wolfgang Goethe. Eminent figures of the period such as Goethe and Herder treated the Bible as a sublime artifact equally available to all readers, Christians and Jews alike, due precisely to its initial unreachability.

Chapter 2 argues that the making of the Bible into an object that is pertinent to members of different confessions revolutionized reading per se. Authors who took part in the period's aesthetic debates—centered on the comparison of poetry to other forms of art—grounded their arguments in the interpretation of the Old Testament, which they saw both as universally pertinent and as an asset that was lost and needed to be rediscovered. In the mid-eighteenth century, scholars were already arguing that the period had undergone a radical shift by viewing the Bible as an artifact with sublime aesthetic value. I propose a new look at this widely accepted thesis by arguing that eighteenth-century biblical reading did not turn to the Bible as a new artifact to be examined within a pregiven set of principles of literary interpretation. Rather, it invented, shaped, and negotiated new arguments about aesthetics through the redefinition of the Bible as an aesthetic asset.

This leads me to examine, in Chapter 3, a major problem concerning theology in the late Enlightenment. The growing view of the Bible as equally available to all readers was incongruous with the ongoing dissemination, consumption, and interpretation of holy texts in religious communities—the prime example being Jews' continued study of Hebrew (and its overall comprehension). The comprehension of Hebrew as a component of one's ethnic or religious identity drew attention to diverging reading cultures in modernity, unearthing their basis in distinct religious belongings. The communal study of the language thus challenged the period's new theory of interpretation.

Chapter 3 develops this problem as a driving force behind Mendelssohn's interventions into various fields of philosophy. At the center of the chapter is Mendelssohn's conceptualization of scriptural reading as compliant with both a Kantian approach to aesthetics and traditional notions of holy texts in Judaism. Mendelssohn reiterates some tenets of such authors as Robert Lowth and Herder in their appeal for the Hebrew Bible's universal merits, but at the same time, he grounds the Bible's relevance for humankind in arguments from traditional Jewish scholarship. Mendelssohn can thus be said to inform a situated universalism. He promotes the Bible's relevance as a global asset while also striving to conceptualize this relevance in terms that preserve the Bible as a pillar of traditional Judaism. Mendelssohn's contributions to modern interpretation thus show the permeability of the political sphere to values of religious minorities. Modern interpretation, I argue, has responded both to universal Enlightenment ideals that were steeped in the globalization of religious notions and to the traditionalist need to adhere to religious rituals that center on Scriptures. Notwithstanding the universalism at the core of Enlightenment theories of comprehension, the Bible therefore continues to be conceived as the sociocultural pillar of the community, a standing that has been honed in the context of traditional reading cultures.

A clear preference in German idealism for Greek over Hebrew (and for the New Testament over the Old Testament) illustrates a later transformation in modern hermeneutics as this interpretive paradigm became popularized. In such works as *Religion Within the Bounds of Reason Alone* (1793), Kant distinguishes between moral religion (which pertains to the individual's natural inclinations) and the authority of the church (which can cultivate these inclinations but not control them). Chapter 4 reconsiders the work of Heine from the 1820s through the 1840s as a response to the conception of scriptural interpretation as a universal measure of human subjectivity in German idealism. Of special interest to me is Heine's presentation of Jewish institutions as determining believers' epistemic choices. In considering his fragment *The Rabbi of Bacharach* (1840), I explore how he portrays liturgical reading as a prism for perceiving and interpreting reality under the auspices of a secluded religious community.

In Chapter 5, I examine hermeneutics in nineteenth-century thought through an analysis of Hegel's "The Spirit of Christianity and Its Fate" (1798–99). Representing dominant tendencies of German idealism at the time, Hegel's essay depicts Christian epistemology as emerging from an ancient, stagnant mode of thinking that is embodied in the Jewish spirit and in Biblical Hebrew. Against Hegel, I read Droste-Hülshoff's canonical novella, *The Jews' Beech* (1842), as a reaction to the detachment of interpretation from its traditional theological contexts. With its perplexing narrative form and its prominent inclusion of a mysterious Hebrew sentence, the novella calls attention to the transformation of the Bible into an object that is no longer understood as the product of a divine revelation.[11] Since they reveal diverging cultures of interpretation with different moral codes, the novella's momentary breakdowns of interpretation prompt reflection on the religious dimension and history of modern hermeneutics. Nineteenth-century literary texts allude to ritual in moments that disrupt the coherence of the narrative;

these moments interrupt attempts to solicit meanings that rely on the narrative's apprehension as a lucid system.

Literary Theory and the Critique of Secularism

Demonstrating the interrelation of secularization and modern interpretation, this book traces the conditions of modern political participation in a community that opts to transcend confessional difference. Hermeneutics and aesthetics construct a realm where interpretation is detached from its anchoring in traditional relationship to holy texts and is thus rendered secular. As Benedict Anderson has pointed out, the spread and circulation of Martin Luther's German translation of the Bible was integral to the emergence of the modern state, owing to the importance it ascribed to cultural production in the vernacular.[12] Modern readership made evident a public that witnesses together the process of reaching the ultimate meanings of the text. Examining the tensions at the core of this enterprise, I argue for the need to understand the Enlightenment's legacy as the outcome of an essential conflict: the motion toward inclusion of "others" in the Enlightenment society of interpreters, despite the eradication of confessional difference.

As Pascale Casanova claims in *The World Republic of Letters*, the rise of national literatures is entangled with the concurrent emergence of vernaculars as a source of cultural capital.[13] Casanova stresses Herder's theory that literature represents a nation's distinct spirit as a main influence on the emerging system of world literatures. *Secularism and Hermeneutics* expands this claim, as it investigates the importance of Herder for literary studies in view of eighteenth-century political transformations. Herder reads the Hebrew Bible as presenting a universal ethos—a reading grounded in the idea that the nation will represent all citizens and the corresponding expectation that those citizens will share his vision of a universal religious ethos. He grants the Hebrew Bible this special status amid efforts to forge the Scriptures into a universal asset that can, at the same time, elucidate the particular character of each nation and culture. The question of how to read Hebrew evokes the particularity of "the Hebrew nation" and juxtaposes it with the living presence of literacy among Jews.

Casanova's depiction of world literatures has become a topic of critique in works that reject broadscale, normative depictions of world literature, such as Emily Apter's *Against World Literature*.[14] Opposing a facile understanding of intercultural transmission, Apter develops the notion of "untranslatability," which presents the difference between national literatures as irreducible to mere cultural differences or gaps. She takes secularism (which she understands in relation to Edward Said's identification of the term with colonial tendencies in modernity) as a key example of the fallacies of translatability and locates the tradition of untranslatability in the traditionalist resistance to the abstraction of the biblical word through the act of translation. She thus contrasts Harold Bloom's presentation of biblical translation as a formative principle of translation with Muslim perspectives on reading.[15]

The fascination with the Hebrew Bible as a cipher of translatability, as I demonstrate in Chapters 1 and 2, is an enduring legacy of Romantic aesthetics and its reception. Apter's position—especially her emphasis on how biblical translatability has constantly been questioned in the history of textual transmission—parallels my own intervention into the historiography of literary hermeneutics. The Romantic idealization of the Old Testament as a cipher of textual transference is an always incomplete project whose incoherence, I argue, is evident in both Enlightenment theology and its afterlives. The status of the Hebrew Bible as a cipher is due not only to its having been marked as the divine gift of transference but also to the Old Testament and the Hebrew language themselves having become ciphers of tensions ingrained in the secular reinscription of biblical reading.

In her turn to Islam as a current of untranslatability, Apter draws upon Talal Asad's inquiry into the religious presumptions that guide modern state politics. Asad's work has become representative of critiques of the Enlightenment's secular legacy.[16] In his *Formations of the Secular*, Asad presents the emergence of German higher criticism as a transformative moment for the social functions of religion in modernity. Biblical critics conceptualized biblical reading as universal, a transition that, Asad argues, mobilized the modern perception of the Scriptures through Romantic aesthetics and its focus on human sensibilities: "My concern is primarily with a conceptual question: What were the epistemological implications of the different ways that varieties of Christians and freethinkers engaged with the Scriptures through their senses? . . . How did Scripture as a medium in which divinity could be experienced come to be viewed as information about or from the supernatural? Alternatively: In what ways did the *newly sharpened opposition between the merely 'material' sign and the truly 'spiritual' meaning become pivotal for the reconfiguration of 'inspiration'?*"[17]

This strand in literary criticism and critical theory—which includes Apter, Asad, Michael Allan, Saba Mahmood, and Michael Warner, among others—demonstrates how fundamentally the critique of secularism informs the historiography of reading, literary theory, and world literature.[18] *Secularism and Hermeneutics* addresses two central claims that these critics have made, claims whose interrelation is central to my account of modern hermeneutics. Asad's depiction of Romantic divine inspiration and Apter's critique of translatability focus on the interpersonal connection between readers and authors (or between translators and authors). The new notion of the Bible as having human authors ("poets," in the terms of Romantic aesthetics) replaces divine revelation with inspiration, which arises from a universal idea of affect and interpersonal communication.[19] The globalization of theology ingrained in literary interpretation the objective to decipher an author's feelings, to which empathy was central.

In viewing the history of the distinction between "uncritical" and "critical" reading, this strain of criticism also stresses an utterly different aspect of modern readership.[20] The ability to perform a critical interpretation of literary texts—and, by extension, of other cultural objects—is expected from mature political agents. It is a skill embedded in the Western conception of individual autonomy and rationality seen as human nature.[21] The making of the Bible into a human book—an enterprise that fueled the search for the Hebrew origins of humankind—established the ideals of interpersonal identification between readers and authors and of critical interpretation of literary texts.

In the late Enlightenment, becoming a member of the emerging political community required, first and foremost, autonomous subjectivity. The subject's responsibility in making epistemic decisions and choices was essential to the attainment of spiritual convictions. The decline of revelation narratives and their replacement with the Romantic vision of interpersonal exchange coincided with the emergence of this subject position. This transformation shaped the view that engaging with the Bible via reflection is a means for spiritual development through believers' subjective utilization of their cognitive and affective capacities. As I shall demonstrate, the divine merits of Scripture came through the processing of a text, rather than through the perception that the Bible is a direct gift from God. This transformation of the Bible into an aesthetic object was foundational to the birth of literary reading. Honing reading skills through the affective attachment to texts, literary hermeneutics grew out of the detachment of interpretation from the historical authenticity of the Bible.[22]

The contemporary critique of secularism can be applied to German-Jewish encounters in the German Enlightenment, an exemplary moment when a traditional religious group entered the general republic of letters. *Secularism and Hermeneutics* contends that the globalization of religious norms does not exclude the influence of religious minorities through symbols, ideals, and practices. The book does not inquire, therefore, whether the dialogue between Germans and Jews is or is not possible. Rather, it explores the symbolic cultural function of this dialogue in construing a political ethos.[23] A model for cross-cultural investigation, Biblical Hebrew presents an invitation into a community of readers—a summons that simultaneously includes and excludes traditionalist believers, making their presence essential to Enlightenment political institutions. At the same time, this invitation sets affective and ideological conditions that define these believers' belonging to the collective of readers (and citizens).

The foundational texts of modern politics established the toleration of religious minorities as the pillar of political secularism. Such works as Hobbes's *Leviathan* (1651), Spinoza's *Theological-Political Treatise* (1670), and Locke's *A Letter Concerning Toleration* (1689), promote critical scrutiny of the Scriptures as essential to political agency. Specifically, they attempt to show how the Scriptures accommodate competing religious doctrines. The contradictory view—that the Bible dictates one true set of religious rules—consequently emerged as a tool of political autocracy. The emergence of modern hermeneutics as a standardized paradigm epitomizes the effort to constitute a new modern subject: one who is aware of how the Scriptures give rise to coexisting religious practices.

As Jonathan Hess has written, from their beginning the debates over emancipation in Germany "were as much about theology as about the politics of universal citizenship."[24] Because its author belonged to a religious minority, Mendelssohn's *Jerusalem* can be read as a formative contribution to these debates. The question of whether the Jewish subject could approach the Bible in a way that would foster, rather than jeopardize, religious toleration was crucial for late Enlightenment political theory. Mendelssohn presents Judaism as a rational religion that facilitates its believers' political engagement. At the same time, he reinforces the perception that ritual law remains important because of its continuous practice since the giving of biblical law. Subsuming the religious credo of Jewish law under the new separation of church and state, Mendelssohn's position allocates religious conduct to the private sphere.

In his correspondence with Herder, Mendelssohn adds new tenets to hermeneutics as he advocates his political agenda. He is lobbying for toleration toward Jewish worship—that is, toward a confessional context that views the Old Testament as the product of divine revelation and certainly not as an object whose meanings were lost. Mendelssohn compliments his interlocutor for his command of Biblical Hebrew and suggests that Herder's efforts to comprehend a foreign culture should be applied to relationships between individuals (*Mitmenschen*).[25] As will be elaborated in Chapter 3, this suggestion gives rise to a certain irony: Herder conceptualizes his interpretive apparatus to a large extent as a means of overcoming a gap between reader and author. The paradigmatic example of this gap is the unreachability of the Old Testament for Christian readers. (The Jews are a damaging factor that causes this breach.) Mendelssohn, in contrast, attempts to use key notions of textual interpretation while circumventing the cultural background for their emergence.

The rise of hermeneutics as a universal practice neutral to one's confession served diverging political agendas. I examine Mendelssohn's use of interpretation in propagating the separation of church and state to show that enacting toleration was by no means exclusive to Protestant thinkers and institutions. Rather, adhering to toleration as a universal value promoted competing religious principles and their claims to compatibility with egalitarian political participation. Using the new umbrella of hermeneutics and its appeal to universal skills, capacities, and values, Herder's philosophy of history, informed by his Pietism, and Mendelssohn's portrayal of Judaism as exemplary for religious toleration promoted diverging religious ideologies. Modern hermeneutics and its reliance on the view that the Bible is an asset with all-human pertinence has thus accommodated, in effect, the claims to universalism made by both reformers and traditional believers.

Alternative Enlightenments

The majority of studies on theology during the Enlightenment have observed Jewish scholarship as a realm separate from Christian theology. This book relies on a different vantage point, following major Protestant and Jewish intellectuals whose debates in the public sphere centered on various presentations of the Bible as a cultural asset that transcends confessional difference. This investigation narrates an Enlightenment where the politics of toleration emerged not through a Christian enforcement of religious values on minority groups but rather through the rise of norms of political secularism—such as the understanding of scriptural reading as a cultural practice—that were porous to different religious ideologies.

The notion of German-Jewish exchange helped constitute the universal community of readers, turning it into an asset of political secularism. Instrumental to this transformation, in the late eighteenth century the Hebrew language became a signifier of higher understanding. This was achieved through depictions of Hebrew as an *Ursprache*, the instrument of creation, and the primeval tongue of humankind. Examination of the intersecting positions of Hamann, Herder, and Mendelssohn in their writings on the Hebrew Bible shows that their references to Hebrew shaped major presumptions of the emerging field of textual interpretation. Reading Hamann's and Herder's respective writings and correspondence throughout the 1760s sheds light upon the role of the Old Testament (and specifically the Genesis stories) in the development of a new, collective historical consciousness for readers. The idealization of Hebrew as a transcendent object rid the Bible of its status as an object of worship in the context of a discrete religious community. The importance of learning Hebrew within the Jewish community was exemplary of the communal attachment to holy texts. As a result of the Enlightenment reconceptualization of the Bible, both Jews and non-Jews had to reshape this traditional training into a practice that pertained to a private identity—ethnic, confessional, or other—and not to the believer's overall ability to function as a reader and interpreter of texts.

My examination of this transition builds on work in German studies that describes a new tendency in eighteenth-century European literature and criticism: an emphasis on representation grounded in semiotics over the production of imitation.[26] More recently, critics have drawn attention to new facets of late eighteenth-century aesthetic sensibilities, including the period's shaping of new disciplines and forms of scholarship, the changing awareness of the senses in the German republic of letters, and the ways in which the period's literary theory made use of new conceptions of politics through the image of the body.[27] Critical accounts of Europe's cultural capital, which I will elaborate below, have shown Herder's influence on the establishment of the notion of world literature, a concept dependent on the vision that there is a system of national literatures that fosters each nation's culture as embodied in its national language and folkloric and mythical sources.

In my account of the interrelation of theology and modern hermeneutics, I rely on studies in literary theory, German studies, and philosophy that have shown Herder's centrality to the Enlightenment shift toward a popular, egalitarian, and inclusive practice of interpretation. One may ask why an inquiry into modern hermeneutics should focus on Herder's intervention into theology. Such a question would imply that the emphasis on Herder stems precisely from his extensive engagement with the Old Testament and the Hebrew nation. Scholarly preoccupation with world literature as a discipline in its own right and with transnational textual circulation has recently brought attention to Herder's role as a forefather of interpretation theories. *Secularism and Hermeneutics* grounds my focus on Herder in this research on his prominence in the history of textual interpretation. Studies on Herder's legacy in literary theory turn our attention to a philosophical interpretive tradition that posits the translation of texts as emblematic of comprehension. This tradition, which links Herder's views on translation to those of Schleiermacher and Walter Benjamin, shows translation to be ingrained in a theological set of debates. Continual and contingent religious polemics have modulated the linking of translation to the study of human comprehension.

In her analysis of the role of theology in the German Enlightenment and, more particularly, in the history of Orientalism, Suzanne Marchand has presented cogent criticism of methodological biases in scholarship on European interest in Eastern cultures. She argues that the popularity of Said (which goes hand in hand with that of Michel Foucault) has encouraged scholars to approach Orientalism as a monolithic and global exercise of power over the East. This genealogical approach, she argues, obscures the need for an extensive investigation of different authors, texts, and tendencies in European Orientalism, which at times may reveal multifaceted ideologies and motivations. In her study of German Orientalism, she found not imperial motivations but various attempts to justify and support long-standing religious interests.[28]

Like the inquiries to which Marchand refers, *Secularism and Hermeneutics* seeks to trace some major principles of modern politics to Enlightenment philosophy. But with Marchand's criticism in mind, I ground my examination in a broad array of historical sources and disciplinary categories, building upon Sheehan's intervention into Enlightenment historiography in *The Enlightenment Bible*. That study draws a substantial connection between transformations in the status of the Scriptures since the early modern era and current critiques of political secularism. Sheehan has shown that the "Enlightenment Bible" became a universal asset as a result of the large number of biblical translations during the period. His study relies, therefore, on the exploration of how a personalized approach to the Scriptures became widespread—a trend that he detects in diverging appropriations of the Bible. In this respect, his book's argument converges with its methodology in that the author detects the globalization of the Bible through the consideration of manifold sources that represent various agendas, motivations, and needs.

Ongoing research on the "religious Enlightenment" also informs my examination of religious practices within Jewish-Christian interreligious exchange. Counter to depictions of the Enlightenment as antagonistic toward religious practices, David Sorkin has depicted Enlightenment theology as conducive to religious polemics and exchange. His book, *The Religious Enlightenment*, challenges the notion that religious toleration per se is the Enlightenment's theological heritage.[29] Rather, according to Sorkin, what tied together different confessions was a set of religious notions and practices common among all members of the political community. His prominent example of such equality is the idea, shared by both Christian Pietists and Jewish readers of the Bible, that engagement with the Bible relies on affect in the process of reading.[30] I build upon Sorkin's insight when I argue that the decline of confessional separatism was the defining factor of public participation and polemics (even in the field of theology) in late Enlightenment Germany. Individuals' emerging characterization of themselves as belonging concurrently to humankind and to their confession is the point of departure for this book.

Detecting Secularism: Diverging Routes

With this theoretical aim, I wish to keep in mind Hans Blumenberg's critique of quests after religious bias in modern political models. In a famous section of *The Legitimacy of the Modern Age*, Blumenberg responds to Karl Löwith's examination of modern history through the notion of *Heilsgeschehen*.[31] For Löwith, the term, in its claims to distinguish itself from theology, exposes a bias in modern historiography. The stakes of this bias lie in the "theodicy" that Löwith locates in some historiographical perceptions of modernity. Modern historiography, he claims, encompasses an inherent conundrum: it relies on a Christian perception of time, but since Christianity does not have a critical historical consciousness, descriptions of events that are salient to modern historiography—particularly those pertaining to the notion of human progress—wear an eschatological cloak.

Responding to the gesture of uncovering that lies at the core of Löwith's project, Blumenberg questions the methodology behind such attempts to uncover the religiosity of secular politics. Blumenberg questions the assumption that notions of cultural inquiry are mobile or transferable from one period in human history to another. Against this assumption, Blumenberg suggests that an investigation of secularism in modernity requires a self-reflective perspective. Such an investigation would ask not only how religious notions manifest in various times and places but also how the observation of history itself and the assessment of its development and transitions absorb religious categories. Blumenberg questions, therefore, the attempt to expose the so-called duplicity of political secularism (or to suggest that the promise of toleration is false). The alternative is to examine how hermeneutic categories and practices were shaped in the course of secular modernity. According to Blumenberg, any dislocation of religious values from one epoch to another is faulty, since it ignores the continual development of historical consciousness, which exerts this ongoing discursive influence in different historical epochs.[32]

To that end, *Secularism and Hermeneutics* scrutinizes the particular routes that the transformation of hermeneutics took as it became a secular phenomenon, most crucially how it circumvented the specificities of religious beliefs and the identities of religious believers. The stakes of this examination echo recent scholarship, such as Charles Taylor's eminent work *A Secular Age*, that has examined the exchange between theology and secularism as instrumental for modern politics and particularly neoliberalism.[33] In his review of this book, Martin Jay criticizes what he sees as Taylor's obliviousness to Blumenberg's criticism.[34] Jay takes issue with Taylor's project of finding unifying or universally valid religious notions in political secularism, claiming that Taylor performs a move similar in structure to the attempts to uncover religious tendencies in modern politics. He accuses Taylor of trying to "discover" in the religious realm precisely those tenets whose merits are often identified with the secular, thus overlooking Blumenberg's critique that such arguments about secularism presuppose that historical consciousness itself is neutral to religious notions. According to Jay, such scholarly investigations as Taylor's present themselves as able to trace the transferring of religious values from one epoch to another without acknowledging that the scholarly account itself contains vocabulary that is intertwined with the cultural reception of secularism, especially the notion of progress.

This critique is discordant with Taylor's turn to religion for the universal values that he considers to be much needed in contemporary politics. Such is the ability of religion to unify an egalitarian human community through the shared feeling of hope and a sense of meaningfulness. Jay recapitulates this view and counters it:

Religion can both embolden some believers to think that they share in divine wisdom and remind others that there are mysteries that they, as imperfect creatures, are unable to solve. It can therefore serve as stimulus to both arrogance and humility, both confidence and doubt, and the historical record abounds with examples of each. For a committed believer like Taylor, the scales are weighted in one direction, toward the possibility of meaningfulness, although he is reflective and self-critical enough to acknowledge they can easily tip in the other. For other less hopeful readers of that record, there is ample reason to worry that the post-secular age, if indeed it is upon us, has some very unpleasant and, alas, meaningless surprises in store, no matter how eagerly they are folded once again into the lessons of a divine pedagogue, whose previous teaching evaluations, alas, leave a great deal to be desired.[35]

Jay compares Taylor's insistence on the need to preserve the mystery of reality—the human inability to comprehend the logic behind history—to Benjamin's reading of Franz Kafka's fable as a comment on human hope. The lesson we learn from Kafka, according to Benjamin, is that the world is full of hope, but this hope is alas not meant "for us." The lesson we learn from Taylor is that "there may be meaning, but it is not for us."[36]

A "liberating" global conception of religion lies, according to Jay's reading of Taylor, in a global notion of spiritual meaning that exists beyond the reach of human capacity. I would add that it lies as well in eliminating a kind of individuality that thrives in the context of a traditional religious community. The liberal "us" knows that meaning exists out there, but the discovery of this meaning is contingent upon the participation in discrete, specific religions of revelation and, hence, in practices of faith that are at odds with global visions of religion. My attempt to reconstruct the history of hermeneutic thinking aims to recover the "us" who are disinherited of the option of soliciting meaning from the world due to the failure to embody the "we" at the core of modern interpretation.

Chapter 1

Rescuing the Text

The notion of a world literature emerged during the late German Enlightenment, when intellectuals began to evaluate the artifacts of different cultures and historical periods on a common scale and attempted to delineate an all-encompassing world history. As this chapter will show, unprecedented interest in the Old Testament in Germany during the 1760s and 1770s influenced this dynamic. Prominent figures in late Enlightenment Germany attempted to construe the Hebrew Bible as a new universal asset, and in doing so, they encouraged readers to bridge the gap between themselves and foreign cultures. Johann Gottfried Herder, in particular, referred to the Old Testament time and again in his writings on textual interpretation. Herder's references to the Hebrew Bible as an exemplary cultural asset promoted a major principle of his theories of aesthetics and of history. Herder advocated reading texts with special attention to the cultural norms that led to their production because, in his view, a literary canon expresses a nation's spirit. The literary asset reflects the transformation of a nation's language and the life of the nation in the course of history.

This new approach to literary interpretation was representative of a larger intellectual climate. The late eighteenth century accommodated historical approaches that promoted the application of philology in scriptural interpretation. Yet the period concurrently gave rise to antagonistic approaches that saw scriptural reading as grounded in an all-human effort to gradually comprehend a text. Theologians not only insisted that the Bible be read as addressing human comprehension but also put this new form of reading into practice. As a result, they created a parallel between the Bible and literary texts. The conceptualization of scriptural reading as grounded in the human experience of trying to comprehend a text or to make it cohere played a fundamental role in modern interpretation. Late eighteenth- and early nineteenth-century theologians revolutionized the treatment of the Bible as a text by humans for humans. Instead of looking to the Holy Scriptures for God's word, readers' attention turned to the task of understanding the culture that had produced the text, evincing a new appreciation of the Bible for its historical testimony.[1] Ultimately, the period's theologians shifted their focus away from the *conclusions* or moral of scriptural reading—and thus from whether the biblical texts are valid historical testimonies of past events—toward the *process* or conduct of reading.[2]

This chapter considers how debates about reading the Old Testament shaped early philosophical positions in German idealism. This examination requires engagement with the writings of Johann Georg Hamann, a theologian whose writings, despite their esoteric style, greatly influenced German philosophy. Hamann's influence is visible in Herder's early writing about the Bible, especially his *Oldest Document of Humankind* (*Älteste Urkunde des Menschengeschlechts*, 1774), which presented a mythical view of poetry as manifesting God's power. In this text, Herder offered an idealized view of Hebrew as the language of creation, which was similar to Hamann's presentation of the language.[3]

Herder's later work marked a transition from these early tendencies. There, he sought an understanding of the Bible—the pertinent example being Biblical Hebrew poetry—based in the comprehension of the concrete historical and cultural circumstances behind its production. As I shall demonstrate in the discussion of Herder's hermeneutic paradigm in this chapter and in Chapter 2, Herder's later work urged readers to decipher the Scriptures based on his more established theories of textual interpretation and historiography.

With this transition in his work, the Old Testament became a platform for Herder to introduce his notion of cultural inquiry. In his later work, he replaced the confessional perceptions of the Bible as an object of worship with a new notion of the Bible as pertaining to universal human faculties and to a new world history. The Scriptures could regain their original meanings through an act of reinstantiation that built on the reader's penetration of the cultural and historical circumstances that led to their composition. My presentation of Hamann's and Herder's respective views of the Old Testament—as well as Herder's divergence from Hamann—will explicate the process through which the Old Testament became emblematic of this project of textual restoration. Notwithstanding their differences, both Herder and Hamann advocated a new approach to the Old Testament: treating the Bible as an object whose supreme quality stems from its affective rapport with its readers, which it achieves through its unique textual form. The transformation of Scripture into a universal artifact, a crucial step in the creation of a global community of readers, required these thinkers to reconceive Hebrew as an artifact that could be approached by all readers in an equal manner. Treating Scripture as an artifact that inherently transgresses obstacles of confessional difference replaced reading the Bible as an embodiment of God's word and perceiving it as an object of worship.

Building on the analysis of Hamann's theology and its manifestation in Herder's early writings, I examine the interrelation between the making of the Old Testament into a universal asset and the new view that humanity shares common origins. To understand the ramifications of this interrelation, I follow Erich Auerbach's famous description of world literature, according to which "the presupposition of *Weltliteratur* is a *felix culpa*: mankind's division into many cultures."[4] Auerbach takes the notion of world literature to presume that national cultures are distinct divergences from a shared beginning. Whereas both advocates and critics of world literature in literary studies note its reliance on the idea of national spirit, researchers have yet to provide a detailed account of the theological history that shaped the term. Critiques of world literature have largely overlooked Herder's investment in theology, as well as the role of his interlocutors in debates on exegesis, among them Hamann, a central figure for aesthetics discourse during the late eighteenth century.

Studying Enlightenment Theology

The new perspective on the value of Scripture had a formative influence on modern hermeneutics, a paradigm that I define as the systematic examination of texts guided by the understanding that the relationships among authors, readers, and literature are embedded in a gradual process of comprehending a text's original meaning.[5]

Late Enlightenment Germany featured a special preoccupation with the Old Testament, whose transmission and form had long been an emblem for readers' confusion.[6] The identification of the Hebrew language with Jewish liturgy, and therefore with a distinct group of believers, encapsulated challenges for the emerging conception of interpretation as a universal ability, open to all religious confessions. Readers of Scripture, regardless of their confessional affiliation, deemed the comprehension of Hebrew a "problem," giving rise to a conception of the language as a universal cipher. In response, theologians explored readers' individual experience, affect, and efforts as they encountered the Old Testament. The Old Testament, and particularly Biblical Hebrew, thus became a laboratory for evaluating the human faculties in the wake of German idealism.

Hamann's provocative manifesto *Aesthetica in nuce* (1762), a key example of this strand of writing on the Scriptures, proposes an aesthetic theory based on scriptural reading. A central principle of Hamann's approach to Scripture is the reader's engagement with the text as an inspirational process of filling in the gaps. Hamann derides his contemporaries for attempting to recover the original meaning of Hebrew words. For him the merit of Hebrew lies precisely in its linguistic incomprehensibility because it necessitates the reader's dynamic engagement with the biblical text.

One implication of this reconceptualization was the emergence of the Bible as a test for new approaches to textual interpretation. In the second half of the eighteenth century, a wave of biblical translations pluralized the Scriptures, as the decision to translate the Bible became increasingly linked to an individual translator's own motivations. According to Jonathan Sheehan, the catalyst of biblical translation was a pietistic project that cultivated an "inspirational model of biblical translation."[7] Theories of textual interpretation enabled the engagement with the Scriptures to be turned into a subjective undertaking and thereby played a key role in the transformation of the Bible into a cultural asset.

Sheehan's argument exemplifies a scholarly trend that portrays theology as a salient part of the Enlightenment. Until the last two decades, the dominant stream of scholarship on the German Enlightenment held that the period's investigations into human reason were intertwined with secularization, broadly understood as the decline in the status of religious affiliations.[8] David Sorkin's 2008 book, *The Religious Enlightenment*, offers an alternative portrayal of the period: "Contrary to our secular master narrative, the Enlightenment was not only compatible with religious belief but conducive to it. The Enlightenment made new iterations of faith. With the Enlightenment's advent, religion lost neither its place nor its authority in European society and culture. If we trace modern culture to the Enlightenment, its foundations were decisively religious."[9]

Sorkin demonstrates how theological practices were transformed during the period so as to make them compatible with different faiths and diverging confessions, as well as how the broad scope of the religious Enlightenment across countries, religious groups, and social strata paralleled the modern notion of political secularism, a principle that enables individuals to relate to holy texts on personal terms.[10] The emergence of the notion of the public sphere enabled the establishment of religious tolerance within the Enlightenment's distinct national regimes. With the key example of religious toleration, Sorkin shows how the proliferation of religious practices during the Enlightenment was congruent with the ideals understood to be the Enlightenment's heritage.

As I argue below, Herder's revision of Hamann's scriptural interpretation popularized Hamann's vision of personalized reading. Herder promoted scriptural reading as a subjective, affective experience at the same time that he advanced the view that readers should seek a deeper understanding of the Bible by reflecting on its historical and cultural origins. This latter imperative, which has become pivotal in both theology and modern interpretation, perpetuates the view of biblical interpretation as a revelatory experience but combines it with the philological aim of attaining objective historical truth.[11]

Biblical Language and the Hebrew Nation

A major aspect in the pluralizing effect of biblical reading is the abstraction of biblical language from its confessional association. Hamann's and Herder's diverging approaches to Hebrew are emblematic of their respective positions on Enlightenment philosophy, particularly the role of reason in language. Hamann's theory of imaginative reading and Herder's efforts in his late works to contextualize cultural artifacts offer two ways of confronting the view of the Hebrew language as Jewish knowledge.

The respective positions of Hamann and Herder to scriptural reading should be examined in juxtaposition to the enterprise of Johann David Michaelis, a prominent philologist who provocatively advocated the study of the Scriptures through linguistic prisms detached from theological institutions and the study of theology. According to Michaelis, the culture of the ancient Hebrews exerted a major influence on legal and political norms in contemporary Germany. Michaelis argued that the Hebrew language should be treated as a historical object.[12] He advocated the study of Hebrew through comparative philology, claiming that consideration of other ancient languages, such as Arabic, would deepen the understanding of Hebrew.

Because Michaelis saw himself as primarily a philologist and not a theologian, he understood his primary task to be the contextualization of biblical sources. In his influential *Mosaic Law* (*Mosaisches Recht*, 1770–71), he calls for understanding the laws of the Israelites in the light of Eastern cultural norms. He contends that legal norms had been determined by the area's climate, tribal customs, the influence of other Oriental populations, and other factors. Seeing the Bible as centered on the Mosaic laws, he scrutinizes the premises and cultural norms that led to Moses' legal treatise: "It is necessary that I mention here the way of life on which Moses founded his entire state and, at the same time, indicate how its laws relate to the other forms of life. We can adequately understand neither the form of government nor what I have previously said concerning some basic principles of the state if we do not know the Jewish citizens, the people who constituted the fabric of the state."[13] For Michaelis, Moses' treatise holds a reciprocal, dynamic relationship to the norms of the culture in which it emerged. It seeks to foster a certain way of life, while at the same time, it is itself shaped and informed by other ways of life. By extension, laws are constantly shaped by the people they govern.

Michaelis's emphasis on the Hebrew Bible's legal aspects and his method of interpreting the Old Testament were both much at odds with the positions of other figures in the late German Enlightenment. Michaelis's endorsement of an academic, philological approach to Scripture gained significant attention because of the opposition it provoked. One key disagreement was the view, shared by Hamann, that the Bible should be open to readers regardless of their philological or theological training. Indeed, much of Hamann's writing on biblical interpretation set itself in opposition to Michaelis's work. Michaelis's view that Biblical Hebrew should be restored via philology served as a point of departure for Hamann's alternative conceptualization of Hebrew as a catalyst that sparks the human imagination in the course of reading.

Describing the biblical language as the language of creation, Hamann's *Aesthetica in nuce* opens with the identification of biblical poetry as primordial language; poetry is "the mother tongue of humankind."[14] This assertion proves to be a major premise guiding Hamann's philosophy of language and approach to Hebrew, which inspire, in turn, his understanding of the hermeneutic act: the drawing of initially unapparent meanings from a text. Hamann's interpretation theory rests on a key theological recognition: that the moment of the formation of human beings was the pinnacle of the creation process, as man stands at its end as the model, or the copy, of divine characteristics: "God crowned the sensual revelation of His greatness with the masterpiece: man. He created man in the divine image."[15] Hebrew is taken to be a secret language in the sense that its incomprehensibleness is constitutive of human experience. This conception of language reconstitutes biblical reading as a universal practice by inviting readers to engage with the language as an esoteric object.

A prominent aspect of Hamann's approach to Hebrew is related to his use of the word "Kabbalah"; the subtitle of *Aesthetica in nuce* is *Eine Rhapsodie in Kabbalistischer Prose* (A rhapsody in Kabbalistic prose). As John Betz notes, "The word ['Kabbalistic'] is very suited for Hamann's sense of humor, evoking such notions so antithetical to his 'enlightened' contemporaries, as 'hermeticism,' 'esotericism,' 'cryptography,' and, above all, 'darkness.'"[16] Despite its status as a cryptic language, the language of Scripture does not exclude the possibility of human comprehension but is in fact tuned toward it. Hamann develops the notion according to which the Bible should be read as intended for human eyes: "For Hamann the humility of Scripture has another, plainly practical purpose, being suited precisely to accommodate our sensible nature and our intellectual weakness. This is why Scripture is written in a narrative form, and why Christ himself speaks in parables."[17] The Bible represents an invitation to exercise faith in God through a dynamic reading process. Biblical interpretation transforms the inability to understand—a so-called human weakness—into a higher mode of understanding a text.

Hamann explicates this perspective by opening his text with two epigraphs: the first from the book of Judges (specifically, the Song of Deborah) and the other from the book of Job. The choice of these excerpts underscores Hamann's approach to the Bible's alleged ambiguity. Taken from biblical poetry (a genre of biblical writing that is often archaic or archaistic), the citations are enigmatic to readers of Hebrew and biblical scholars, for they use several words in a manner at odds with their lexical meanings. And yet Hamann includes no translation of the epigraphs:

Buch der Richter 5:30

שלל צבעים רקמה

צבע רקמתים לצוארי שלל

[Book of Judges 5:30
spoil of dyed stuffs embroidered,
two pieces of dyed work embroidered for my neck as spoil]

Elihu im Buch Hiob 32:19–22

הנה בטני כיין לא־יפתח

כאבות חדשים יבקע:

אדברה וירוה לי

אפתח שפתי ואענה:

אל־נא אשא פני־איש

ואל־אדם לא אכנה:

כי לא ידעתי אכנה

כמעט ישאני עשני:

[Elihu in the Book of Job 32:19–22
My heart is indeed like wine that has no vent;
like new wineskins, it is ready to burst.
I must speak, so that I may find relief;
I must open my lips and answer.
I will not show partiality to any person
or use flattery towards anyone.
For I do not know how to flatter—
or my Maker would soon put an end to me!][18]

Hamann begins his own text with a performance of obscurity, typical of his entire oeuvre, which features parables, wordplay, and allusions to biblical sources that animate Hamann's critiques of his intellectual rivals.[19] A third epigraph follows the first two: a citation in Latin from the poet Horace, "Odi profanum vulgas et arceo" (I hate the mob and distance myself from it).[20] By playing familiarity against unfamiliarity, Latin against Hebrew, the text excludes precisely those readers who think that they understand a text by means of comprehending the language in which it is written. Hamann's many references to Michaelis in his oeuvre suggest that the target for his critique of the "mob" is this prominent philologist.[21] John Hamilton has argued that both the act of choosing to open his text with Hebrew fragments and the transition he makes to the Horace citation embody the language philosophy that Hamann develops in his essay.[22] As he points out, Hamann dispels the ease associated with the feeling of understanding a language: the Latin-literate but Hebrew-illiterate readers are made to feel that they are part of the vulgar crowd. At the same time, Hamann's transition away from Biblical Hebrew in the text is a cipher of the shift from obscurity to clarity (or, at the least, the belief in such clarity). Dispelling this impression, the Latin epigraph is followed by Hamann's attack on the period's philologists: "Heil dem Erzengel über die Reliquien der Sprache Kanaans!" (Praise the archangel of the relics of the language of Canaan!). Treating Biblical Hebrew as relics that can be restored, as does Michaelis, overlooks an essential aspect of God's work. The artifacts that mark godly activity in the world are living evidence of His continual presence rather than monuments to His impact on humanity.

Importantly, the "obscurity" of Hebrew emerges here as a cultural convention with which the reader is presumed to be familiar. The subsequent process of transcending the written letter builds upon the presumption that textual gaps act as a barrier on a cognitive level, jeopardizing the understanding of the text for all of its readers. Because of the universal validity of human apprehension of objects, Hamann sees reading Hebrew as relevant to the general audience. For Hamann and, as we shall see, also for Herder, the Hebrew Bible is a platform for explicating reading techniques in a general theory of cognition, and Hebrew is no longer meant to be apprehended in the scholarly, philological sense of the word. For Hamann, Hebrew is a mechanism for demonstrating his theory of reading, but it also continually challenges the confidence of the universal reader of Scripture. The initial inability to comprehend biblical language makes one strive for the meaning that lies beyond the literal sense of the word. As the following will demonstrate, Herder, on the other hand, turns the difficulties of the biblical texts into a call for readers to engage with deciphering the original cultural, historical, and religious context in which the texts were produced.[23]

The turning of Hebrew into a symbol for obscurity does not, of course, presume that every reader will attempt to learn the Hebrew letters and penetrate the Hebrew text and its secrets. It also does not imply that every reader has the potential to acknowledge the status of the secretiveness of the Hebrew language and subsequently to understand Hamann's performative theory of reading. Betz argues that Hamann's notoriously obscure writing style was influenced by Robert Lowth's aesthetic approach to Biblical Hebrew. Lowth's *Lectures on the Sacred Poetry of the Hebrews* (1753) deeply resonated with German theologians. Lowth was both a bishop of the Church of England and a professor of poetry; accordingly, he examined the literary devices in Hebrew poetry, such as its parallelism, rhythm, and rhyme.[24] It was not only Lowth's methodology of reading the Bible that was received enthusiastically by German theologians but also the premise behind it: the contention that Hebrew poetry is a refined aesthetic creation.[25] Against the backdrop of the period's description of human reason as universal, Hamann develops an alternative view: that readers of the Bible may share an experience of initial obscurity.

Importantly, Hamann composes the text as an aesthetic manifesto that connects his theory of an affective connection to the Scriptures with a theory of reading in general. Already in his early writings, Hamann declares enthusiastically, "Gott ein Schriftsteller!" (God [is] an author!), comparing the act of divine creation to writing.[26] *Aesthetica in nuce* thus begins as an attack on attempts to recover the world of the Bible—especially to the Old Testament—and shows through multiple references to Psalms that the work of God the Creator is evident in creation's fragmented structure. The Creator's Hebrew text is the epitome of His work.

Hamann's text portrays reading as a process that continually challenges common assumptions about the reader's identity and efforts. Hamann views the Bible not as a divine object free from errors but as a human transmission of the word of God in which errors, fragments, and gaps create moments of incomprehension. The gaps in human understanding elicit a higher mode of conceiving cultural objects.[27] Hamann's theory of reading, which stresses the importance of both the reader's imagination and belief in God, could portray him as a forerunner of religious existentialism. It bears noting that the Danish philosopher Søren Kierkegaard, the most notable representative of this stream of thought, quotes Hamann in an epigraph to his seminal text *Fear and Trembling* (1843). Hamann's theory of reading the Scriptures centers on the personal inspiration that emerges in the act of reconciling textual gaps and difficulties through the one's creativity and faith. This way of reading Scripture through confronting the lack of human knowledge might be described as a "leap of faith"—a notion most readily associated with Kierkegaard's philosophy.

To Hamann, the interpreter of the Bible must have the courage to become a "Kabbalist"—that is, to say more than the text does, not to express himself but rather to articulate what the author leaves unsaid. From the Kabbalah, Hamann derives the notion of imaginative reading of the Bible. In his version of Kabbalistic reading techniques, interpretation is therefore motivated by a spiritual quest that yields the powerful, creative, and inspirational connections to texts. This dynamic interaction with the Bible always relies on the biblical text. At the same time, however, the power of Scripture lies in its position as model object in kindling the reader's imagination, an idea already present in Jewish practices of reading.

The recognition that the Bible is not perfect is of central importance to the establishment of this perspective on textual interpretation. The perception of Scripture as imperfect is a precondition for Scripture's role as a mediator of godly communication.[28] By and large, Hamann's text contributes to a long tradition of hermeneutic approaches that oppose the idea that the inability to understand a text is either a sign of the text's own flawed character or of a certain deficiency in its readers. Hamann regards this individual engagement as a praxis that reciprocally constitutes both the reader and the Bible. This radically human perception of divine language is, in effect, what mediates and enables Herder's famous claim that the Bible must be read as a human text. Hamann takes Biblical Hebrew as an atemporal marker of the relation between man and God. Thus, he argues, the aim of reading the Scriptures is not to make the text more coherent. The text's fragmented nature and the ambiguity of Biblical Hebrew are constant reminders of the reader's connection to God, a connection forged in the experience of reading the Scriptures. The vagueness of certain biblical passages is a prominent example of the text's merits in stimulating the reader's engagement with God.

This inspirational theory of reading encompasses the conviction that every reader can engage in interpretation, as the "holy language" is now taken to facilitate a common (if yet idealized) starting point for all readers. Thus, ironically, *Aesthetica in nuce* presents a provocative theory of religious conduct based on inspirational imagination that further constitutes a collective with a shared vocabulary taken from religious conventions in their reference to the reading of Hebrew, the secretiveness of the letter, and faith in God. It is precisely the esoteric and obscure character of Hebrew that invites a universal readership to grapple with its meaning. The biblical language construes a paradoxical notion that is yet salient to the Enlightenment heritage: that of a collective individuality.

Herder's Bible and the Roots of Restorative Reading

In his pursuit of a career in the church, Herder moved several times—to Riga, Weimar, and other cities—and was exposed to the period's rapid transformations in philosophy, literature, and aesthetics. He dominated these fields thanks to his companionship and intellectual correspondences with prominent intellectuals, such as Johann Wolfgang Goethe and Moses Mendelssohn, which will be examined in Chapters 2 and 3, respectively. Herder's wide-ranging writing included attempts to unfold world history, polemics on the period's aesthetic theory and literature, poetry, and translations of the Bible and other texts that he esteemed for their supreme literary style.

While Herder contends that the context of the Old Testament's production is important to its understanding, he also acknowledges that erudition or philological expertise are not sufficient to grasp ancient Hebrew culture. That would require an empathetic rapport with the authors of the text. In his approach to Biblical Hebrew, Herder seeks to reconcile two things: Michaelis's perspective that the Hebrew texts can be restored through the comprehension of their historical setting and Hamann's emphasis on individual engagement with the text. In sum, Herder presents scriptural reading as a process of close affective engagement with the Hebrew text, during which modern readers put themselves in the shoes of the ancient authors in an attempt to understand the norms and worldview of ancient Hebrew culture.[29] Frederick C. Beiser describes the influence of Hamann on Herder's philosophy and legacy thus: "If we were to describe in a word how Herder assimilated Hamann's thought, then we would have to say that he secularized it. In other words, he explained it in naturalistic terms and justified it in the light of reason."[30] This process of secularization crucially involved personalized reading as a process of restoration. Hamann's view of scriptural interpretation as a revelatory experience played a central role in this intervention into theology. Herder, who incorporated Hamann's views into general Enlightenment discourse, transformed scriptural reading into a manifestation of humanity's common historical origins.

For both men, the initial obscurity of the encounter with Scripture grants the Bible a new status as universal object, but whereas Hamann relies on this premise to develop a theory of a subjective and imaginative engagement with the Scriptures, Herder portrays Hebrew's enigmatic nature as a catalyst for reflection. In Herder's interpretation theory, Hebrew demonstrates the need to understand a foreign culture in its historical and ethnographical context so as to hone our knowledge of its cultural objects. In this conception of the Bible as a cultural object of universal relevance, cognition is embedded in the process of deciphering an object foreign to the reader's culture.

Herder's inquiry into the artifacts of foreign cultures has long been associated with empathy.[31] In fact, Herder's notion of interpretation as bridging a gap between readers and authors may have been the result of Hamann's presentation of the principle of empathy in his early work on biblical interpretation as seminal to reading in general. Inspired by the experience of a sudden religious conversion during a visit to London in 1758, Hamann wrote that the Scriptures' stimulation of human feelings should be a leading principle in terms of how they are read. Affect is transferred between author and reader through what Hamann defines as "the necessity to immerse ourselves as readers in the feeling[s] of the author whom we have before us, in order to come as close as possible to his state of mind."[32]

Hamann's belief in *Einbildungskraft* (force of imagination) and empathy influenced Herder's better-known contention that the ancient, biblical text can and should be understood in the context in which it was composed. Despite the Hebrew Bible's fragmented nature and linguistic obscurity—and notwithstanding the discrepancy between its cultural background and that of modern times—the text can be made approachable to the modern reader. Affective identification plays a seminal role in this process for Herder as well. A major difference between the two thinkers lies in Herder's view of biblical reading as a process that yields progress toward an objective truth, insofar as the reader gets closer to the authors' original meanings.

This difference is reflected, for instance, in Herder's *Fragments on Recent German Literature* (*Fragmente über die neuere deutsche Literatur*, 1766–67). Engaged with textual interpretation in general, the essay explains how the meaning of a text changes over time. Herder posits that languages develop from "childhood" to maturity and that the early stages in any language's development parallel the earliest stages in the life of the nation that produces that language.[33] Hebrew provides a key example for his argument. The antiquity of Hebrew results in a language whose meanings cannot immediately be apparent to the modern German reader. With the vocabulary available to them, the ancient authors of the Bible scrupulously expressed their surroundings—such as animals and nature—but much of what they intended is no longer accessible.[34]

According to Herder, the ancient Hebrew audience was naturally suited for oral poetry.[35] Hebrew is a reminder of a lost sensuality and sensitivity, which humankind possessed during a mythical phase of oral culture. Hebrew poetry is wild and primordial, the epitome of the very spirit of poetry. Although Herder believes that any kind of poetry should be considered a divine gift from God, he considers the Hebrew Bible to be exceptional in its ability to recount the beginning of language and to unfold the history of its own medium of transmission.[36]

An important principle that Herder shares with Hamann is the idea that the Bible is a text written for humans by humans and that it should be read and interpreted as such. Herder develops an elaborate commentary on Hebrew poetry, applauding its aesthetic and historical value. His broad engagement with the topic, which extends over several volumes, is at pains to maintain the divine stature of the Bible and, at the same time, to construe a new, historiographical approach to the text. The divine, in this project, is experienced in two ways: through the process of apprehending the thoughts of the ancient authors and through witnessing God's greatness in His ability to materialize in human form through the text of the Bible.

At the beginning of his *Oldest Document of Humankind*, Herder writes, "With God, everything is an eternal and perfect thought, and in this sense, calling a word or a thought from the Bible 'divine' is the grandest hyperbole of anthropomorphism."[37] Reading the Bible as God's literal words would be "nonsense, the divinization of the human soul."[38] With no means of understanding the divine, readers should instead seek a better understanding of the human aspects of the text: "As long as we do not have a godly grammar, logic, and metaphysics, we want to interpret [everything] in a human manner. Language, time, customs, nation, authors, context—everything, *just like in a human book*."[39] The Bible can thus be grasped through a process of reflection that requires no prior knowledge. For Hamann, the Scriptures evoke a relational coexistence with God. In his religiously esoteric and quasi-Kabbalistic principles, Hamann suggests humanity is a community of readers. For Herder, the view that the Bible holds the key to its own reading results in a rational reading process, a subjective progression that strives for objectively true findings.

As I will discuss in greater detail in Chapter 3, the principle according to which human reason can be exercised by reading the Scriptures dates back to Baruch Spinoza's *Theological-Political Treatise*. The success of Herder's hermeneutics lies in its ability to reconcile this idea with the religious view of the Bible as a divine artifact. According to Herder, both factual and fact-like descriptions depend upon the conditions of the text's writing, to which the spirit gives right.[40] Through this new, historically grounded reading, he grants factuality and fiction the same ontological status as he sustains a reading based on the text's divine right.

This principle supports the vision of philological recovery that Michaelis had proposed. In accordance with his position as a Protestant theologian, Herder's theory of biblical interpretation applies to each and every reader of the Bible. The general reader is also capable of emulating Herder's aesthetic readings of biblical poetry by attending to such features as parallelism, repetition, and rhythm. Accordingly, Herder's examinations of Hebrew do not necessitate philological knowledge of the language in order to understand their conclusions. They impart the idea that any reader can interpret the Bible, regardless of scholarly training, thanks to commonsense apprehension of the circumstances in which the text was written.

Hebrew was at its aesthetic peak, Herder explains, when it functioned as a national language and lost its beauty with the advent of the Diaspora. In many of his texts, and most famously in the *Treatise on the Origin of Language* (*Abhandlung über den Ursprung der Sprache*, 1772), Herder describes linguistic ability as relying upon the embodied linguistic apparatus. The distinct structure of a race—influenced by many factors, including climate and geography—shapes the singular structure of a national language. When he says that contemporary or medieval Jews do not use the same language as the ancient Hebrews, he marks them as inherently different from the ancient Hebrews.

Because of Hebrew's theological status, the inquiry into the origins of the language does not entail merely the investigation of one culture among many. Herder's reading of the Old Testament develops a dual status for the Hebrew people. On the one hand, he portrays the Hebrew language as a particular cultural artifact to be interpreted in light of the nation's specificities: its cultural norms, its aesthetic conventions, and the historical and cultural circumstances that produce a text. On the other hand, the interpretation of the Hebrew Bible is a paragon of cultural study in general. This impression emerges in *The Oldest Document of Humankind*, particularly in its discussion of the Genesis stories. There, Herder cites the story of the Tower of Babel as an explanation for the divergence of national languages from one another. According to the Babel narrative, one language alone cannot prevail on earth for long; its fragmentation into various languages is inevitable. Indeed, Herder continues, differing languages are a necessary and natural phenomenon since they reflect the manifold of dissimilarities (physical, cultural, and others) between their speakers. Distinct ways to utter a language can develop into diverse physical features that are contingent upon gender and upon diverse physiological constructions of the *Sprachwerkzeuge* (language apparatus): the throat, the palate, the tongue, the teeth, and the lips.[41]

This interpretation assigns Genesis a poetic awareness, both as historiography that pays special attention to the role of language in the creation of the world and as literature whose text alludes to its own status as such. Through his writing, the Hebrew poet replicates the creative act of naming. The naming of the woman is done *in the moment of* (or *through*) the act of narrating the origins of humankind. Heavily influenced by Hamann in this early work, Herder contends that the creative act of naming is parallel to the act of innovative narration. Both naming and narration reveal the human ability to find a creative, linguistic shape for one's own reality, a capacity that draws equivalence between a person and God.

In *The Oldest Document of Humankind*, the self-reflective nature that Herder ascribes to the Hebrew Bible takes the form of an elaborate theory of the Hebrew language—a theory that presents Hebrew as possessing special semantic qualities. Examined in its historical context, Herder's later description of the Hebrew people's unique writing system appears as an apologia. The text responds to *The Divine Legation of Moses* (1738–42), in which influential British theologian William Warburton developed a theory of hieroglyphs. For both Warburton and Herder, the Hebrew language elicits the emergence of a new writing culture.[42] Whereas Warburton sees Hebrew as a degraded stage in the development of languages, Herder contends that the poetic style of the Hebrew Bible is like a speaking hieroglyph.[43] God's ability to create the world in seven days, according to Herder, forms a pattern that resembles script: the seven days of creation being equivalent to seven letters with which the world was "written." Unique among world nations, the Hebrews granted a unique spiritual meaning to the number seven.[44]

The attempts during the 1760s and 1770s to reimagine and idealize biblical language were initial and essential steps in the establishment of a grand narrative of a world system of nations. Diverging and even opposing approaches to the Hebrew Bible were combined with one another, creating an infrastructure that tethered interpretation (as a universal set of cognitive capacities) to a model of global religion. As modern hermeneutics was becoming a dominant cultural practice, biblical interpretation served as the ground on which to establish reading as a form of interpersonal deciphering. The belief in every person's aptitude to read and interpret—which disguises the other conditions that are required for cultural dialogue—sustained the appeal of modern hermeneutics.[45] Through attention to the text's style, its literary devices, and the historical circumstances of its writing, the Bible became a model for interpretation because it could be perceived equally by all.

World Literature and the Search for Humanity's Origins

Inquiries of diversity as an ideal that guides the comparative examination of national literatures have been pertinent to literary studies, particularly in discussions about the validity and effectiveness of world literature as an interpretive paradigm. Erich Auerbach described world literature as a normative statement about chronology. According to Auerbach, an understanding of the world as a system of cultural assets that develop separately yet in conjunction dictates the understanding of humanity as having a common history.[46] Auerbach considered humanity to be the product of "the cross-fertilization of the manifold," meaning that behind all notions of world literature stands the ideal of *felix culpa*: the division of mankind into numerous cultures.[47] He nonetheless challenged the view that literature, by representing civilization's entry into modernity, could teach us that humankind progresses in a linear direction toward universal toleration.[48] To the contrary, he saw that during his lifetime humanity was shifting toward nationalism and separatism. But rather than revoke the term "world literature" altogether, he offered a conceptual modification: to replace what he saw as Herder's influence on the term with Giambattista Vico's more self-reflective model of historicism and cultural relativism, which was less likely to invite nationalism. Auerbach thus presented Herder's influence on world literature as both powerful and perilous.

Pascale Casanova's *World Republic of Letters* similarly considers Herder's influence on the concept of world literature. According to Casanova, Herder's theories "brought about the first enlargement of literary space to include the European continent as a whole."[49] He conceptualized world literature not as a preexisting resource that belonged to eminent nations but as a concept that enabled the appreciation of cultural assets previously seen as inferior. The enthusiastic reception of Herder's philosophy of history, she explains, had the effect that various national literatures—whose literary value had previously been ignored—came to be seen as holding "literary legitimacy" due to their function in a national tradition: "By establishing a necessary link between nation and language, [Herder] encouraged all peoples who sought recognition on equal terms with the established nations of the world to stake their claim to literary and political existence."[50]

Central to Casanova's new paradigm of world literature is Herder's contention that artifacts of a foreign culture should be viewed with respect to their origins, particularly if they belong to distant cultures. Casanova fails, however, to address some aspects of Herder's enterprise, especially its theological context and that context's persisting influence. A major facet of Herder's attempt to "rescue" texts previously deemed to be of inferior literary quality was his declaration that the Old Testament contained superb national poetry.[51] The theological agenda behind Herder's interpretation theory and his interrelated view of the world depend upon a system of nations. The reception of this system in the literary world follows the allocation of national literatures to world territories.[52] This reception has therefore reiterated a Protestant vision of the division of the world's nations into geographical territories that sees world structure as a divine plan and promotes a new notion of the Bible. The Bible's ostensible aesthetic merits in capturing a specific national culture allowed it to become an object of interpretation regardless of its readers' confessional belonging.

Herder's *This, Too, a Philosophy of History for the Education of Humanity* (*Auch eine Philosophie der Geschichte zur Bildung der Menschheit*, 1774) advocates a central principle for the interpretation of foreign cultures: the attempt to put oneself in the shoes of human beings utterly different from himself or herself.[53] Herder addresses his reader with the imperative: "Fühle dich in alles hinein!" (Feel yourself into everything!). Literary texts address the sensibilities, tastes, and preferences of a certain historical group of people. Focused on standardizing the readership of the Scriptures, Herder develops a new notion of civilization that can meet the challenges put to a universal vision of scriptural interpretation.

As we have seen, the Hebrew language emerges in this process as a unique particular. It is unique like any other specific national artifact, but it is also unique as a cultural symbol unusually laden with meaning. Accordingly, Herder views the Hebrew Bible not merely as an object of study to which he may apply his interpretation theory but also as a history of the different components upon which his theory relies. Herder's engagement with the Genesis stories exemplifies this composite approach to the Old Testament. They emerge as a collective, universal ethos of the origins of humankind. Because of the importance it assigns language, aesthetics, and the emergence of different nationalities and national languages, the Hebrew Bible is an especially strong collective source.

Herder's description of the world system of nations is central to his notion of historiography. In his monumental *Ideas on the Philosophy of the History of Mankind* (*Ideen zur Philosophie der Geschichte der Menschheit*, 1784–91), Herder describes human history from its beginning. To the questions "Where is the homeland of man? Where is the middle point of earth?," he replies that the worldly center of human existence can be found everywhere—in any place inhabited by humans.[54] He replaces the expectation that one nation (or geographical location) could be defined as superior to others with his revolutionary conceptualization of the world's nations as a self-contained system defined by each one of its members. This perception promotes the view that the Bible should be read in a human way and that, when reading the Scriptures, the purpose should be the transmission of the divine message into human words. In his apologia on biblical poetry, Herder's goal is not to establish cultural relativism but rather to standardize a genealogy of humankind. The basis of this genealogy would be the primordial aesthetics of the Bible, which could be appreciated by all readers from within their respective national and cultural positions.[55]

The notion of a people's singularity also plays an important role in the development of languages. The childhood of a nation is reflected, as Herder establishes in his *Fragments on Recent German Literature*, in the first linguistic utterances of its early cultural stage. In his *Treatise on the Origin of Language*, he describes all human languages as originating from one primordial mother tongue. Over time, the different national languages have developed in accordance with the specificity of the people who speak the language: a singularity that reflects their respective processes of cultural maturation.

Normative Theology

By constituting a homogenous world history, Herder established a universal concept of religion with the Bible at its center as a hermeneutic object that offers itself to the interpretation of all readers. I turn now to the cultural context of Herder's thought in order to show how his ideas emerged in relation to the period's development of personalized engagement with the Hebrew Bible. I look at two poets—Friedrich Gottlieb Klopstock and Salomon Gessner— and their adaptions of Genesis stories.

As part of their admiration of the Old Testament, late eighteenth-century German thinkers displayed a fervent interest in Biblical Hebrew. Prominent figures in this period's republic of letters, such as Goethe and Herder, wrote extensively about the Hebrew language, often debating with one another about the proper way to conceive of it.[56] New aesthetic enterprises—such as those of the Sturm und Drang authors—widely employed specific genres of biblical literature, such as prophetic speech and the idyllic poetry found in the Psalter. Familiarity with the Scriptures, as well as with such authors as Homer, Horace, Dante, and Shakespeare, proved an author's erudition and established his cultural prestige. Functioning as a catalyst of the narrative, the Scriptures were linked to the reminiscences of a lost past. Biblical images reappeared in the poet's memory through encounters with images in reality, which reminded him of scriptural scenes. Germany's celebrated poet Klopstock represents this poetics.

Critics credited the poet for his deep understanding of the Bible, which they saw benefiting his work. In his 1749 biography of the poet, Johann Jakob Bodmer considered Klopstock's acquisition of Hebrew at a young age as having provided him a poet's natural asset.[57] *The Death of Adam* (*Der Tod Adams*) appeared in 1757, after Klopstock had become a well-known poet.[58] The adaptation of the paradise story for the stage introduced a new genre to Klopstock's oeuvre.[59] A tragedy about the death of the first human being ever created, the drama places the subjective identification with the Bible at its center. The play's tension culminates as Adam awaits his impending death. In a speech, Adam confesses his strong feelings in view of his passing from the world:

> Blessing is far from me; I cannot give it:—Pains unfelt before, And thousand deadly thoughts of bitter anguish, Croud on my mind:—e'en now before me rise. The blest ideas of my early days, And form a contrast that o'erwhelms my soul. The thought of immortality once more springs on my mind, and makes me shudder.—Ha! Where am I now? 'tis darkness now no more, and sight returns agen but to behold the champian vast distain'd with reeking blood. Ye ghastly dead, look not with hideous glare on me. . . . It was her only child.—See mangled limbs, and there a trunkless head;—away, away, Ye fearful objects

hence.—Alas, my children, with pity's soft concern behold your father, and kindly lead him from those plains of woe.[60]

The anticipation of death paradoxically provokes signs of vitality. Adam recalls his first living moments, whose eternity "moves in [his] bones." This morbid livelihood appears again when Adam reconciles with Cain. In an abrupt meeting, the two sinners recognize their parallel fates: Cain, the murderer, has paid for his sin by being condemned; Adam faces death as a result of God's punishment. The Genesis story is special in that it reflects upon the personal fate of its main character. At the same time that the dramatic demise of the individual reveals details specific to that person, it also invites the recognition that the fate of the first man on earth is bound to a universal human character.

In *The Death of Abel* (*Der Tod Abels*, 1758), the popular Swiss poet Salomon Gessner also depicts paradise as a liminal space between the particular and the universal. He tries to emulate such a close connection to the Scriptures by situating the Genesis stories in an idyll. Abel's death is the contingent outcome of the protagonist's character and vices, but this contingency conveys the universal pertinence of the Genesis stories: the patriarch's personality parallels that of the reader, who could imagine himself or herself in his shoes. In this sense, the poet strives to provoke an affective resonance that transports readers to a primordial scene with which they are already familiar.

Whereas Klopstock's exposure to Hebrew had its roots in his early education, Gessner's case was just the opposite. Gessner took the Genesis story to establish himself as a literary persona *tout de suite*. His use of images from the Bible was not the fruit of erudition but a blunt attempt to hide the fact that he lacked the familiarity with the Scriptures expected from a poet at the time. His previously published idylls were popular, but they were seen as lacking a serious theological statement.[61] A theological theme catered to the taste of the prominent critic Bodmer, whose translation of Milton's *Paradise Lost* was well known. Gessner's contemporary, the great novelist Christoph Martin Wieland, was displeased with Gessner's occupation with images from Greek mythology; he preferred shepherds who adhered to monotheistic beliefs.[62]

Gessner opens *The Death of Abel* with an apologia on the literary adaptation of the Scriptures. He confesses its boldness from the start: he has taken on, he admits, a "more sublime subject" than those in his previous work.[63]

He dismisses those who have read the biblical stories but have not found beauty or usefulness in them; holding a dialogue with such readers would be as useless, he notes, as carrying a lamp before a blind person.[64] According to Gessner's line of argument, the acknowledgement of the Bible as supreme goes hand in hand with viewing its poetry as sublime. To his mind, preventing poets from using biblical materials is a crime against poetry and contributes to poetry's decline (*Verfall*), since the merit of poetry lies precisely in its ability to make us aware of everything that is beautiful.[65] His use of biblical stories thus conveys to believers the power of religion through the craft of his poetry. Gessner ends his prologue by noting that every nation through time has adapted the Bible. Biblical alteration is a common practice because, since antiquity, great poets have referred to and adapted historical events, with Homer as the most prominent example.

Gessner further argues that the use of ancient materials does not negate their historical validity. His apologia presents a provocative perception of the Scriptures; his professed apologia according to which poetic adaptations do not harm the Bible's status is typical of the period's new conception of the Bible's status as a historical document. The Bible's validity as a historical document is put forward as an agreed-upon fact drawn not from the authority of religious institutions but from cultural relevance.

In Gessner's adaptation of the Genesis stories, the murder of Abel is the high point. The tragedy depicts the loss of a unique individual to a sin whose gravity lies in the fact that every individual is the reflection of God's image. Both in Klopstock's and in Gessner's works, the tragedy is a human one: the protagonist laments his sin, without which punishment and suffering would not have entered the world. In their adaptations, the prominence of the Scriptures as a true account of humanity's conception is replaced with the idealization of the Bible as a platform for a creative and individualistic quest. The death of the individual (Adam or Abel) becomes the primary scene detailing humanity's mythical origins. With its appraisal of the re-writing of the Bible not as a sign of heresy but as a token of faith, literature allows, solicits, and advocates the further rewriting of the Scriptures.

This perspective enhances the reconciliation of the literary and the historical by means of understanding the circumstances in which the text was written. According to Hans Frei, "Hermeneutics [was] clearly on its way toward a notion of explicative interpretation in which a biblical narrative makes sense in accordance with its author's intention and (before long) the culture he exemplifies. And the meaning of the narrative is the subject matter to which the words refer."[66] In the same manner that his poetic adaptation of the Bible reaffirms its aesthetic merits, the reader's personal relationship to the Bible confirms its status as ontologically supreme. The Bible's adaptation to one's time bolsters the truth value of its descriptions. The endpoint of interpretation is no longer the solicitation of scriptural tenets; rather, it is the subjective, revelatory, and dynamic engagement with the text. Hamann's and Herder's respective investigations into interpretation equate, as we have seen, this approach to scriptural interpretation with interpretation in general.

Herder's view of the cosmos requires a distinct geographical location for each nation.[67] As we saw above, climate and geography shape a people, the corporal and linguistic apparatuses, and thus the national language. Since each geographical location stands, according to Herder, at a fixed distance from the sun, the cultural divergences between peoples are a derivation of the cosmic structure. The attempt to define a universal history encompasses different epochs as well as diverging cultural perspectives. Discerning national particularism then leads to the understanding of humankind's chronological development.[68] The Hebrew Bible becomes emblematic of humankind's common asset; it proves that humanity shares historical origins, the inclination toward national belonging, and the psychological apparatus that enables the recognition of both.

Herder's innovations in scriptural reading shaped two interrelated notions at the root of modern readership: the view of reading as a gradual restoration of an original text whose meanings are not immediately apparent to the reader and the conception of a system of diverging traditions that should be examined in their respective cultural contexts. By presenting the Hebrew Bible as the product of a certain national culture, Herder made it into a pertinent asset to society, not because of its perfection as God's word but because of the need to restore and rescue it from harmful influences.

Through Hamann's construal of obscurity as Hebrew's absolute trait, literary adaptations of Genesis that present their relevance to all readers, and Herder's call to decipher the Scriptures through the understanding of the culture that produced it, late Enlightenment philosophy relied upon transformations in scriptural reading. The manifold perspectives on Biblical Hebrew ultimately yielded two major philosophical positions: Hamann's invitation to endorse faith as an inseparable part of the human apparatus and Herder's model of adhering to affect as a companion for reason. Herder managed to consolidate a concept of textual restoration that built on a subjective engagement with the Scriptures while adhering to the text as historical documentation. Herder established an influential model of constructive intellectual reasoning, which designated a central role for intellectual achievement, interpersonal exchange, and human empathy.

Biblical Myth and the Critique of Modernity

Inquiries into the origins of language have informed not only Enlightenment theories of comprehension but also their critiques in later philosophical writings, as is evident in the oeuvre of a foremost critic of modernity: Walter Benjamin. One way in which Benjamin's writings exhibit their originality is their engagement with cultural artifacts from different epochs: ancient classicism, baroque drama, modernist poetry, and so forth. In the milestones of Western civilization, Benjamin traces repetitive manifestations of humans' understanding of the world. However, he seems not to have offered an equivalent investigation of the Enlightenment, the epoch that popularized systematic explanations of how human beings perceive their surroundings, interpret them, and communicate their impressions to one another. For the remainder of this chapter, I would like to examine an early essay, "On Language as Such and on the Language of Man" ("Über Sprache überhaupt und über die Sprache des Menschen," 1916), which I see as containing Benjamin's reflections on the Enlightenment. These reflections can be found in his discussion of theological myths that are relevant to the Enlightenment and to its legacy in modern hermeneutics. "On Language as Such" shows the pertinence of the Bible, and especially the Genesis stories, for theories that seek to depict linguistic enunciation and its interpretation as collective human experiences.

"On Language as Such" touches on several philosophical tropes that would become seminal to Benjamin's later philosophy of language. Consider, for instance, Benjamin's essay "The Translator's Task," ("Die Aufgabe des Übersetzers," 1921) which famously contends that "no poem is intended for the reader, no image for the beholder, no symphony for the listener," distancing the artistic artifact from the audience exposed to it.[69] "On Language as Such" makes a move toward this view by stressing the medial nature of language and portraying it as inherently conflicted. The essay develops the idea that linguistic utterances involve an inherent tension. The naming of objects is charged, on the one hand, with a deep belief in the immediacy of the human grasp on reality through the senses. On the other hand, linguistic utterances always recall the instrumentality of language, thus dispelling the urge and motivation to have a direct grasp of the objects that one names. Tracing these two tendencies is central to Benjamin's philosophy of language, as demonstrated in his influential work on translation. "On Language as Such" ponders the role of theology in linguistic usage and describes biblical myth as a salient influence on the belief in the communicability of ideas.

Written in a cryptic style, "On Language as Such" discusses at its beginning the attachment of words to world objects. The ability of language to convey a speaker's impressions of the world is accompanied by a further trait: the arbitrary and necessarily indirect connection between signifier and signified. Language is irreducible to its denotative quality so that the daily use of language to name objects is a practice that establishes man as an omnipotent being.[70] Worldly objects seek to transmit through language an essence that Benjamin defines as their inner core or spiritual essence. Benjamin suggests that "the name" transmits the essence of objects and thereby exposes the divine quality of man: "[The] view is the bourgeois conception of language, the invalidity and emptiness of which will become increasingly clear in what follows. It holds that the means of communication is the word, its object factual, and its addressee a human being. The other conception of language, in contrast, knows no means, no object, and no addressee of communication. It means: in the name, the mental being of man communicates itself to God."[71] With his ability to name objects, man evokes the godly image that was given to him during creation. He appears as "the master of nature," who transmits through words the quality of worldly objects in his surroundings.[72] The mythic notion that God used an original language (Ursprache) in His act of creation perpetuates the theological notion that man was made in God's image, which in turn fixes this theological conviction in linguistic structures.

The biblical creation stories, which depict how man emulated God by naming the objects around him, ingrain in many human languages a metaphysical contention regarding man's role in the world: "Man can call name the language of language (if the genitive refers to the relationship not of a means but of a medium), and in this sense certainly, because he speaks in names, man is the speaker of language, and for this very reason its only speaker. In terming man the speaker (which, however, according to the Bible, for example, clearly means the name giver: 'As man should name all kinds of living creatures, so should they be *called*'), many languages imply this metaphysical truth."[73] With this reflection on the theological presumptions behind language use, Benjamin suggests that the myth *of* language becomes entrenched *in* language. The influence of biblical myth is manifested in the belief that the speaking subject is able to capture the essence of objects through the act of naming them.

Particularly relevant to *Secularism and Hermeneutics* are Benjamin's references to Hamann, specifically Hamann's blunt attacks on Enlightenment thinkers over their perception of language. Hamann criticizes his contemporaries for perceiving language as a means to an end: that is, as the interpersonal exchange of messages that are open to the receiver's interpretation. As we have seen above, both the adherence to reason in exegesis and Hamann's opposition to an instrumental approach to the biblical language constitute readers as a collective audience of autonomous individuals. In a similar vein, Benjamin sees Hamann's thought as authenticating the efficacy of linguistic signification rather than eliminating it. Benjamin could have attributed the belief in man's power to communicate his thoughts to Gottfried Wilhelm Leibniz, Christian Wolff, or Immanuel Kant; his choice of Hamann demonstrates the intricate interrelation of Enlightenment notions of interpretation and theology. Following his reading of Hamann, Benjamin observes that theological myths exist not in an antagonist relation to major Enlightenment notions but in a dialectical one. In doing so, he shows eighteenth-century theology, particularly its strands that were critical of the unwavering faith in reason, to have been constitutive of hermeneutic thinking. This early essay is thus a stepping-stone for Benjamin's own philosophy of language, which would later challenge global and instrumental portrayals of linguistic usage.

To Hamann, as we have seen, all linguistic utterances encompass the reminiscences of the biblical scene of God's creation of the world and man's emulation of God in Adam's naming of the animals. For Hamann, the moment of creating man is the pinnacle of the process of creating the world. Man's divine traits are shown first and foremost in his ability to create new objects in the world.[74] In Benjamin's reading, Hamann cites, as well as perpetuates, the Ursprache myth. The original language, which builds upon human sensual input, had an immediate, visceral connection to worldly objects: "Hamann says, 'Everything that man heard in the beginning, saw with his eyes, and felt with his hands was the living word; for God was the word. With this word in his mouth and in his heart, the origin of language was as natural, as close, and as easy as a child's game.'"[75] The idea of a language of origins fixed in the Bible suggests the notion of an aesthetic Bible. According to this perception, the Scriptures display truisms about the function of human language and historical evidence for the birth of language. Biblical myth extends into the everyday linguistic structures of many national languages. Linguistic communication necessitates a constant belief that the name given to an object transmits its essence. At the same time, linguistic theory entails—and reveals—that this belief implicates the lacking nature of language. Language is a medium that cannot fulfill its promise of mediation and bears the risk that Benjamin describes as the abyss that threatens language philosophy.[76]

In showing that the Enlightenment's legacy owes its relevance to its dialectic with theology, Benjamin offers a second step. His essay discloses an alternative theological conception of language, one that would build on the view of meaning as ungraspable in language. He suggests that fostering this alternative theological approach to language situates speakers at a distance from the belief in linguistic signification as the unwavering representation of reality. Benjamin's portrayal of theories of language as existing in dialectic with theology would become central to his own intellectual project.

Chapter 2

Hermeneutics and Affect

In 1731, the philosopher Christian Wolff famously wrote, "The interpretation of the Holy Scripture lies in the application of logics."[1] Eminent figures of the Enlightenment republic of letters would later contradict this assertion as they adapted biblical stories into poetry and drama and praised the Bible's aesthetic merits. Friedrich Daniel Ernst Schleiermacher's hermeneutics would come to rely on the Sturm und Drang movement's appraisal of the Bible as literature. This literary preoccupation with the Bible had the effect that all Enlightenment readers—every citizen of this new collective—were expected to be able to acknowledge the supreme poetic merits of the Bible.

Herder and his contemporaries took on the question of why biblical poetry was a supreme aesthetic artifact, but they did so by presenting a new argument. Herder, Friedrich Gottlieb Klopstock, young Goethe, and others reclaimed the Bible as an object whose merits are revealed through reading, a process of reflection that every person can perform. They presented poetry as a divine gift to humankind, even if they simultaneously saw the Bible as a text written by humans for humans. In a larger aesthetic conception of literature, the Bible's aesthetic merit became the token of its supreme nature. Their claims for the aesthetic merits of Hebrew poetry relied on the traditional view of the Bible as a historical account of the origins of humankind, but under aesthetic conventions, they maintained that reading was a procedure of spiritual discovery, and to do so, they had to construe the Bible as human—or secular.

This new sense of what made the Bible divine emerged through debates over the existing view that art stimulates unique manifestations of human experience. Scholars commonly hold the view that Klopstock, Herder, and Goethe, by praising the aesthetic merits of the Old Testament and emulating biblical poetry in their own poetic writings, promoted the reading of the Bible as literature.[2] Research, however, has overlooked that the conception of the Bible as literature emerged in an intellectual circle that was neither passive nor neutral with regard to how it defined literary interpretation. This chapter will argue that these authors in fact developed new approaches to textual interpretation with the ostensible claim of *applying* pregiven methods of literary analysis to the Bible.

Even as these authors engaged extensively with the Holy Scriptures, their work focused on a certain part of the Old Testament: the Hebrew Bible. To make the Bible into a model for textual craftiness, they not only had to reconcile the divine text with a secular world but also had to shape that divine text into a universal object of human cognition, equally accessible to all people despite their different systems of faith. The particularity of the Hebrew Bible—that is, its association with a religious minority—had a decisive influence on their new conceptions of literary interpretation.

The transformation of the Hebrew Bible into a collective asset of Enlightenment readers is one conceptual root of literary hermeneutics. It both utilized and advanced the interpretive turn from aesthetics to hermeneutics in the German literary scene of the late eighteenth century. The discourse around the Bible as literature addressed readers in the emerging modern political sphere and, in effect, constituted such readers as a public. They formed a collective able to discern that the Bible's merits were its universal aesthetic and historiographical importance and that the Bible was detached from a spiritual or religious identity.

As we considered in Chapter 1, the Hebrew Bible was seen as proof of Jewish interference and the ill transmission of the text.[3] What role then would a religious minority have in transmitting a text that was becoming a universal cipher? In light of the association of the Hebrew Bible with Judaism, hermeneutics had to become a recuperative effort—a cognitive procedure that could rescue meanings from their loss; texts from the damaging influence of time; and objects from cultural ignorance and decay. But at the same time, the role of biblical poetry was a unique expression of affect in literature. William Robertson Smith argued in 1912 that the new attitude toward the Bible in the eighteenth century resulted in a new conception of poetry: "The true power of poetry is that it speaks from the heart to the heart. True criticism is not the classification of the poetic effects according to the principles of rhetoric, but the unfolding of the living forces which moved the poet's soul. To enjoy a poem is to share the emotion that inspired its author."[4]

This principle of reading, which pertained to the Bible and specifically the Old Testament, is a forthright description of major characteristics of the eighteenth-century interpretive turn from rhetoric to hermeneutics. The debates on how to read the Old Testament credited readers with an empathetic yet distant relation to the author of a text that would help them attend a text's original meanings.

The Hebrew Bible became emblematic of the hermeneutic turn through three conceptual steps. The first was to distinguish between the ancient Hebrews and the Jews. The period idealized ancient Hebrew poetry, but contemporary Jews were treated with suspicion and occasional contempt. This discrepancy required a second step: the favoring of Hebrew as a trope of sublime aesthetics and the concurrent repression of its material and ritual presence. Then, as we will see in Chapter 3, the praise of Hebrew reached its a third climatic step. With a view of reading practices and education as universal, Jews received the conditional promise of being considered competent readers. As a modern German-speaking national culture was emerging, Judaism was both the raison d'être of hermeneutics (Jews corrupted the text that should now be restored) as well as the signifier of its accomplishment (Jews are able to interpret like Christians through the universal apparatus of human cognition). But this purported accomplishment of inclusion is exactly what exposes the original presumption of hermeneutics—the need for restoration—as invalid. This duality parallels the period's larger political transition.

This chapter analyzes eighteenth-century debates on how to read Hebrew in order to show how these debates shaped the period's model of literary interpretation. The German republic of letters had a deep interest in the Bible as a resource for the poetic imagination of both the individual and, by way of homology, the emerging national culture. Tying the Hebrew Bible to key notions in early Romanticism—childhood images, imagery and language acquisition—helped authors such as Goethe and Herder to ponder the emergence of national languages and literatures.[5] Their efforts, however, also exposed the differences between the authors with regard to a German-speaking national culture.

Robert Lowth's *Lectures on the Sacred Poetry of the Hebrews* (1753) will serve as my main example of the debate over biblical and literary reading in the mid-eighteenth century. Praised for his attentiveness to the Hebrew Bible's literary devices, Lowth strives for an affinity with the Hebrews through masterful comprehension of the Hebrew Bible's aesthetic merits. In *On the*

Spirit of Hebrew Poetry (*Vom Geist der ebräischen Poesie*, 1782–83), Herder appears to adapt Lowth's ideas in his insistence on historical, cultural, and anthropological relativism.[6] But whereas Lowth identifies the Hebrews as an early stage in the development of aesthetic merit, Herder argues against such a linear chronology of aesthetics and for an understanding of cultural particularity as relational. Then, in order to contextualize Herder's interventions into textual interpretation and aesthetic theory, I review research on the shift from aesthetics to hermeneutics in the late German Enlightenment. My goal is to trace the beginning of hermeneutic thinking on cultural objects in writings that praise Hebrew poetry as aesthetically supreme. I discern the role of the Hebrew sublime in Herder's emerging perception of poetics, noting how his choice to translate the Song of Songs advanced his intervention into the aesthetic theories of Gotthold Ephraim Lessing and Alexander Gottlieb Baumgarten.

In some of the eighteenth century's most vibrant poetry and treatises on poetics, Pietism became the means of unifying the citizens of the modern state, not despite but exactly because of its separatist zeal. The fascination with biblical poetry promoted intimacy with God and religious experience through aesthetics. In its energizing power, Pietism exhibited religious enthusiasm even if not in the form of religious practice. Pietistic ideas therefore offered a possibility of social and national integration. David Sorkin has thus analyzed Pietism not as the locus of separatism between Christian hegemony and religious minorities but rather as enabling different religious groups to find spiritual common ground. He shows how the work of Siegmund Jakob Baumgarten, which centers on Pietistic principles such as the benevolence of God and the obligation of contributing to society, in effect enables Jews and other non-Christians to found a common religious ideology that justifies and mobilizes new constellations of national coexistence.[7] Sorkin's original explanation offers a new perspective on the role of Pietism in constructing Germany's religious ideology. Through its amalgamation with nationalism, Pietism granted the members of different religious Enlightenments both the recollection of religious separatism and the ability to participate in a unified society.

The spread of this religious faith throughout Germany's intellectual elite explains the influence of Pietism on the emerging national culture. Kant's background and education as a Pietist can be seen as evident in his advocating of the "religion of reason" in a text such as *Religion Within the Bounds of Reason Alone* (1793). In that case, Pietistic ideology serves not so much as the content of Kant's explicit ideology with regard to religious models as the motivation that stands behind it. Pietistic influence is also evident in the literary experimentation with the poetic speaker's self-aggrandizing *I*. This poetic persona parallels the advocacy of reading as both an individual capacity and as the grounds for the unity of the nation.

The Hebrew language had become, in this process, a trope connoting the unity of the nation under the umbrella of an aesthetic experience detached from traditional textual comprehension. The process of turning Hebrew into a sublime artifact made Hebrew poetry, which had been a marker of Jewish faith and of the concrete ritual practice of a religious minority, incongruous with the new model of a universalistic experience of reading texts. The Hebrew sublime is a constant reminder that the cognitive process that aesthetics elicits suppresses religious and ethnic differences and, in turn, ingrains this suppression in the infrastructure of the modern nation. This loss is a continual and disturbing recollection of that which is left behind.

The Hebrew Bible and the Language of Childhood Memories

Theories on the Hebrew Bible have long intersected with, reflected on, and confronted depictions of the nation. Some theorists have commented on the people that originated the Hebrew language. In his *Essay on the Manners and the Spirit of Nations* (*L'Essai sur les Mœurs et l'esprit des Nations*, 1756), Voltaire writes that there is nothing "fine" in Hebrew poetry since there can be no artifact of beauty from "the crude nation of the Hebrews."[8] Spinoza's *Theological-Political Treatise* takes a critical view of ancient Israel as an authoritarian state (as will be discussed in the next chapter in relation to Moses Mendelssohn). Significantly, Spinoza presents the Hebrew Bible as a text that is meant to function, first and foremost, as a legal constitution.[9] His analysis of the so-called fallacies of the text—its gaps, fragmentary passages, and inner contradictions, as well as descriptions that do not accord with reason, such as those of miracles—portrays the Hebrew state as a political power primarily occupied with securing its ascendancy through textual falsification and populist antirationalist tropes. Through means such as censorship, textual circulation, and redaction, the Hebrew state focused on securing its power through its ongoing transmission of the Bible. Spinoza thus fuses political and textual corruption, creating, like Voltaire, a parallel between the text and its producers based on a critical view of both. Such positions reiterate that of Gottfried Wilhelm Leibniz, who does not give a special place to Hebrew in his historiographical account of the development of human language from its beginning.

But late seventeenth-century Germany also featured alternative accounts of the Old Testament. These relied on the aesthetic merits of the Hebrew Bible to draw an affinity between German poetry and the ancient Hebrews. This affinity was grounded in the identification of the Hebrew Bible as the prehistoric source of poetry and of the Israelites as the nation that brought forth aesthetics. The new perception of the Bible as an aesthetic artifact was followed, in the eighteenth century, by extensive interest in Luther's Bible, which widely inspired German-speaking poets in their establishing of a new alternative to classicism. This assumption relied on the acceptance of the Bible's cultural significance as a condition for its entrance into the collective sphere.[10]

In his investigation of the birth of modern national cultures, Benedict Anderson scrutinizes the stimulating effect that Luther's biblical translation had on print (and, vice versa, on the importance of print to the circulation of the translation).[11] Anderson famously shows how the rapid circulation of texts in the vernacular stimulated the emergence of nation-states in the eighteenth century. The focus on hermeneutics offers a new nexus with which to understand the influence of the circulation of the Bible on the development of modern nationalism. It is not merely the influence of the Bible as a national epic or its reciprocal affinity with "print-capitalism" that established the Holy Scriptures as the crucible of the emerging nation-state.[12] The Bible's preeminent role was the relational affinity it had to all texts, establishing nationalism not on the idea that texts belong to the same community but rather on the idea that there is a community that can interpret cultural objects in a similar manner.

Late eighteenth-century Germany approached the Hebrew Bible as a new platform for the prevailing wave of affect that resonated with theological convictions. In the Sturm und Drang movement, the broad emulation of the style and themes of the Hebrew Bible served as a major expression of a new nationalistic tendency: an emerging affiliation of the German nation with the Hebrew state.[13] The sweeping embrace of Hebrew thus stemmed from the circumventing of other aesthetic models, such as ancient Greek poetry (which was already used in German classicism) and Latin (which by then was a recognizable cipher of French nationalism). The choice of Hebrew to separate the German state from preexisting aesthetic models and national movements signaled the emergence of modern German nationalism.[14]

The Hebrew sublime emerged amid debates on poetry in eighteenth-century Germany. In response to his contemporaries' interest in the Bible, Goethe's autobiography, *From My Life: Truth and Poetry* (*Aus meinem Leben: Dichtung und Wahrheit*, 1833), depicts the role of theology in Germany's literary scene as he retrospectively maps the emergence of new poetics. Aware of the form that German national literature had taken, Goethe explains how arguments involving Hebrew had brought to the fore tensions between different Enlightenment figures, such as his and Herder's agonistic views on religion and human passions.

In the seventh book of his autobiography, Goethe names the qualities that a good poet should have, as perceived at the time. He shows that the influence of Johann Christoph Gottsched's *An Essay in Critical Poetics* (*Versuch einer kritischen Dichtkunst*, 1730) on the period's poets was great, but in addition to the formal knowledge of poetry (such as that of rhythm) explicated in Gottsched's influential aesthetic manual, poets were expected to possess a certain erudition and good literary taste.[15] The erudition demanded from the poets included "human history," of which the Bible was an important part. More than any other book, the Bible was considered pregnant with meaning, a quality that made it especially suitable for use in the reflection on "human things," which Germany poetry had been missing.[16] What is more, the belief that the Bible was a divine gift designated it as a cultural object of importance to humanity as a whole. In effect, the Bible turned humankind into a unified entity:

> For hitherto men had received it as a matter of implicit faith, that this book of books was composed in one spirit; *that it was even inspired, and, as it were, dictated by the Spirit of God.* Yet long ago already the inequalities of the different parts of it had been alternately cavilled at and apologized for by believers and unbelievers. English, French, and Germans had assaulted the Bible with more or less violence, acuteness, audacity and wantonness; and just as often had it been taken under the protection of earnest, well-minded men of each nation. As for myself, I loved and valued it: for almost to it alone did I owe my moral culture, and its events, its doctrines, its emblems, its similes, had all stamped themselves deeply upon me, and had influenced me one way or another.[17]

Goethe's description is telling. The Bible's status as a text with universal relevance was due not to its being praised but rather to its being attacked from
all sides ("by Englishmen, Frenchmen and Germans") because of its fragmented nature ("the inequalities of the different parts"). Consequently, the
Bible had to be defended—and, in the act of its defense, cherished—by "men
of each nation." A welcoming environment for debate, contestation, and
apologia solicited the Bible's repetitious appearances in the eighteenth
century's public sphere. For eminent Enlightenment figures, theology was not
about the sweeping reception of the Bible's higher ascendancy. Rather, by way
of the period's new concept of pluralism, the Bible was becoming an organizing principle of the political entity that was to become the nation-state. The
debates on the Bible in every nation and the competing religious ideologies
that they employed created the sense that it was of universal importance.[18]
Situating the nation in the global system, or community, of world nations,
these debates represented the importance of the Bible for each individual nation (each in itself a microcosm of biblical readers).

The role that Goethe ascribes to the Hebrew Bible when defining, pondering, and developing his persona as a writer is especially illuminating. The
ending of the paragraph introduces the question of readership and textual
circulation as a driving force of modern nationalism.[19] The republic(s) of letters used identification with the Bible as part of growing national reading cultures, and the Romantic reception of the text made the Bible an influential
source for mobilizing readers to identify their role in the national community. Goethe "loved" the Bible, as he testifies about his early life, because of
the text's rich contents in which every man could find what he was looking
for. The view of Hebrew as the language of childhood imagination, which in
turn sparks poetic vocation, was widespread in Goethe's time. A prominent
example is in the work of Klopstock, arguably Germany's most celebrated
poet at the time, who relied on biblical forms and motifs, as we have already
seen, to enhance his poetic expression.

In the background of young Goethe's encounter with Hebrew was the notion of poetic vocation relying upon and being driven by biblical forms and
motifs. In the fourth book of his autobiography, Goethe describes his attempts
to study Hebrew as a youngster. This account, itself a part of the performative
unfolding of Goethe's poetic persona, touches upon Goethe's poetic formation,
literary imagination, and apprenticeship as a reader and writer. Having
had some knowledge of Yiddish, which he picked up by strolling in Frankfurt's Jewish quarter, Goethe turned to ancient Hebrew to get a better hold

of the Hebrew script so as to transcend the corruption of the language in its modern usage.[20] He justified this choice to his father with the widespread conviction that command of Hebrew leads to better comprehension of the Old Testament—and that command of the Old Testament leads to a better understanding of the New Testament.[21]

His attempt failed. After several lessons with Doctor Albrecht, a churchman and the rector of his gymnasium, Goethe quit studying Hebrew. The medieval addition of punctuation to the script and other peculiarities of the language, such as writing from right to left, overwhelmed him.[22] Because the original signs (*Urzeichen*) are followed in Hebrew by an overwhelming presence of auxiliary signs, the transmission of the language appalled him:

> It had also been taught, that the Jewish nation, so long as it flourished, really preferred the first signs, and knew to write and read in no other. Most willingly then would I have gone on along this ancient, and, as it seemed to me, easier path; but the old man declared rather sternly, that we must stick to the grammar as it was authorized and approved; that reading without these points and strokes was very hard, and could be accomplished only by adepts; and I must therefore learn these little characters without more ado. But the thing perplexed me more and more. Some of the larger primitive letters, it seems, had no value in their places, in order that their little neighbours might not be utterly useless where they stood. Now they indicated a gentle aspirate, then a guttural more or less rough, and anon were mere prefixes or affixes. But, finally, when one fancied that he had noted every thing, these personages, both great and small, were rendered inoperative, so that the eyes always had much, and the lips little to do.[23]

To the young reader striving to explore idyllic biblical stories and images, the encounter with the Hebrew script as a medium reached its peak with a bodily rejection: the marking of the breath as fluctuating between soft breathing and guttural sounds resulted in a complete discordance of the eye-mouth relation.

Friedrich Kittler has traced the origin of Romantic reading to a mother reading to her child, an act in which she fulfills her moral and civil duty. For Kittler, the Romantic conception of script evokes the presence of the voice behind the word. Reading is fundamentally phonetic, such that the child becomes a reader of the "mother tongue."[24] With this image in mind, Hebrew seemed to embody for Goethe a conundrum of mediation. Whereas its complicated grammar system exposed it as foreign to German, its script comprised primordial signs. Not a part of the original script but yet necessary for its articulation, Hebrew punctuation disrupted his ability to utter—or even imagine—the voice behind the script through reading. What was so disappointing, according to Goethe, was the constant rejection embodied in Hebrew. The collective aspiration of his age for an intimate connection with the language required that he command its grammar, but the closer he got to the language, the more evident its mediated nature became. Ironically, only those already well trained and erudite were able read the language in its original form and make its punctuation redundant.

Goethe's writing about Hebrew contains multiple references to Herder. His relationship with Herder emerges in Goethe's biography as fluctuating between admiration and derision, making palpable the tensions between the two men. In his *On the Spirit of Hebrew Poetry*, Herder writes that one needs to learn Hebrew to understand the Old Testament and, ultimately, to better understand Christianity—a statement undoubtedly meant to create interest in the essay.[25] Learning Hebrew poetry thus entails an objective of restoration. For Herder, since Hebrew was spoken during early human history, studying it shows one's recognition of the importance of that period. One of the interlocutors in Herder's dialogue confesses, however, that because of its tedious grammar, the study of Hebrew in one's childhood leaves a bad taste in the learner's mouth. *On the Spirit of Hebrew Poetry* intends to renovate Hebrew's reputation. As will be elaborated in what follows, the essay presents Hebrew as a vivid, rich, and enjoyable object of study.

On the Spirit of Hebrew Poetry presents the collective childhood embodied in the language as a joyful and vivid recollection that can be detected through the close examination of Hebrew's features. The essay replaces the studious formation of the humanistic reader with the reminiscences of the Hebrew people's vitality. When, in *Truth and Poetry*, Goethe presents Herder's call for a childhood imagination of Hebrew as didactic, in spite of its ostensibly liberating content, he alludes to the religious motivations behind Herder's depiction of Hebrew. Goethe's disappointment and ultimate distaste for institutionalized religion resonate in the failure of his study of Hebrew. For Goethe, the self-stimulating nature of the childhood recollection is constantly at odds with the obstacle of mediation embodied in Hebrew.

Thus, in the final analysis, in Goethe's post-Romantic reflection on Sturm und Drang poetry, the childishness of the period's Hebrew nostalgia manifests as German nationalism confessing its failure to find original material for its emerging national literature:

> The Germans sought everywhere for the materials which, in this manner, gave more or less determinateness to form. They had handled few national subjects, or none at all. . . . The tendency to idyl extended itself without end. Gesner's [sic] want of distinctive character, with his great gracefulness and childlike simple-heartedness, made every one think that he could do something of the same kind himself. Just so those poems which should have portrayed a foreign nationality, were built out of no materials but such as belonged to the whole human race in general; for instance, the poems founded on Jewish pastoral life, principally those on the patriarchs, and whatever else relates to the Old Testament.[26]

The German poets consented to the lack of originality with the "childish joy" in which they embraced their lack of character. The fathers of national German poetry failed to attain their own role as patriarchs because, ironically, they turned time and again to patriarchs of another nation whom they figured as the patriarchs of humankind. By attaching a symbolic role to Hebrew punctuation—as the disturbing reminder of the concrete presence of a foreign nation—Goethe exposes the utopian presentation of Germans as ancient Hebrews. From within that mature position, Goethe rejects a universal creation story that positions one nation at its center while attempting to empower a German national project. Goethe's account discredits Herder's cultural pluralism and its recurrent attempt to found, through biblical aesthetics, an immanent principle with which to justify its raison d'être: to establish the observing subject on the basis of a religious model of divine creation and revelation.

Biblical Aesthetics

As discussed briefly in Chapter 1, Herder's own attitude toward childhood and nation-building figures prominently in his *Fragments on Recent German Literature* (1767–68), where he draws parallels between children's early stages of language development and those of a national language. To Herder, the early life of a national language features poignant sounds that transmit the speaker's blunt reactions and raw feelings:

A language in its infancy, like a child, will burst forth with monosyllabic, rough, and high-pitched sounds. A nation in its earliest savage beginnings, like a child, marvels at all things before it; terror, fright, and thereupon, wonder, are the only emotions both are capable of, and the language expressing these affects is sounds—and gestures. To utter the sounds their voices are yet unpracticed; as a consequence, the sounds are high-pitched and full of forceful accents; sounds and gestures are symbols of passions and emotions; consequently, they are urgent and strong. . . . [T]hey are also better able than we are to understand the language of affect, since we know that age only from later reports and inferences; for as little as we have of early childhood recollection through memory, so little evidence is obtainable of that age of language when one did not yet speak, but uttered sounds.[27]

This account of language acquisition in the childhood of a nation resonates with Herder's famous opening to his *Treatise on the Origin of Language* (1772), where he provocatively distinguishes himself from both Johann Georg Hamann and Kant by refusing to take a position on their dispute. Herder's ascription of language in its primary stage to animalistic drives (the most basic of which is pain) is at odds both with Hamann's idea of language as God's gift and with Kant's view of language as the accomplishment of human reason. Later, Herder's project of recovering the childhood of language—perceived as a reflection of the emergence of a nation—turns, in his *Fragments on Recent German Literature*, from the detection of the nature of literature in Germany at that time to an exploration of the emergence of the ancient languages of the *Morgenländer* (the Orient).[28] That is to say, his inquiry turns to the childhood of humankind as a whole. These languages—of which Hebrew receives the fullest account—embody a wild beauty that is no longer fully accessible. He explores these lost traces of ancient languages in a description of Hebrew synonyms, which, according to Herder, were not synonyms when ancient Hebrews spoke; then, they were signifiers of distinct objects. The immediacy of the Hebrew characterization of world objects has been lost, which presents a major problem for biblical translation.

The Hebrew sublime emerged along with frequent references to the Bible as a literary asset and a supreme aesthetic artifact. But this common characterization of mid-eighteenth-century biblical reading needs to be amended. At the center of these discussions was not the Bible as a whole but only one part—the Hebrew Bible—which had been deemed damaged or lost. The question of how to comprehend the Scriptures through new universal categories of human cognition took shape against a background of deliberation on the possibility of Jewish emancipation in Germany. The potential integration of Jews in European society made the attempts to reconceive the Bible as an all-human asset pertinent.

An important example of these efforts is found in a text widely circulated in Germany, Lowth's *Lectures on the Sacred Poetry of the Hebrews*. As Jonathan Sheehan demonstrates, Lowth's apologia for Hebrew poetry served as a seminal model for Enlightenment figures as they began to use the Bible for the coining of new aesthetic ideals and reading practices. The originality of Lowth's text derives to a large extent from his unique and bold approach to the translation of the Old Testament. He argues that translations do not have to repeat the rhyme and rhythm of the original text.[29] Herder and Schleiermacher's later theories of translation echo Lowth; for all three, cultural inquiry and textual restoration are to be achieved not through the text's original content and form but through free translation and a focus on the spirit (*Geist*) of the text.

In this way, Lowth's reading of the Old Testament seeks to repair the relationship between the contemporary reader and the author of the original Hebrew text. He proposes a model of reading wherein the reader attains an emotional identification with the author. The attentive investigation of Hebrew culture will result in such emotional identification as readers follow in the footsteps of the ancient authors: "We must endeavor as much as possible to read Hebrew as the Hebrews would have read it. . . . [H]e who would perceive and feel the peculiar and interior elegances of the Hebrew poetry, must imagine himself exactly situated as the persons for whom it was written, or even as the writers themselves."[30] The ability to transfer emotions from one soul to another and to criticize or analyze the thoughts of another was a revolutionarily new conception that emerged with modern hermeneutics and became central to it. It involved a new notion of sharing between reader and author. In his scrupulous reading of the Old Testament, Lowth praises its aesthetic merits. His analysis relies on several premises, the most important of which is the distinction between the ancient Hebrews, who are not held responsible for the corruption of the text, and the Jews, who are responsible for it. This distinction allows the reader to make a connection to the ancient Hebrews but also to elude the corrupted medium through which their work has been transmitted. This idealization of Hebrew poetry elicits a strong motivation to bridge the gap that lies between the reader and the text.

According to Lowth, it is therefore important that poetry be analyzed through the attempt to penetrate the authors' emotions. But it is also important that poetry be written in view of this anticipated effort of its future audience. Hebrew poetry, with its appeal to the human passions, is the historically important emblem of this aesthetic effort at the core of poetic creation. Due to its long-lasting circulation, Hebrew poetry substantializes the short-lived project of the Greeks to regulate and sustain a participatory civil order by addressing the senses. Lowth's intention is to show that Hebrew poetry has a unique virtue. The role of poetry in general is to "improve the bias of our nature," and Hebrew poetry has the merit of its "natural splendor," which helps its readers hone their virtues with great effectiveness.[31] Because of its sublime beauty, Hebrew poetry has the power to maintain noble feelings, which are a testimony to human accomplishment: "The human mind can conceive nothing more elevated, more beautiful, or more elegant; in which the almost ineffable sublimity of the subject is fully equaled by the energy of the language and the dignity of the style."[32] Hebrew thus emerges as an ideal language that refines the noblest feelings of humankind.

Lowth's third lecture takes up illustrating Hebrew's aesthetic merit with an inquiry into the metrical and rhythmical sophistication of its poetry. Hebrew's meter differs from that of Greek and Latin, languages whose poetic merits are well known. To illustrate the particular poetic devices of Hebrew, Lowth first argues that although passages of Hebrew poetry may not appear coherent, this is because their coherence derives not from their meaning but from the alphabetic order of the last letter of each stanza. Second, he argues that the obscurity of Hebrew poetry was the poetic intention of its authors. Similar to other authors who are confined to verse, the Hebrew poets often used words in ways that transgress or even oppose their conventional usage.[33] The outcome is not only the unique versification of Hebrew poetry but also its lexical diversity. Hebrew elevates the common use of language through the introduction of foreign words and irregular or uncommon usage.

While these characteristics of Hebrew poetry support its new claim to being a unique poetic language, Lowth also admits that of the three ancient languages that demonstrate poetic excellence (Greek, Latin, and Hebrew), Hebrew has been the most severely corrupted. The foremost evidence of Hebrew's corruption is the fact that we do not know how Hebrew poetry should be pronounced. Lowth's claim that the Jews have corrupted Hebrew's sweetness is one that was prevalent in eighteenth-century writing on Hebrew. It manifests in Herder's later distinction between the Israelites as an ideal nation and the Jews as a group antagonistic to the refinement of human virtues through the engagement with aesthetic artifacts. Herder's preoccupation with accent, dialectal features, and sound sensitivity is a major aspect of this contention.

On the Spirit of Hebrew Poetry and on Poetry in General

Herder's *On the Spirit of Hebrew Poetry* reiterates Lowth's search for the text's original meanings through the reader's identification with its author. Like Lowth, Herder also extols the supreme aesthetic value of Hebrew poetry. With Johann David Michaelis's philological inquiry into Hebrew, on the one hand, and Lowth's praising of the historical aesthetic achievements of the language, on the other hand, Herder is pushed to adapt a different approach to Hebrew: one that discerns its merits in the specific context of the culture in which it emerged. This approach avoids the assessment of Hebrew poetry on a universal scale of aesthetic principles. Therefore, it also objects to the view of this poetry as a historically significant contribution to the progress of poetic creation. In the very first line of his essay, Herder acknowledges the need to distinguish his position from Lowth's.[34] The key differences between the two authors mark a path that leads from the commentary on the Hebrew Bible to the shape of literary interpretation under the influence of Herder's particular interventions in the field of aesthetics.

On the Spirit of Hebrew Poetry discusses the merits of Hebrew poetry in the form of a dialogue between Alciphron, a young and skeptical scholar passionate about gaining knowledge of ancient peoples, and Eutyphron, an older scholar who is convinced of the superior merits of Hebrew poetry. Eutyphron believes this excellence should grant the language a supreme status as a cultural asset. In Herder's text, the so-called faults of Hebrew become evidence of its literary qualities. At the beginning of the essay, Eutyphron alerts his interlocutor that the ostensible deficiencies of Hebrew in fact illustrate its supreme aesthetic nature. He thus responds to several major problems that Alciphron finds in the language. The latter complains that it has too few adjectives and prepositions; its tense system is irregular, unclear, and disorienting; it lacks adjectives; and it often derives formulations from different roots, leading to artificial collocations and far-fetched images. Additionally, he criticizes its parallelism—the setting of sentences or clauses in conjunction with one another in such a way that presents them as equivalent—which he finds dull. With respect to this laconic repetition, the language's tone appears monotonous, and its sound unpleasant. Alciphron saves to the very end of his attack a most infamous attribute of Hebrew: its vowels were added to the language very late in its history. As a consequence, Hebrew's pronunciation remains unknown, and the language appears like a "dead hieroglyph."[35]

Eutyphron's answer to Alciphron rehearses some of the arguments that Herder presented in *The Oldest Document of Humankind* (1774). He begins with praise for the dominant presence of verbs in Hebrew, explaining that its relatively small number of adjectives, nouns and prepositions works to highlights the verbs in the language. Here, Herder is applying relativism in structural analysis, but instead of comparing languages, he is comparing parts of speech. In Hebrew, nouns derive from verbs, making the language especially animated. The poetic nature of Hebrew rests on the inherent vividness of its verbs, which, as opposed to the more static nature of nouns, embed in the language a feeling of liveliness and constant action.

Herder's characterization of Hebrew through the anthropological detection of its origins presents the language as a communicative medium. In striking opposition to Lowth's claim that the poets who composed the text were considered divine ("the ambassadors of heaven") at the time of writing, Herder casts them as humans addressing their worldly circumstances.[36] For him, the Bible is divine not because its poetry, in its materialization through perfect transmission, is the word of God but because its divine message takes the form of a flawed human medium.[37] Its divine aspect is the ability to transform a godly message into an utterly human form. Herder's evident philological erudition makes his analyses cogent, but since de facto they do not require a similar knowledge of the language from readers, who are able to follow Herder's conclusions without such knowledge, Herder's praise of the language turns Hebrew into a new trope that is beyond the literal understanding of the word.

This means, further, that it is the human medium that reveals Hebrew's merits and not the other way around—that the objective beauty of the Hebrew reveals the Bible's spiritual essence. Herder describes the particularity of the language's medium in the context of eighteenth-century debates on aesthetics. Biblical Hebrew features an abundant use of verbs, which, according to Herder, grants the language unique vividness. The more verbs a language has, the livelier it is:

> [Eutyphron.] So the language, that abounds in verbs, which present a vivid expression, and picture of their object, is a poetical language.

The more too it has the power of forming its nouns into verbs, the more poetical it is. The noun always exhibits objects only as lifeless things, the verb gives them action, and this awakens feeling, for it is itself as it were animated with a living spirit. Recollect what Lessing has said of Homer, that in him all is bustle, motion, action, and that in this life, the influence, the very essence of all poetry consists. Now with the Hebrew the verb is almost the whole of the language. In other words every thing lives and acts.[38]

To acknowledge what is at stake in this characterization of Hebrew poetry, one needs to consider Herder's broader engagement with and contribution to aesthetic theory. For Herder, the inference of nouns from stems, a known feature of Hebrew, establishes Hebrew as a language that is built upon verbs (in Hebrew grammar, the primary function of stems is the construction of verbs). Hebrew thus comes across as a language in constant motion. Here enters the picture another contemporary thinker from whom Herder now assiduously tries to distinguish himself: Lessing.

The elegance and natural energy that Herder attributes to Hebrew in its function as a communicative medium situates the language as an important trope in view of eighteenth-century discussions about language and art. Herder's dialogue namely reiterates the discussion about the dynamic and static features that are to be found in art and poetry, which was captured in the famous correspondence between Johann Joachim Winckelmann and Lessing.[39] Lessing's essay *Laocoön: An essay upon the limits of painting and poetry* (*Laokoon oder Über die Grenzen der Malerei und Poesie*, 1766), which seeks to establish fine art and poetry as incomparable, reacts to Winckelmann's classicist approach to art, which considers art's connection to reality as mimetic and direct. Lessing's *Laocoön* rejects Winckelmann's assertion that pain was not represented through sculpture since it would not suit the noble, unbreakable Greek spirit. In contrast, Lessing offers a theory that distinguishes the differing features of media. He argues that the expression of human emotions depends on the respective properties of the art and, particularly, on the differences between fine arts and poetry. Whereas poetry unfolds a narrative in time, sculpture does that in space.

To Herder, poetry strives to escape its spatial limits. To show this, he presents a critical account of Lessing's *Laocoön* in his *Critical Forests* (*Kritische Wälder*, 1769). Lessing maintains that poetry and fine art cannot be compared since the former depends on time and the latter on space. Herder's criticism of Lessing leads to his original contribution to aesthetic theory. First, Herder considers the question of whether art necessarily exists as a means for imitation. The statue of Laocoön cannot capture pain in an aesthetic manner, since the expression of pain would make the sculpture forever ugly, and because of this, there appears to be a fault in art.[40] If art cannot represent, the whole discussion is meaningless. Instead, Herder suggests looking at the way our minds operate when observing works of art.

But what about arts other than sculpture and poetry? Herder establishes that there are "energetic" arts in which the work unfolds a narrative and works in which everything appears at once. Herder distinguishes energetic arts, such as music, poetry, and dance, from sculpture and painting, but he still separates poetry off into a further category. What is it that differentiates poetry from the other energetic arts and primarily from music, the art that Herder brings as a counterexample to Lessing's binary distinction between poetry and fine art? Poetry is more than sounds, Herder claims, because it transforms sounds into words and creates segments of meaning whose intricacy derives from the arbitrary nature of this transformation. Poetry is therefore not just about the senses, whereas in music, sound is the most central aspect of a work. This difference gives the poet more possibilities than the artist. In the face of manifold options, poetry obtains meaning not through time or space but through what Herder calls "force," a characteristic that combines the synchronicity of sound, temporality, and movement.[41]

According to Herder, Lessing shows that the essence of poetry is its "motion," which induces the feeling of vividness. This view guides the apologia on Hebrew, which relies not on the denial that the language is poor but rather on the grasp of its inherent characteristics in relation to one another. Since verbs are the most essential part of Hebrew, as Alciphron is happy to admit, Hebrew is shown to be especially suitable for the creation of poetry (on his part, Eutyphron concedes that Hebrew is not suitable for the abstract thinker or the philosopher). A correct examination of the language requires a comparison of its inner properties (e.g., the relatively large number of verbs and the derivation of nouns from verbs). The logic of such an assessment changes the perspective from what Hebrew lacks to what it contains, and it leads to the identification of Hebrew's "symbolic value": its dynamic or poetic essence.

That said, Eutyphron's first move in defense echoes Herder's predominantly anthropological perspective on aesthetics, which he elaborates in essays, translations, and correspondence. This principle, which Herder lays out most extensively in *Critical Forests*, determines that one culture's beautiful artifact cannot be compared to another's. Cultural artifacts should be evaluated only in the context of the specific time and culture that produced them. In *Critical Forests*, Herder situates the relativist principle in a scientifically based description of the physiological development of humankind. Poetry is the most emblematic expression of this principle. Herder claims that cultural artifacts are aimed at addressing the sensual needs and drives of the people who produce them. Thus, whereas ancient peoples were sensitive to tones (*Töne*), humankind has lost this ability and can only respond to sounds (*Laute*). Herder insists on the power of a synchronic cultural inquiry over a diachronic one.

Taking an opposing approach to the idealization of a specific moment in the history of aesthetics, Herder claims that aesthetic beauty cannot be compared between cultures, since every culture has its own aesthetic ideals. The text reconciles two agonistic arguments on cultures. It describes Hebrew as one of many cultures that fulfills its singular role in the history of humankind. At the same time, the uniqueness of the sounds of Hebrew recalls the primordial and special vividness of its poetry, which makes it emblematic of all poetry. *On the Spirit of Hebrew Poetry* idealizes Hebrew as it once again positions the language as the originating source of human cultural efforts and, specifically, poetics.

Herder's *Volksgeist* theory and the relativism it encompasses thus yields an important divergence from Lowth. For Herder, empathy for the ancient authors is not the outcome of self-identification with their legacy. One should feel empathy for the culture even as it is entirely separate from one's present circumstances. Yet, at the same time, one should acknowledge that, in its relativity, Hebrew (as any other culture) occupies a unique place of beauty in the world's system of aesthetic artifacts, language, and sensibility. Because of its primordial nature, Hebrew is the emblem of this empathetic reasoning. And yet, Herder's perspective does leave space for a comparative and diachronic account of beauty insofar as the representation of the *Volksgeist* is a variable proof of aesthetic merit. Herder offers the Old Testament, Homer, Ossian, Klopstock, and also Shakespeare as examples of supreme texts, because they all responded well to the needs of their day. *On the Spirit of Hebrew Poetry* explains that Hebrew responded especially well to an extreme sensual stage of humanity—a stage that has since been lost.

Hebrew therefore exemplifies a tension present throughout Herder's work: the conflict between universalistic ideals and a relativist understanding of different cultures and historical periods. Aiming to understand the context in which Hebrew emerged should yield an understanding of the ancient perception and primordial origins of poetry. Herder shows that the Enlightenment's standardization of taste in accordance with national collectivity—as evidenced by Lessing's seminal theory of media difference—enriches and is enriched by literary hermeneutics and the political order that this paradigm construes. Universalistic theories of cultural interpretation accelerated certain political transformations to which those theories were responding. The new globalization of the Bible reflects the new standardization of a cultural and temporal conception of national languages and literatures. This standardization stands in a reciprocal relationship with the emergence of a new political sphere. The seminal role—and conflicted position—of the Hebrew Bible in the globalization of the Scriptures shows that the new theories of medium and of language, and the new relativist consideration of cultures, were charged with the attempt to define one universal asset that would function as the pillar of the system of world nations.

Herder's inquiry into the sublime nature of Hebrew poetry presents the distinction between Hebrews and Jews as decisive. The supreme characteristics of ancient Hebrew stand alongside the acknowledgment that the language has been corrupted and degraded and has regressed. Because Hebrew has not been enriched through time, as opposed to languages spoken by other *Morgenländer*, such as Arabic, a certain suspicion toward the Jews arises. To Alciphron's note that the language is not a dead one, since the rabbis have continued speaking it, Eutyphron responds that they have not made it into an aesthetic language. Although his defense of Hebrew involves proving that its faults in fact reveal its strengths, Eutyphron's apologia does not extend to the ritual usage of Hebrew that marks its continual transmission. Furthermore, it is exactly Eutyphron's line of argument that in effect necessitates the critique of the Jews. Eutyphron presents Hebrew as a dead language that is alive only in its nature. The greatness of Hebrew, in Herder's apologia, rests then on readers' ability to bridge the gaps of time—an effort stimulated by their enchantment with the language's natural vividness. The harming influence of time, the fact that the language lacks natural development, and the insufficient knowledge of Hebrew in the present all prove its remarkable ability to stay in circulation.

Despite the important role that Hebrew plays in Herder's aesthetic theory, he concerns himself with only a brief phase of the language's history, which he defines as the golden age of Hebrew poetry. This marking off of Hebrew as a dead language grows out of Herder's perception of modern-day Jews, who are responsible for the linguistic hybridism that disrupts the correlation of language to national culture.[42] Their daily use of the vernacular influences their liturgical usage of Hebrew, thereby corrupting the ancient language and weakening Hebrew's ancient national grounding.[43]

A certain quality of Hebrew allows it to transcend the damages of time: its genuine reflection of the language of nature, to which the sounds of the language hold direct, mimetic connections. In view of this linguistic feature, Alciphron wishes that the Hebrew nation had composed its writings in such a way that they had made transparent this nation's unique contribution to humankind. The failure to do so shows this people's faith, which is intertwined with their national spirit, to be exclusive of others:

> The belief in providence, which you lately unfolded to me out of the writings and from the history of the Hebrew nation, and which you extolled as a flower full of beauty and interest for the human race, has no adversary in me. I could wish rather, that the writings of this people had in fact unfolded in a form unmixed with national peculiarities and interesting to the whole human race. But has it been done in this form? Was not this belief among them a mere national faith, so narrow and exclusive, that it might rather be considered offensive and hostile, than friendly to the race.[44]

Eutyphron's response restates the aesthetic value of the Hebrew language to be this people's contribution to humankind. Despite its emergence having occurred in a specific cultural and historical setting, Hebrew contributes to humanity because it resonates with humanity's primordial roots. The language's intimate connection with nature, which Herder pointed out in his *Treatise on the Origin of Language,* has survived and is still echoing in the biblical language, despite the harmful presence of the Jews.[45]

Commenting on this presence, *On the Spirit of Hebrew Poetry* considers more specific complaints against the rabbinic transformation of the language. For example, to Alciphron's comment that the rabbis have continued speaking the language, his older companion responds by refuting the view that Judaism preserves the beauty of Hebrew, insisting that the rabbis speaking the language have only contributed to its corruption, since their speech has produced "nothing valuable" (literally, "no pearls"): "Of nothing valuable however, nor in accordance with the genius of its original structure. When they wrote, the nation was sunk in poverty, and dispersed over the world. Most of them conformed their mode of expression to the genius of the languages, that were spoken around them, and thus produced a sorry medley, not to be thought of in a discussion like this. We are speaking of the Hebrew, when it was the living language of Canaan, and of that too only during the period of its greatest beauty and purity."[46] The Hebrew that Herder wants to return to is therefore a dead language. The effort of putting oneself in the shoes of the Bible's authors—an effort that became the model of the hermeneutic tradition—is always a restorative one. For the hermeneutic enterprise that emerges from Herder's philosophical anthropology to be achievable, a rupture has to be made noticeable between ancient Hebrew and its continual circulation in the Jewish tradition. The legacy of identifying with the Hebrew poets shaped modern interpretation by way of the recurring correspondences between how we read literature and how the Bible should be read in its universalized status as a cultural asset. As hermeneutics prompted the emergence of new aesthetic ideals, these same ideals were in turn reforming biblical hermeneutics and societal positions toward the Bible. Insofar as it relied on the aesthetic features of the Bible, the beginning of the hermeneutic tradition also relied on the distancing of the reader from the Jews in order to reconnect with the Hebrews.

The intensive preoccupation with Hebrew in the Sturm und Drang circle took place under the auspices of the relation that the movement drew between spiritual stimulation and the experience that art generates within its observers. The emergence of a national culture was ingrained not only in the contents that literature wished to utter but also in the genres that this literature accommodated or gave rise to. The Jewish "shepherd songs" that Goethe mentions as the trademark of Hebrew poetry were taken by other authors as a major influence on genre and style. Important in this regard was the genre of the ode, which during the period manifested patriotism, most prominently in Klopstock's poetry.[47] The consideration of Hebrew poetry as dictating a certain aesthetic model, which Klopstock emulates in his poetry, resounds in many of his odes. These often present a poetic speaker who expounds a prophetic monologue as would one of the Hebrew prophets. The theme of prophetic speech and its use in pronouncing German nationalism is a major example of biblical adaptation. It is a motif that becomes a genre and a speech-act that is presented as exceedingly individualistic and that strives toward collective affect. As we have seen in the previous chapter, Klopstock's works that build on theological vocabulary often revisit biblical stories and detail new incidents in the life of the world's first inhabitants. Such texts "interpret" the Hebrew Bible by filling in gaps in the text with the psychological motives and dilemmas of the patriarchs. With adaptation and emulation of the Hebrew Bible, textual forms—such as a self-aggrandizing speaker's monologue that mimics prophetic speech—are detached from the Bible insofar as they are no longer perceived as objects of worship in the concrete sense of the word.

A two-Bible model is celebrated in the framework of this attempt: the Bible as is conceptualized as both a superior object and as a variable source. This move shapes the power of the Bible as a cultural object that is familiar to the general reader and continually constitutes its status as such. Yet ironically, the radical transformation of the Bible repudiates its status as an unchanging source. Revisions, alterations, and dialectics make the Bible an object that is changeable. What is more, the ability of readers to recognize biblical motifs (such as the passionate belligerence of the Psalms) and biblical forms (such as long prophetic monologues) make the Bible's adaptability its unique virtue. The Bible's Pietistic alterations mark it as an object whose so-called singular merit stems, ironically, from its versatility and malleability. The process of universalizing the Bible presumes not only its inherent merits but also the ability of every reader in the Enlightenment's emerging reading culture to recognize biblical forms and motifs despite their alteration. Thus, in the same motion with which the Pietists undertook the mission of "speaking" the Bible in their individual voices, they also assumed a collective that could comprehend the text as a universalized cultural asset as was the ability to recognize references to the Bible in a literary text.

As poets were establishing the new aesthetic paradigm in which sensitivity to another person's emotions became part of a collective practice, nationalism and the celebration of the Hebrew Bible went hand in hand. New ways of comprehending the Bible idealized the ancients at the same time as they dictated the correct emulation of them. And by facilitating the state's address to a public of biblical readers, these new interpretations of the Old Testament also shaped an ideal view of the modern state. As the basis for a better command of the New Testament, the Old Testament was taken to be an asset precisely because it created an obstacle of mediation that elicited a new understanding of script and the role of poetry.

Hermeneutics of the Senses

These new aesthetic approaches to the Bible emerged from a circle of authors across various movements and pursuits. Klopstock, Lessing, and Herder engaged with poetry both in the form of original essays on art and its interpretation and in their own poetic compositions. Critics have claimed that these authors' consideration of texts through aesthetic theory led to the transition toward hermeneutic thinking. David Wellbery's *Lessing's Laocoon* argues that eighteenth-century discourses on art elicited a new semiotic awareness that became essential to a hermeneutic view of art and of the world. He contends that the focus on successiveness in representations—the gradualness that creates the beauty in a work of art—results in a new perception of the aesthetic effect as ontological rather than psychological.[48] He draws this conclusion from the lively debates surrounding Lessing's essay, especially those involving Georg Friedrich Meier, Herder, and Mendelssohn. These polemics demonstrate the ontological shift toward semiotics, an understanding of objects as signs that bear socially contingent meanings. Art became central to a model that saw interpretation as a new mode of deciphering the world.

In a more recent book, Lothar van Laak offers a different view of eighteenth-century approaches to aesthetics, in particular how the Sturm und Drang movement prepared the ground for hermeneutics.[49] He identifies the foundation of modern hermeneutics in a new appreciation of the sensual. The movement emphasized the sensual effects of texts, especially those that are provoked through oral transmission.[50] The irony, or the counterintuitive aspect of this preference, lies in the eighteenth century's esteem for rhythm and musicality, *Bildlichkeit*.[51] This preference for *lebendige Schrift* (lively or dynamic script) did not lead to a focus on readers' individual emotions but rather to a fresh critical approach from which to view texts. Critics conceived of the literary text as an artifact to be transmitted orally, and in this process, they brought to the fore the perception of the text as plot.[52] Herder advanced a performative and historically grounded concept of *Bildlichkeit*, formulating poetics as communicative utterances rooted in a certain historical moment. As it unfolds in the reading process, poetry achieves unique status as a cultural artifact that both embodies ontological essence and contains traces of cultural specificity.

This hermeneutics of sensibility was claimed to have reached its climax in Herder's anthropological perception of aesthetics. Some scholars place this perception and its implications within a disciplinary shift and see Herder as an initiator of disciplinary classification. Robert Leventhal detects the emergence of modern hermeneutics in a disciplinary shift expressed predominantly in the period's move toward semiotics: "Herder's writing . . . ruptures literary-aesthetic discourse by subverting precisely the notions essential to the 'aesthetic' paradigm; subjectivity, the totality of the text, the primacy of spirit (Geist), the systematicity of argumentation."[53] Leventhal sees Lessing, Herder, and the early Romantics sharing with Martin Heidegger a suspicion against "a theory of interpretation grounded in a transparent, self-identical subject, or any substrate that might provide an ahistorical ground for understanding." This leads him to argue that hermeneutics emerged between 1770 and 1800 as a self-referential interpretive turn that relied not on a privileged status of comprehension but on the awareness that comprehension and incomprehension are interdependent: "As a form of text itself, hermeneutics is subject to the same historical exegesis that it itself allows us to perform on texts that are not readily translatable into our own idiom."[54]

Rüdiger Campe's *Affekt und Ausdruck* takes a yet different approach to the rise of hermeneutics. Through an extensive consideration of transformations in physiology, psychology, and medicine, Campe describes an eighteenth-century shift from a "rhetorical" culture to a "hermeneutic" one.[55] He depicts the emergence of modern interpretation as gradual and not the result of contingent interventions by major works of poetics and criticism. For him, the late eighteenth century signals the final stages of a shift toward the understanding of the author of a literary text as a poet rather than as a theoretician.

The literature on the history of literary interpretation agrees that the publication of Lessing's *Laocoön* proved consequential to the birth of new approaches to poetry and the arts in the German-speaking territories. To Wellbery, *Laocoön* is the high point of the period's interest in semiology, the first step of which had been the classification of different kinds of signs according to a hierarchy of ontological status. Wellbery distinguishes between representation-semiotics and expression-hermeneutics, the latter of which he identifies with Herder and early Romanticism.[56]

What is common to both Lessing and Herder, however, is the strong emphasis they both put on affect when describing encounters with art. In his *Critical Forests*, Herder's most comprehensive contribution to the field of aesthetics, he engages the Winckelmann-Lessing debate, drawing from it the tenets of his own interpretive endeavor. There, Herder's discussion of Lessing's essay recognizes and consequently advances its cultural importance. Herder assumes that aesthetic experience intensively activates the various faculties of humankind. In his analysis of Greek and other traditions of ancient art, he investigates how human faculties can be examined through the analysis of aesthetic experience both synchronically (how art activates various physical and psychological mechanisms that are inherent to the human aesthetic experience) and diachronically (how observing art from different periods reveals not only these mechanisms but also their historical evolution). The premise of the essay thus affirms Ernst Cassirer's claim that Herder viewed aesthetics as key to the founding of a new, anthropological philosophy.[57]

Herder's account sheds light on his invention of the Hebrew sublime. The role of Hebrew aesthetics in mobilizing the new hermeneutic reading of poetry entailed first and foremost the advancement of anthropological consideration of cultures and texts. As we saw in Chapter 1, the Hebrew language served thinkers in establishing philosophical positions at the dawn of German idealism. The encounter with Hebrew was a platform for reconceptualizing affect and reason, and engagement with the Genesis stories demonstrated for readers how to foster a dynamic and personalized engagement with the Bible. As I argue in this chapter, Hebrew provided the basis for a new interpretive endeavor (examining cultural artifacts as discrete and autonomous systems), which in turn involved scrutiny of the conceptual origins of poetic creation in the language. But the focus on the affect created by the Hebrew sublime involved two other major assumptions of the new hermeneutics: that the analysis of texts should discern the gradual process in which they unfold representations and that all readers are capable of situating a text in its historical context in order to perform such analysis. Hebrew—the biblical language rendered as ideal for the writing of poetry—became a new model for the reading of poetry of all kinds. The religious meanings that infused biblical reading during that time bled into the discourse on how affect should be made comprehensible and how everyone should be capable of undertaking this endeavor.

The transition from a focus on rhetoric to a focus on the ability of art to unfold representations depended on new ways of perceiving signs and texts. But in order to trace the social transformations in which this transition was embedded, we need to look at the notion of the reader that these shifts formed. In his review of the emergence of literary criticism in eighteenth-century Germany, Klaus Berghahn applies Kant's notion of critique (as developed in his 1781 *Critique of Pure Reason*) to the period's new conception of readership.[58] He cites Reinhart Koselleck's *Critique and Crisis* (1959), which argues for the neutralizing effect of readership in light of the consignment of intellectual pursuit to the private, nonpolitical realm.[59] For Koselleck, critique is the ability of the masses to scrupulously observe a text as well as the circumstances of its writing in order to solicit from it meanings that are not immediately apparent. Regardless of whether they describe the aesthetic shift in the interpretation of texts as continuous or discontinuous, theorists of the Enlightenment agree that it is the contextual ground from which modern hermeneutics emerged. Among them, several make a certain counterintuitive assumption: that the enhanced presence of literary affect in eighteenth-century Germany signaled a new stage in the status of the sign, a stage that entailed the transformation of rhetoric into a new critique that can be pursued by all (and not the dispelling of rhetoric by means of establishing an immediate emotional connection with texts). This new stage resulted from the all-encompassing presence of affect in the new model of the self. Affect did not eliminate distance from the text. Quite the opposite, it prompted a new distance from the text by way of the novel observation that literary devices produce emotion. The new textual analysis both sublimated and relied upon rhetorical practices. As I will discuss in more detail toward the end of this chapter, the idea that texts provoke emotions through critical analysis rather than through revelation carries with it political implications.

In *On the Spirit of Hebrew Poetry*, Herder establishes that the Hebrew language is unique in its unfolding of a representation and that this unfolding evokes a supreme aesthetic feeling in readers. This presentation of Hebrew eliminates the Bible's status as a ritual object precisely because of the sublime and spiritual nature attached to the Bible's aesthetic merits, which are taken to be accessible to all readers. The wave of biblical translations in the late eighteenth century vividly demonstrates how the Bible was adapted for individual and group identities and how its prevalence now drew on its status as an asset of every citizen of the modern state.[60] It is crucial to note that Herder's essay assumes an audience that includes no readers of Hebrew—that is, the concrete language, with its unique alphabet, vocabulary, and grammar. His project presumes no philological or religious training on the part of his readers. In the prologue to *On the Spirit of Hebrew Poetry*, he writes, "With mere learning and the characters of a foreign language, I could not consent to burden my pages. To the unlearned they are of no use, and the scholar who has the original language and the ancient translations at hand, can easily accommodate himself with them."[61]

Since Hebrew is a language in which verbs are the most prominent parts of speech, it is a language uniquely suited to develop a plot. Hebrew poetry, a unique *national* poetry, nevertheless embodies the aesthetic ideal of poetry *in general*, and it pushes the reader to acknowledge the power of the poetic artifact. That unique power arises from its musicality (sensual trait) and semantic flexibility (cognitive merit).

The Song of Songs and the Aesthetics of Sensuality

By the 1770s, the revolution in Germany's aesthetic discourse was already evident in commentary on the senses' role in creating the modern citizen. The period's religious trend had been fundamental in fashioning the new members of the emerging national community as autonomous individuals. Representative of these shifts, the period featured a distinctive phenomenon of engagement with the Scriptures: a wave of translations of the Song of Songs. The refashioning of the Song in these translations drew upon the notion of a human affective apparatus as central to the engagement with texts.[62] These translations also showed the specific, if varying, ways in which key authors portrayed the role of the Hebrew sublime in the Protestant state. The translations amalgamated these new poetic and political stances based on the cultural influence of Pietism.[63] Pietism relied on representations of physicality, employed in striking ways, to emphasize the human ability to follow the unfolding of an aesthetic work. The Song's sensual nature made it an especially suitable text for this emphasis.

Herder's engagement with the Song (he published two translations, in 1776 and 1778) reveals his attention to the text's literary devices and aesthetic rapport with readers. John Baildam describes Herder's translations of the Song of Songs as a prevalent and inherent part of both his theological and literary reflections: "In an age which considered Hebrew poetry barbaric . . . Herder was unique with his plea that poetry in general was divine revelation, and that the Hebrew poetry of the Bible was the epitome of all poetry, the pinnacle of which was the Song of Songs."[64] Herder's approach to the Song, Baildam argues, should be understood in the context of his broader view of the Bible: "He saw the Bible as reflecting directly all the experiences of mind and body with which God had endowed mankind. Of these experiences the most important was love, the prime bond between mankind and God, and between human beings. For Herder the sole theme of the Song of Songs was human love between a man and a woman."[65]

Herder's engagement with the Song alludes to Alexander Gottlieb Baumgarten's definition of aesthetics. Baumgarten, whose writings Herder had studied assiduously throughout the 1760s, defines artistic creation as the finest stimulator of the human faculties. To Baumgarten, the soul naturally integrates varied perceptions into a whole. *Felix aestheticus* is one who manages to "think beautifully." Unifying one's perceptions into a perfect whole achieves self-governance and openness to the world. Thus, to Baumgarten, a valuable (or beautiful) representation is one that, with the perfected order that it encompasses, can "provide human beings with that centering of subjectivity that had previously been the function of the transcendent being."[66]

Herder's presentation of the Song as a supreme manifestation of poetry needs to be understood in the context of his reconceptualization of aesthetics and in the larger shift from aesthetics to hermeneutics that he significantly advanced. In Herder's conception, aesthetics can advance the exploration of human cognition by investigating its various functions:

Aesthetics exercises our capacity to grasp reality in all its concrete individuality and complexity. It celebrates the confusion of sensory knowledge, its particularity, vibrancy, and plenitude, precisely those qualities which are necessarily lost in translation from the specific to the general but embodied in exemplary fashion by works of art. Poetry, for example, which for Baumgarten was the paradigmatic form of artistic expression, does not pretend to discover universal laws or principles but lucidly represents individual things, persons, or situations, and the greater the vividness, richness, and inner diversity, the greater the value of the poem.[67]

With this new aesthetic effort in mind, the attractiveness of the Song for Herder and for other translators—who were in dialogue with one another— was due not only to its sensuousness but also to the ways in which it discloses human sensation. The Song's imagery unfolds in a gradual manner, often through scenes that name each sense one after another and arouse them in this process. Another stimulating device is the dialogic form of the text, which exhibits what Herder finds to be an inherent characteristic Hebrew poetry: a lively narrative or plot.

But Herder's most notable preference in relation to the cultural reception of the Song is his elimination of the allegorical from its interpretation. In Wilhelm Dilthey's overview of the emergence of modern hermeneutics as a restorative effort, he classifies interpretation as the individual ability to reflect but not to make free associations. This move requires disqualifying the eminent religious reading practice of allegory.[68] The intense engagement of Herder and his contemporaries with the Song and especially its human topic, sensual love, is emblematic of the hermeneutic movement as a whole. Interpretation becomes a form of support for the human imagination. The comprehension of the text unfolds like a journey through a particular imaginary world. Beauty, sensuality, and imagination help the reader to occupy the protagonist's position. This secular charm of the sublime, experienced in the unfolding of the text, replaces allegorical, mystical, and other ways of comprehending the text by means of one's own initiative or imagination. This charm takes shape in the way that the Song centralizes the object in the eyes of the observer. These lines from Herder's 1778 translation express this unique characteristic of the Song while adhering to the syntax and literary devices of the original (Song of Songs 1:2–3):

> Er küsse mich
> Mit seines Mundes Küssen:
> Denn deine Lieb' ist lieblicher, denn Wein.
> Wie deiner süssen Salben Duft,
> So ist zerfliessender Balsam
> Dein Name . . . [69]

He kisses me / with the kisses of his mouth / since your flesh is lovelier than wine / Like your sweet ointment-scent, / so is the flowing oil / Your name . . .

In Goethe's and Herder's respective translations of the Song, the strong influence of two salient aesthetic theories can be detected: Baumgarten's *felix aestheticus* and Lessing's theory of media relativism. Herder's ability to explore both concepts within the Song's fertile, synesthetic images explains his fascination with the text. Note, for example, Herder's adherence to alliteration in the above excerpt from his translation (*Lieb'* and *lieblicher, süssen* and *Salben*). Keeping this feature of the original text preserves its enhanced sensuality, both in content and form, as the musicality and semantics combine to spark the audience's imagination. The excerpt from Herder's translation demonstrates his overall adherence to the Hebrew sentence structure, which comes across as foreign in the German. His choice to emulate the original sentence structure preserves the flow of the original plot, which is reflected semantically in the text's many references to the flow of fluids.

The opening of the Song expresses its synesthetic quality, evoking taste, touch, and smell simultaneously in such a way as to blur the distinction among them. The kisses of the mouth are compared to wine by means of their common feature: their sweetness. Yet as the paragraph continues, the imagery of the sweet flowing fluids becomes the center of the scene. The first line uses the wine metaphor to allude to—and, at the same time, to conceal—the bodily fluid that is exchanged during the kiss. But as the picture unfolds, a common feature of the Song emerges: the flexible replacement of metaphors with the objects they signify.[70] The point of the Song is thus not to merely present erotica but to provoke within readers the experience of desire through allusive and evocative poetic description.

In addition to being favored as Greek-like pastoral poetry in the Hebrew Bible, the Song of Songs also typified the national fascination with the Old Testament. During a twenty-year period, the figures who translated the Song included the young Goethe, Hamann, Herder, Friedrich Heinrich Jacobi, Mendelssohn, Lessing, and other prominent late eighteenth-century authors.[71] The Song's themes and style could be adapted to fit more traditional ideals of beauty. It deals with erotic and scrupulous descriptions of bodies, and it allots much space to nature. The period's fascination with the poem can thus be attributed to its ability to bridge two models of beauty, the Greek and the Hebrew, while moving from the former to the latter. The Song's identification as the new aesthetic sublime typified the appropriation of themes, genres, and forms from the Old Testament in the emerging sentimental style of early Romanticism.

Goethe's translation of the Song (1775) is part of his continued polemical engagement with Herder. Involving himself with the holy text of the Bible creates a conflict with his mentor's more traditional aspirations regarding the Scriptures. Goethe is famous for preferring Homer's writings to the "pagan" stories of the Bible.[72] Spinoza's influence on Goethe, and Goethe's subsequent statements on adhering to the religion of nature, also advanced his opposition to the practice of monotheistic faith. But more important for my discussion, Goethe's turn to the Song is evidence of his references to the Old Testament as a text that, if taught didactically, can enrich human self-reflection and national unity.[73] He undertook the task of translating the Song not simply to share it with the public but because it was a supreme manifestation of beauty and he wanted personally to recreate it in the German language. His translation of the Song is an experiment in intentionality that enhances the originality and scope of his own poetic achievement.

Like his older interlocutor, Goethe was not aiming for literal comprehension of the Old Testament. In fact, in disclosing that he lacked knowledge of Hebrew, he proposed engagement with biblical language despite partial understanding. Such partial comprehension required that Goethe frequently turn to Luther's translation and to the Vulgate, transmitting what had already been transmitted: "Like many good translators . . . to transmit transmissions further" (Wie gar mancher gute Übersetzer . . . aus Übertragungen weiter übertragen).[74] Goethe admired Luther's translation of the Bible for how beautifully it captured the Bible in his mother tongue. According to Kittler, the ability to transmit the Bible through coherent style and form was, for Goethe, a search for the perfect signifier.[75] Goethe's interest in translation as a medium overtook his belief that signifiers correspond to singular content. Turning to the Song, with its stimulating sensual and synesthetic effect, gave Goethe the opportunity to illustrate what he believed translation fundamentally to be about.

Goethe's translation of the Song is therefore not a transmission from Hebrew into German as much as it is a transmission of the old translations into a new one. While the former practice transmits an object between two languages, the latter extends the act of translation. This endeavor both references and performs the continual medial presence of translation in the reading of the Bible. Because he was less concerned than Herder with following the original, Goethe eliminated much of the alliteration that had appeared in previous translations and stayed closer to the German sentence structure:

Küss er mich den Kuss seines Mundes!
Trefflicher ist deine Liebe denn Wein.
Welch ein süser Geruch deine Salbe,
ausgegossne Salb ist dein Nahme . . . [76]

He kisses me with the kisses of his mouth / your love is more splendid than wine / what a sweet smell your ointment has / your name is flowing oil . . .

Goethe combined a translation from Hebrew into German with a "translation" from German into German. In doing so, he echoed Luther's earlier project to "Germanize" (Verdeutschung) Hebrew in his influential vernacular translation of the Bible.

The Song of Songs sparked the interest of both Herder and Goethe through its poetic qualities and its manner of expressing the passions. The ostensibly single voice of the Hebrew culture, which emerges from the Bible as the voice of tradition, became a sort of muse to a new German culture.[77] Both men solicited from the Song a way to reflect and evoke the human passions in order to transcend temporal and cultural distance, thereby adopting the Hebrews' national voice. They read the Song as an invitation to playfully and enthusiastically adapt the Hebrew passions. As discussed above, the Hebrew sublime both reflected and advanced Herder's contributions to aesthetics, and its imagined orality came to represent a decisive transition from aesthetics to hermeneutics. Lyric poetry that emulates the unique musicality of the Hebrew Bible was a new idea in German literary culture. Reading Hebrew became a cultural praxis, the idealized nature of which demanded that translation be rethought. In regard to orality as the source of Hebrew poetry's beauty, Wellbery has argued that "Herder is historically such a decisive and influential critic not because of the accuracy of his observations and judgments, but because he formulated a *new imaginary of language and literature*. . . . Herder imagines the collectivity of oral culture as a single individual that, in the inwardness of its audition, hears its own voice, the originary song of its language."[78] The translation of the Song was a platform for competing attempts to animate a new, unique national culture manifested in the German language, and Herder's translation exemplified a major component of his aesthetic vision: the eminence of orality as the pillar of collectivity.

The Hebrew Sublime and the Lyric "I"

In his *Formations of the Secular*, Talal Asad reflects on the eighteenth century's emerging discussion of the Hebrew Bible as an aesthetic artifact. He analyzes the period's sweeping admiration for Hebrew poetry as a major step in the advancement of exegetical reading techniques as universal pillars of modern textual interpretation: "Not only was it conceded that prophets and apostles were not superhuman, they were even credited with an awareness of their personal inadequacy as channels of revelation. In the romantic conception of the poet, the tension between authentic inspiration and human weakness allowed for moments of subjective illusion—and thus accounted for evidence of exaggeration and insufficiency. . . . *What mattered was not the authenticity of facts about the past but the power of the spiritual idea they sought to convey as gifted humans*."[79] In Romantic notions of authorship and readership, human vulnerability was idealized. Insofar as godly attributes such as the ability to create and interpret were manifested in the process of reading and writing literature, theology was not rejected but subsumed into a new set of concepts. Gifted humans, according to Asad, no longer had to experience divine revelation. Instead, the Hebrew sublime promoted a view of inspiration as a neutral aesthetic merit. The Hebrew sublime played a prominent role in establishing the universal stature of the Bible, but the dependence of the aesthetic merits of Hebrew also entailed a negotiation with the Jewish faith. This dilemma shows the Hebrew sublime as fundamental to the universalization of the Bible through the mutual dependence of Pietism and patriotism. As the Bible lost its ritual standing and became an abstraction, every citizen could take up ardent faith and enthusiastic nationalism as the morality that it now embodied.

Equivalent claims can be found in scholarship on the nationalist character of early Romanticism in the German-speaking world. In his seminal study of Goethe's lyric poetry, Wellbery has claimed that the young Goethe's poetry created a new literary and idyllic model for lyric poetry, a transformation that happened within what Wellbery named "the lyric phantasm."[80] Wellbery thus argues that the eminent role of divination in hermeneutic theory is a main catalyst of that effect of Goethe's early lyric: "*The authentic utterances of the lyric call forth a hermeneutic identification* such as we find developed in Romantic hermeneutic theory from Herder to Schleiermacher, the inventor and canonizer, respectively, of the concept of divination in its hermeneutic sense. Thus, the lyric appropriation of the idyll evidenced in the juxtaposed texts engenders an entirely new form of cultural communication. Textual processing unfolds no longer as the playing of a social game, but rather as the reactualization by the reader of a subjective mode of being articulated in the text."[81] Hermeneutic theory has changed the position of readers of lyric poetry, providing them with a new model of textual identification: the lyric "I." This shift illustrates the radical changes that the paradigm of literary hermeneutics brought about in Enlightenment reading culture. For Wellbery, Goethe's case illustrates how this new reading method, with its religious origins, was establishing what lyric poetry was supposed to be about. In Wellbery's subsequent analysis of Goethe's poems, he considers the emergence of hermeneutics and of the sublime to have shaped such poetic figures as the *ich*, *du*, and the "community of readers," as well as the role of poetry in articulating religious views to the community of readers.[82] Herder's definition of the *Volk* as the basis for mythical production also became a germane presumption for the figurative role of poetry. The invention of the lyric thus embodied both Herder's imaginary and idealized notions of orality and mythical production as practices associated with collectivity and origins. The role of the Hebrew language, and themes and motifs from the Hebrew Bible, cannot be overlooked when tracing the paths by which hermeneutics gave rise to the new, all-encompassing position of the lyric "I" that became a universal subject position.

The prominent influence of Pietism translated into aesthetic and cultural phenomena. The religious movement had a major impact on the seminal values and objectives of the Sturm und Drang movement, namely: the movement's emphasis on texts as a means for evoking intense feeling within readers, the importance it granted to sensuality (*Sinnlichkeit*) and sensitivity (*Empfindlichkeit*) in its aesthetic model, and its establishment of the lyric "I." Hebrew facilitated the adherence to these values as it transitioned into a sublime equally available to all readers, and it embodied these same values in its references to a primordial stage of humankind as a collective entity.

As major Sturm und Drang figures referred to Hebrew as culturally ascendant, the perception of the Hebrew Bible as the mythical origin of humanity became a major part of the shift toward literary hermeneutics. This turn to Hebrew, Ilany has argued, corresponded to the attempt to find an aesthetic model that would represent the ideals behind the poetry of the Sturm und Drang.[83] The identification of the German classicists, such as Winckelmann and the young Friedrich Schiller, with the ancient Greek tradition and of French authors with the Latin tradition presented an opportunity for Hebrew to stand as an alternative ancient tradition. Ilany argues that the eighteenth-century turn to Hebrew signified a new political trend in Germany.

The ability to analyze one's own poetic efforts—whether as reader or author—presumes pondering in one's soul the impressions created in that of another. This technique is the outcome neither of a self-aggrandizing poetic speaker nor of the emphasis on readers' emotions. Rather, this major precondition for hermeneutic thinking builds on the consideration of aesthetics as a means for measurement, prediction, and analysis. Aesthetics deploys and reaffirms the universality of human aptitudes, thereby establishing an affinity between individuals (i.e., between authors and readers). The aesthetic position of the modern hermeneutic movement thus highlights certain generic constructions and motifs as religious because they emerged from the newly universalized interpretive and semantic legacy of Lutheranism.

As I showed at the beginning of this chapter, Goethe's view of Hebrew poetry emerged from an all-encompassing enthusiasm that he would later disavow in his account of the immaturity of a German national poetry that

strived for plain imitation of biblical poetry. Goethe's dismay at the punctuation of the Old Testament continually brings to mind Jewish interference
with the now-lost primordial Hebrew Bible. On a last account, he rejected
Herder's attempt to conceive the national reader as a divine creation and humankind as unified through a shared epos. For Goethe, it was exactly this
struggle to establish a unique national character and a corresponding poetic
model that defined that nation as individual. That individuality emerged in
an indirect manner: through the reflection on the medial nature of aesthetic
creation and through the individual's recognition of the poetic emulation of
primordial orality.

Odysseus's Scar Revisited

Erich Auerbach's magnum opus, *Mimesis*, has been seen as the model for the
field of comparative literature, as well as the humanistic potential behind
the notion of world literature. Auerbach's flight from Nazi Germany to
Istanbul created a mystique around the book that suggested his interpretive
brilliance resulted from unjust sanctions. Because he did not have his library
with him, Auerbach could not use secondary sources or dictionaries, and
his analysis of world literature greatly relied on his memory.[84] The German
Jew produced a work that has been perceived as reaffirming the victory of the
human spirit. Critics have idealized *Mimesis* as embodying the Enlightenment ideals of equality and universal affinity. Its vision of literary analysis
centers on discerning and describing a text's style, literary devices, and linguistic craftiness. It also relies on an extensive, if remote, understanding of a
text's cultural context. The Jewish critic in exile is a model interpreter insofar
as he expertly performs universalistic hermeneutic thinking on literature.

Arguably the most discussed chapter in *Mimesis* is the first, "Odysseus's
Scar." In his comparison of Homer's *Odyssey* to the story of the sacrifice of
Isaac, Auerbach praises the Hebrew Bible for its contribution to Western civilization as a model of succinct and crafty narration. He reveals the conci-
sion of Old Testament narrative by contrasting it with the excessive detail in
Homer's description of Odysseus's scar.[85] Ironically, it was because of his vul-
nerable and disadvantaged position as a Jewish exile that Auerbach successfully produced a Protestant, Pietistic, and Romantic image of hermeneutic
readership.

The sweeping appreciation for *Mimesis* is telling. The book fully embodies
the secular, cultural presumptions of world literature and modern herme-

neutics, transferred to the political circumstances of Nazi Germany. Auerbach proves his command of the humanist and universalist perspective on literature and puts himself in the shoes of many authors as he restores their original thoughts. His admiring reception compensates the Jew for his expulsion from the modern state and the revocation of his equal citizenship. In fact, his precarious position proves the extent to which he commands skill in addressing the Bible as literature. Auerbach's intimate relationship with the Hebrew Bible parallels the relationship between his national, ethic, and religious identity and his idealized position as a critic in crisis. This idealized position culminates in his ostensible rescuing of the Hebrew Bible from falling into a precarious cultural standing.

Hebrew aesthetics is not just an outcome of hermeneutic thinking about literature; it is also, and more importantly, the very ground on which hermeneutic thinkers successfully operate. It is from here that they reaffirm their belonging to a world community of readers and forge empathetic connections to past and present textual artifacts that are assumed to have been partially or fully lost. The early Romantic adaptations of the Old Testament invites the question: what might the field of world literature have become had traditionalist understandings of the Bible and their corresponding perspectives on textual analysis been taken into account as modern hermeneutics took shape?

Chapter 3

Perilous Script

The German Jewish philosopher Moses Mendelssohn was in dialogue with some of the most influential figures of the German republic of letters, including poet and playwright Gotthold Ephraim Lessing and historian Friedrich Nicolai. And yet, despite Mendelssohn's involvement with the German intellectual scene, it remains little known that in 1780, he wrote to the eminent philosopher Johann Gottfried Herder about scriptural reading. The two had corresponded once before. In 1769, after the publication of Mendelssohn's treatise *Phädon, or The Immortality of the Soul* (*Phädon oder über die Unsterblichkeit der Seele*), Herder initiated a correspondence. *Phädon* engages a theme of philosophy since antiquity: the logical justifications for the belief in the soul's endurance after death. Mendelssohn refutes the naturalistic explanation that the soul changes its material status by contending that the soul is an immaterial entity by virtue of being different from the body, which is material. The soul adheres to abstract notions (*Begriffe*) that are separate from the realm of sensibility, and since entities maintain their initial form in nature, the soul would continue in an immaterial form. In their correspondence, Herder accepts that the soul is immortal but opposes *Phädon*'s dualistic perception of the body and the soul. According to Herder's metaphysics, the soul has the power to generate concepts because it is one with the body.

In his 1780 letter, Mendelssohn—attentive to the key role that empathy plays in Herder's interpretation theories—appeals to him to reflect on how his stance on biblical interpretation may provide both standards and tools for courteous interpersonal relationships: "My dear sir, you have shown that you understand Hebrew very well. Perhaps you also have some knowledge of Rabbinic Hebrew. At the least you do not seem to despise it altogether. You own the gift of putting yourself, whenever you wish, in the place and mind-set of your fellow man in order to judge him."[1]

In renewing their correspondence after a long silence, Mendelssohn exchanges the debate on metaphysics for concerns that make clear his belonging to a persecuted minority. Mendelssohn takes up Herder's command of Biblical Hebrew, as demonstrated in his multifaceted references to the Old Testament, as an opportunity to legitimize traditional Jewish scriptural interpretation. He suggests that the Jews' ability to engage with the Bible on their own terms may be an asset to Christian scriptural interpretation, and in so doing, his appeal reiterates traditional apologies for Jewish ritual.

Mendelssohn's reference to Herder's scriptural interpretation in an appeal for interreligious dialogue and courteous sociability is ironic. In presenting Jewish ritual as legitimate, Mendelssohn is working against the anti-Jewish ideology that brought about this very school of interpretation. Herder's extensive writing on Biblical Hebrew, as we have seen, calls for the restoration of the Holy Scriptures because of the harmful influences of its faulty transmission over time. He portrays Biblical Hebrew as a dead language that should be traced back to the time when the nation that produced it was at its zenith. His influential hermeneutics builds on the view that an inherent gap exists between the Hebrew Bible's authors and their contemporary readers because of the Jewish corruption of the text. Mendelssohn's position is greatly at odds with such a view, as he defends the very same tradition that Protestant hermeneutics has attacked. With his apologia on Jewish liturgy, which casts Jews as faithful guardians of the text, Mendelssohn seeks to defend the very tradition that Herder has attacked.

Throughout his oeuvre, Mendelssohn endorses aesthetics as grounded in universal human skills, such as judgment; the preference for mimesis; and the perpetuation and advancement of literacy. As I show in the first three sections of this chapter, these aesthetic positions reinforce his positions on theology. I then turn to read Mendelssohn's seminal political treatise, *Jerusalem, or On Religious Power and Judaism* (*Jerusalem oder über religiöse Macht und Judentum*, 1783), as offering an alternative, universal use of the Hebrew Bible to advance political and social norms. Mendelssohn promotes the political participation of Jews as equal citizens who adhere to Enlightenment values. *Jerusalem* lays bare Jews' affective attachment to the Bible—which Mendelssohn ascribes to prescriptural ritual—and to Judaism's historical legacy. By allocating religious ritual to the private sphere, *Jerusalem* ultimately offers an alternative to the transcendental view of religion as common to all members of the political sphere.

From Mendelssohn's various references to interpretation, this chapter develops a twofold argument. First, I contend that Mendelssohn's views on the Hebrew Bible and his views on aesthetics and hermeneutics are interdependent. Second, I show how this interdependence provokes ambivalence in Mendelssohn regarding the possible grasp of the interpretive community as universal. In that regard, my goal is not to reconcile or explicate peculiar statements that Mendelssohn makes about hermeneutics. Rather, I show that Mendelssohn's ambivalence toward interpretation derives from his multifaceted political motivations, whose contradictions are brought to the fore in his letter to Herder. To a certain degree, the visions of humankind that inform notions of hermeneutic community enchant Mendelssohn because they may promise political advancement and, importantly, religious freedom. Yet, at the same time, the great German Jewish philosopher also wants to defend the insularity of the Jewish community, embodied in the Jewish tradition.

The Social Climate Behind Religious Toleration

If we take Mendelssohn's letter from 1780 as an example of the early reception of Herder's hermeneutics, it indicates a broad view that Herder's interpretation theory promotes interpersonal sympathy. The notion of empathy (*Einfühlung*) is fundamental to Herder's influence on the hermeneutic tradition, particularly in the context of literary studies and philosophy. The term has been taken to represent Herder's perspective on the interpretation of cultural artifacts and to mark his influence on modern historiography. But in fact, Herder never used the term *Einfühlung* as a noun. The attribution of the term to Herder has relied on a passage in *This, Too, a Philosophy of History for the Education of Humanity* (1774) that calls on the reader to "feel yourself into everything!"[2]

Various scholars have associated Herder with turning empathy into a guiding principle for cultural inquiry.[3] These scholars presuppose that texts contain meanings that are obscure at first but that interpretation, by enhancing the relationship between the reader and the author of the target text, can gradually reveal. As a cultural practice, hermeneutics represents the potential for interpretation to improve sociability, because it yields the most interpersonal understanding.

Herder's and Mendelssohn's respective writings on the Hebrew language encapsulate their divergent agendas regarding Jewish-Christian relations. In 1783, both men published influential works that sought to show how the Hebrew Bible was an asset to contemporary Enlightenment society. Herder published *On the Spirit of Hebrew Poetry* (1782–83), his most elaborate account of the biblical language as a supreme aesthetic artifact, and Mendelssohn published *Jerusalem*, which also revisits the Hebrew nation but in a starkly different way. In *Jerusalem*, Mendelssohn reclaims the Hebrew Bible as the record of a time when state law and divine revelation merged into God's revelation on Mount Sinai. He sees the Hebrew Bible first and foremost as a political asset, which distances him from Herder's anthropological examination of world literatures.

Scholars have long debated whether Mendelssohn's contributions to German philosophy represent particularly Jewish positions.[4] Some have argued that Mendelssohn barely integrates traditional Jewish principles and values into the period's political philosophy. But whether or not Mendelssohn's philosophical investigations adhere to traditional Jewish principles, his efforts to be considered an observant Jew are clear. In multiple writings, both in Hebrew and in German, as well as in public polemics around his refusal to convert to Christianity, Mendelssohn describes values that he associates with Judaism and that he considers compatible with major notions of reason in the late Enlightenment.

Mendelssohn sharpened his political positions amid his own insecure status. He and his family could have been expelled from Berlin at any moment, which raised the stakes of his plea to Herder. In a key intervention into the debate around the rights of Jews, *On the Civil Improvement of the Jews* (*Über die bürgerliche Verbesserung der Juden*, 1781), Christian Wilhelm von Dohm makes the suggestion that Jews should take part in society and enjoy equal political rights. Opposing the common view of Jews' inherently corrupt character, Dohm revolutionarily claims that the state authorities are the ones at fault for not integrating the Jews into society. He also argues that Jews can overcome their unproductive character by undertaking such practices as working the land, since their "decadence" is not innate but the outcome of long-standing disregard.[5] In *Jerusalem*, Mendelssohn relies on Dohm's thesis as he further develops the philosophical case for Jewish emancipation. Mendelssohn embraces the idea that Jews should be considered equal members of society and treated by state authorities as such. Mendelssohn differs from Dohm, however, on a major issue: instead of arguing that Jews must be improved to take part in politics, he contends that they are already qualified for political participation and do not suffer from corporeal or spiritual decay.

Lessing's famous play *Nathan the Wise* (*Nathan der Weise*, 1779), commonly seen as a classic statement of Enlightenment religious tolerance, sheds light on the cultural conditions for Mendelssohn's plea for the social integration of Jews. The play presents a conflict among three brothers, who quarrel over one another's right to their father's property. The three brothers represent Judaism, Christianity, and Islam, and the play ends with the father distributing his property equally among them. Lessing presents a myth that may guide, enrich, and foster cultural dialogue among the three major religions.[6] The dialogue between the three monotheist religions assumes that they are different but equal. Religious difference is not merely a potential obstacle to dialogue; their otherness is the reason for the dialogue in the first place. Furthermore, the play lays out specific rules for tolerating a faith different from one's own and shows that dialogue requires a governing authority to make it happen.

Mendelssohn's position on the public participation of Jews highlights his unique role within the German republic of letters. As he advocates for his people's ability to participate in politics, he demonstrates that very ability. His dual stance as both a public figure in the German republic of letters and a Jew gives him membership in two reading cultures and therefore affords him insights into the hermeneutic principles of these diverging communities.

Mendelssohn promotes aesthetics and interpretation as practices that work to cultivate an individual's universal merits. In tandem with these preferences, Mendelssohn depicts in both his German and Hebrew writings the traditional Jewish community as cultivating hermeneutic practices that are a cultural asset for humankind. The Hebrew Bible plays an important role in this presentation. The Hebrew Bible's cultural relevance for educated society highlights the contribution of the Jewish people to humankind due to what Mendelssohn describes as the Jews' merits in honing a loyal transmission of the text. In this way, his attempts to preserve the uniqueness of Jewish reading practices result in a redescription of Jewish liturgical practices that abstracts the traditional binding of scriptural reading to divine revelation. Mendelssohn recasts the role of literacy, interpretation, and hermeneutics in Jewish society to promote the ability of Jews to belong to a universal community by showing their capacity for *Bildung* (the self-cultivation through education that pertains to both individuals and cultures). In so doing, Mendelssohn grounds the Jewish contribution to humankind in a spiritual uniqueness facilitated through this religion's self-government. This facet of Mendelssohn's legitimization of Judaism, which plays an important role in *Jerusalem*, relies on yet another and much different intervention into hermeneutics. In *Jerusalem*, Mendelssohn shies away from the valorization of literacy altogether in order to praise the Jewish tradition for being infused with preverbal ritual that circumvents the hazards of interpretation.

Aesthetics and Virtue

Mendelssohn's entry into the Enlightenment public sphere resulted from his early essays on aesthetics. These essays present an overtly optimistic view of the potential for poetry and art to develop the individual. Through his own essays on aesthetic theory and through his reviews of others' literary and philosophical works, Mendelssohn systematically applied rationalist terminology to aesthetic observation and to language philosophy. At the same time, his dialogue with such figures as Herder and Johann Georg Hamann led him to consider language in a new framework.[7]

Mendelssohn's model of aesthetics foregrounds human agency. For him, human perceptive abilities are the key to the creation of beauty.[8] Unlike art, nature does not intend to create beauty even as it reveals beauty to the viewer indirectly. This distinction between nature and art grants independence to art while sustaining nature's ontological superiority. In his "On Sentiments" ("Über die Empfindungen," 1755), Mendelssohn describes attraction to beauty as an inherent attribute of the senses: "My senses encompass an inclination toward perfection, [like] all thinking creatures, which to some extent I share with God."[9] Mendelssohn's aesthetic theory holds that admiration for geniuses is rooted in the human virtues, whereas the lack of passion (*Unlust*) that may occur during reflection is evidence of human weakness. The greatest artistic representation is consequently one that captures the unity of all its components while still stressing their distinction from one another. Such a work brings attention both to its components and to the overall representation within a short span of time. The feeling of pleasure culminates in the experience of perfection (*Vollkommenheit*), which in turn results in the experience of sharing God's assessment of the world as a whole.

According to Mendelssohn's aesthetic theory, in the moment of artistic observation, the observer of art exercises personal freedom. The agency of the observer of art demonstrates the human capacity for aesthetic contemplation. The role of the critic as an independent individual relies on his or her judgment of the quality of the artwork under examination. The judgment of the aesthetic quality of art became predominant in Enlightenment thought after Johann Jakob Breitinger and Johann Jakob Bodmer claimed it was integral to the engagement with poetry and art in their seminal aesthetic manifesto, *Critical Poetry* (*Critische Dichtkunst*, 1740). Eighteenth-century aesthetic discourse tended to highlight the individual's capacity for judgment as an essential part of defining critique, but in Mendelssohn's aesthetic writings, judgment takes on a new meaning that pertains to social interactions. Taken together, his views that the striving for perfection is inherent to the human senses and that the human senses are inclined to seek the wholeness of beauty constitute a conception of the individual as an independent and autonomous being. Aesthetics appears to parallel political participation because both involve a process of judgment that engages and hones individuals' natural qualities.

The human ability to perceive beauty relies on a clear grasp of the representation's attributes as well as on a distinct portrayal of each of the details of this representation. The clarity of the representation arouses a strong sense of vividness and pleasure within the human soul: "As the presentation of the beautiful object becomes broadly clearer, the pleasure derived from it becomes more passionate."[10] Evident within Mendelssohn's aesthetic theory are his disagreements with the strand of Romantic aesthetics that Herder represents. For Mendelssohn, a salient quality of art is its distance from nature. Stressing that a good aesthetic creation is a constant reminder of that distance, he grounds good poetry in the exact opposite experience than does Herder. Poetry does not aim to remind readers of civilization's early and raw stages, as it does for Herder; rather, it documents and extends civilizational progress.

Mendelssohn sees poetic creation as becoming more refined and advanced over the course of a nation's development. He refers to different nations as refining their virtues throughout their cultural development, a process reflected in the growing subtlety of their aesthetics. This view marks the distinction between Herder's and Mendelssohn's respective views of language. For one, as we have seen, Herder's *Treatise on the Origin of Language* (1772) mourns humans' distance from the original language, as the progress of civilization emptied language of emotion. What had been the catalyst of communication through sound—a primordial and animalistic drive to share a sudden feeling with another—had been "dried out" of language.[11] For Herder, poetic creation, which has the potential to unearth traditions of oral expression, is at its best when it rediscovers language's wild, primordial origins.[12]

In many of his works of literary criticism, Mendelssohn refers to his generation's celebration of Biblical Hebrew literature. These works include reviews of popular literary works by Friedrich Gottlieb Klopstock and Salomon Gessner, which, as we have seen, make use of Genesis stories in staging scenes typical to a modern-day drama. He also engages other instances of the idealization of Hebrew in writings on aesthetics and historiography. In his German writings, Mendelssohn intermittently endorses Biblical Hebrew as an ancient literature with aesthetic merits, alongside critical comments that, for the most part, insist on the need to understand Hebrew poetry on its own terms as a unique historical phenomenon. On this point, Mendelssohn differs from historicist accounts of the Old Testament, which he exposes as biased, as the next section will demonstrate.[13] Although favoring the examination of Hebrew's development over that of other national literatures, the period's new commentaries in effect presume that the poetic enterprises of different peoples reveal comparable modes of development, which are teleological in nature. In other words, the period features unprecedented interest in Hebrew as a national language, recognizing that its unique qualities merit reflection on its origins, but at the same time, the methodologies used to reflect on Hebrew are faulty because they had been used to describe other languages that had, unlike Hebrew, greatly developed with time.

Mimesis and Human Virtue

As David Wellbery has argued, Mendelssohn appreciates poetry when "it exhibits an iconic relationship between signifier and signified, that is, when it *attains to the status of a natural sign.*"[14] This process occurs when a work is perceived as a depiction of an object in nature. The exposure to a representation results in a new perception of reality for the observer of art. According to Mendelssohn, the gradual revelation of works of art shows their unique essence. This quality makes art capable of changing the observer's grasp of the world.

These views on aesthetics should be understood in the context of Alexander Gottlieb Baumgarten's revolution in the field of aesthetics. In his inquiry into human cognition and aesthetic experience, Mendelssohn endorses Baumgarten's view that the science of aesthetics should focus on the reception of outside impressions by the human senses. In Mendelssohn's aesthetics, human agency is to be found in gradual cognitive processing, as best seen in his important essay, "Reflections on the Sources and Connections between the Fine Arts and the Sciences" ("Betrachtungen über die Quellen und die Verbindungen der schönen Künste und Wissenschaften," 1757). Here Mendelssohn presents the observation of art as exemplary for the study of the human senses. He asks, "Which phenomena propel the soul's driving forces into motion more than the effects of the arts?"[15] The work of art exercises a complex effect on the soul, provoking emotional responses that arise from art's proper emulation of nature. For this to happen, art's representation of nature must be faithful to the original and yet at the same time distant from it.

Mendelssohn's innovation in aesthetics includes his view that the perception of reality changes through exposure to art.[16] Through an artwork's unique way of imitating nature, the aesthetic object challenges the preconceptions and cognitive patterns through which the individual perceives reality. According to Mendelssohn's aesthetics, the mimetic effect—the acknowledgment that poetry is not nature but rather the processing of nature—is a stepping-stone toward the cultivation of higher human skills. Herder's and Mendelssohn's diverging aesthetic values, which inform their readings of the Hebrew Bible, reflect their different views of human nature.

Mendelssohn's long review of Lowth's *Lectures on the Sacred Poetry of the Hebrews*, which Mendelssohn composed in 1757, hones some main principles of Mendelssohn's aesthetic theory. At the opening of the text, Mendelssohn commends the new regard for Biblical Hebrew, which he claims has been neglected.[17] Although Hebrew's "beauties" can be found through comparison with ancient Greek and Latin, he argues that the differences between the three languages need to be considered as well. For one, the Hebrew poets did not have the basis of myth on which to build, as did their ancient contemporaries. In the place of myth, Hebrew poetry features representations of objects in nature, which capture the intensity of the Land of Israel's beauty. Mendelssohn stresses the role of literary devices in Lowth's depiction of the divine poet's oeuvre, particularly the count of syllables that characterizes this poetry's use of meter. He finds Lowth's treatment to be equivalent to discussions of Hebrew by Jewish scholars, such as Don Isaac Abrabanel.[18] This means that equally cogent accounts of the biblical language are to be found in traditional Jewish scholarship on the Scriptures. If the Enlightenment turned scriptural interpretation into a technique for all humanity—one that addresses the affective and cognitive apparatus of all readers—Mendelssohn wants it to be known that the awareness of the supreme nature of biblical poetry as a hermeneutic object has long been an attribute of Jewish scholarship.

This is an instance of the situated universalism that characterizes Mendelssohn's oeuvre. "Situated universalism" is a term that has been used in postcolonial studies to capture the interaction of non-Western and primarily Muslim thinkers with modernism. Nils Riecken has recently used the term to understand Egyptian thinkers' attempts to adapt the main notions of Western philosophy—such as the definition of modernity—to their self-identification as a religious and ethnic minority.[19] Situated universalism usefully describes how Mendelssohn appropriated a universal stance in his claims that Enlightenment values had long been rooted in traditional Jewish scholarship. As the above example shows, what enabled Mendelssohn's situated universalism was the contemporary attempt to make the Hebrew Bible into a universal asset.

Susannah Heschel has provocatively suggested that Jewish theologians' writings could be equated with postcolonial efforts to describe history from an outsider's perspective and to subvert Christian universalism.[20] In understanding Mendelssohn through the prism of situated universalism as a practice pertaining to the interaction of religious minorities with the Christian world, *Secularism and Hermeneutics* takes a similar stance. One difference is that in the case of Mendelssohn, there was no coherent party of universalists to whom he responded. As we have already seen, Mendelssohn took after such figures as Kant, Lessing, and Baumgarten, favoring their theories over the views of others who advocated alternative forms of universalism. As will be elaborated on in the discussion of *Jerusalem*, Mendelssohn's situated universalism ultimately aligned with some germane versions of Enlightenment political values already dominant during that time, rather than advancing an outsider's perspective on history. Jonathan Hess has shown that German Jewish thinkers challenged German thinkers' understanding of modernity in universal terms largely based on polemical Christian theology. In his reading of Mendelssohn's *Jerusalem*, Hess argues that the treatise strives to subvert Christian dominance in the field of scriptural interpretation.[21] Although I agree with Hess that Mendelssohn's theological arguments intervene in Christian universalism, I will describe *Jerusalem* not as subverting the Enlightenment's overall tendency toward universalism—a tendency manifested in the appropriation of Hebrew as a global asset—but as weaving some salient Jewish ideas into the universalist portrayals of history.

As we have seen in the previous chapters, Herder's praise of Hebrew poetry gave rise to a wide-ranging effort to account for national literatures. In his *Fragments on Recent German Literature* (1767–68) and *Treatise on the Origin of Language* (1772), he grants the people of the East (the *Morgenländer*) a central role. They are living testimony, according to Herder, of inherent human traits of creativity and creation, and their poetry is a model of poetic creation that addresses an audience whose sensibilities have not yet been tamed.

Against this view, Mendelssohn contends that, through their literary devices, the Hebrew poets transmitted to the reader images (*Bilder*) of the unique views from Palestine. These descriptions reflect the freedom of the Hebrew poets, through which they were able to transmit their impressions of the outside world; this free self-expression is much greater, contends Mendelssohn, than that of the Greek or Roman poets. And yet, even though he reiterates the view that the Hebrew poets were especially close to nature, Mendelssohn distances himself from Herder when he writes that as readers of Hebrew, "we must not compare our artificial and almost unnatural life" to the ancient Hebrews' way of living, as such an act would show us to be wrongful judges of their poetry.[22] Here, Mendelssohn seems to allude to Herder's position that the reading of Hebrew poetry requires readers to put themselves in the place of authors. To this, he counters that the ancient poets' natural lives were different from ours, such that we cannot hope to emulate them.

Mendelssohn's critique of Herder exposes the religious backdrop of the period's debates over aesthetics. In the 1770s, Mendelssohn had already taken interest in Herder's views on Biblical Hebrew. In a review of Herder's *Fragments on Recent German Literature*, Mendelssohn contextualizes their respective readings of Hebrew texts in a broader perception of the world.[23] The author of the *Fragments*, Mendelssohn observes, bases his theory of the evolution of national languages on the transition of linguistic constructs from epoch to epoch. His theory pertains to ancient Greek, which did indeed develop between the epochs in which it was spoken, but Latin and Hebrew did not develop in a similar fashion. Because of that difference, Mendelssohn claims, it would be wrong to describe the work of the Hebrew writers—which he, like Herder, describes as "wild"—as featuring distinct prose and poetry genres.[24]

Importantly, Mendelssohn's review of the *Fragments* concludes with a skeptical reference to Herder's motivations in his praise of Biblical Hebrew. Mendelssohn's critique underscores how their diverging views on aesthetics encapsulate starkly different visions of human virtue. Mendelssohn notes that Herder presumes that good poetry brings humankind back to its wild roots, and he asks, "What do we want from poetry?"[25] His own answer to this question, which he developed throughout his life, is that the point in writing poetry is exactly to escape barbarism and refine human nature. Mendelssohn praises the refinement of language through cultural progress in his essay "On the Question: What Does 'to Enlighten' Mean?" ("Über die Frage: was heißt aufklären?," 1784) which portrays the practical usage of language as complementary to poetic creation: "A language attains enlightenment through the sciences and it attains culture through social interaction, poetry, and oratory. Through the former, it becomes more fit for theoretical use; through the latter for practical use. A language is education when both are found together. Culture in an external sense is called 'refinement.' Hail to the nation whose refinement is the effect of culture and enlightenment, whose external splendor and elegance is based upon an internal, solid genuineness."[26] The reexamination of the Hebrew Bible as a quest for humanity's origins abstracts the classicist model and imposes it on Hebrew poetry. Although he participates in the project of considering the Hebrew Bible a global cultural asset, Mendelssohn dismisses germane ways in which early Romanticism idealizes the Hebrew language and which are pertinent to Herder's work. His objection to the portrayal of Hebrew as a primordial language that can be revived is indicative of his larger conception of human virtue and of poetry as a way to provoke the pursuit of higher skills.

Holy Tongues: Liturgy and Literacy

As David Sorkin has cogently demonstrated, the Jewish Enlightenment (the Haskalah) developed its ideals and its new religious curriculum through its debates with German Protestantism.[27] These interactions resulted in two new approaches to the Hebrew Bible among Jewish scholars: the scientific study of the Bible and the view that the Hebrew Bible, because of its unique aesthetic qualities, elicits affect in readers. Both of these tendencies are evident in Mendelssohn's writings on Hebrew.

Mendelssohn's linguistic competence and training in the study of traditional Jewish sources and Hebrew grammar guided his intellectual and political influence on both Jewish and German culture. As the author of biblical commentaries and translations of the Hebrew Bible, Mendelssohn maintained his engagement with the Orthodox Jewish community while also gradually becoming a recognized thinker within Germany's republic of letters.

Although literacy in Hebrew had long been an important requirement for belonging to a religious community, it started to mark belonging to a national community that transmits its own oral tradition. As Andrea Schatz has shown, Mendelssohn conceptualized the Bible as an asset of the Jewish people and thereby redefined both in his period's terms: Jews became a national group whose historical longevity was perpetuated through a cultural artifact that documented Jews' shared origins.[28] Jewish education was the precondition for maintaining the framework of traditional community through the dismantling influence of modernity. At the same time, it newly construed the Hebrew language as representing a national culture and the act of reading Hebrew as enhancing national belonging. Responding to modern nationalist trends in early German Romanticism and particularly in Herder's notion of national spirit, Mendelssohn made a revolutionary move. He built on the characterization of Hebrew as an ancient national language, which, as we have seen in Chapter 2, was connected to Hebrew's orality during his time. Mendelssohn correlated this asset to the ongoing affiliation with a religious minority that was newly seeking collective traits amounting to the legitimacy of national affiliation.

Mendelssohn's preoccupation with the Hebrew language as a means for introducing the Jewish tradition to modernity was an integral part of his exegesis of Jewish sources. As Sorkin observes, Mendelssohn adhered to the principle of the "profundity of plain meaning," by which he meant "the Bible's unique oral quality as the most effective means to transmit practical knowledge."[29] His translations of the Hebrew Bible were an important part of his engagement with scriptural interpretation. Mendelssohn completed a herculean task when he translated the Pentateuch into German with the use of Hebrew characters. In a 1779 letter to his friend Avigdor Levi, Mendelssohn explains what drove him to undertake this challenge: "I am translating the script to the German language . . . for need of the sons, whom God has spared me. My oldest son died—a curse from God—and I was left only with my son Joseph (may God strengthen his heart with His Torah). I lay the German translation in his mouth, so he would understand through it the simple sense of script, till the boy grows up and understands it himself."[30] Mendelssohn's translation not only continued the tradition of reading the Scriptures but also transformed the Jewish tradition through translation. His translation was a radical intervention into the consideration of liturgy, which Mendelssohn explained as "the need of the sons." His son Joseph represented a generation of Jewish youth who had difficulty reading Hebrew but who, at the same time, could be brought to read the Scriptures and appreciate the beauty of the text. Mendelssohn defined literacy as ingrained in Judaism's traditional values. In this traditional community, the circulation and reading of the Pentateuch is ingrained in a generational relationship that is the pillar of the community. Mendelssohn's apologia evoked the patriarchal lineage of traditional reading practices. Whereas the young Goethe approached Hebrew as the mother tongue of humankind, evocative of the individual's primordial drives, we might say that Mendelssohn saw Hebrew as a "father tongue," in that it embodied the longevity of the patriarchal lineage.

The Jewish tradition is rooted in familial relationships that perpetuate the role of sons as readers. A legacy encompassing a unique awareness of the script's materiality, literacy was integral to Mendelssohn's own identity. He was the son of a scribe (a writer of Torah scrolls) and retained his father's profession. Trained at a young age in orthography, Mendelssohn was renowned among Enlightenment thinkers for his refined handwriting. Mendelssohn envisioned a gradual process of training in Hebrew literacy whereby the beauty of the text, first unveiled in German, makes the readers go through the difficult task of gradually familiarizing themselves with the Hebrew script (the German word *Schrift* denotes both script and the Bible).

Representing a hybrid literacy of Hebrew and German, Mendelssohn's translation stresses the community's attachment to the former, which can be perpetuated—somewhat counterintuitively—only through knowledge of the latter. The community shares command of German, and so German enables the perpetuation of Jewish ritual. As Mendelssohn rightly recognized, the contours of textual cultures were drifting away from the boundaries of religious cultures. In order to maintain communal affinity involving texts, Jews had to choose the language of the nation where they resided and where they had a growing affiliation. Mendelssohn creatively responded to this situation by transforming Hebrew into a national asset, common to Jews in their various places of residency, and by perpetuating the material and lexical presence of Hebrew as a trait of the Jewish community in his German translations of the Bible.[31]

The essay "Or la-netiva" ("Light for the Path," 1782) demonstrates Mendelssohn's presentation of Hebrew as Jews' national language. The essay addresses the Jewish community through Mendelssohn's use of traditional characterization of the language. This text cites the religious presentation of Hebrew as a language distinct from other world languages first and foremost because of its role in the creation of the world. Hebrew is the language in which God first spoke to human beings (i.e., the Genesis patriarchs), and it is the language in which God gave the religious laws on Mount Sinai.[32] Hebrew is also the language in which God spoke to His prophets and to Moses. According to Mendelssohn, these reasons justify calling Hebrew "the holy language." In line with this religious consideration of the language, "Or la-netiva" presents Hebrew as a unique language whose enduring importance is to be found in its singular grammar and syntax and whose circulation has guaranteed its preservation throughout Jewish history.[33] On the one hand, the essay resonates with the idealization of Hebrew among Mendelssohn's contemporaries, but on the other, it diverges from other instances of the idealization of the language described in the previous chapters with its references to the specific context of Jewish theological history. Mendelssohn's is a religious attachment, and that attachment informs his participation in the discussions of Hebrew as a language with universal relevance.

Nonetheless, "Or la-netiva" does not merely present a vocabulary that allows readers to follow both traditional Jewish sources and Enlightenment portrayals of the civilization's common origins. The essay also seeks to define certain religious practices—particularly those pertaining to scriptural interpretation—as in accord with both Judaism and Protestantism. As such, the essay remains close to Mendelssohn's appeal for the recognition of the Jewish contribution to universal values honed through exegesis: *Jerusalem*, his influential treatise published in 1783.[34]

Mendelssohn's theological case for the study of Hebrew reframes the Jewish tradition in a new paradigm for thinking about history, culture, and literacy. The emerging consideration of Jews as a legitimate collective posited Hebrew as one national language and literature among others. Traditional religious laws, however, see religious practice as having a distinct truth value. In order to resolve the tension between these positions, Mendelssohn employs in *Jerusalem* the idea of cultural pluralism and diversity. His presentation of Jews as faithful readers legitimizes Jewish collectivity by stressing the circulation of traditional Jewish sources as the primary trait of this community, marking their unique contribution to civilization.

Jerusalem's Goals

In his influential political manifesto *Jerusalem*, Mendelssohn closely attends to foundational works of political theory—by Hobbes, Locke, Spinoza, and others—that argue that a ruler employs religion to serves his agenda and is not guided by a "true" reading of the Scriptures. In its first part, *Jerusalem* argues for the separation of church and state, based on the premise that religion exists in one's private conscience. Responding to Hobbes's notion that the state controls its citizens by restricting their natural drives, Mendelssohn narrows down the areas in which the state is able to influence the individual. Whereas citizens can renounce the natural rights that relate to their physical existence, they cannot give up any rights that relate to the spiritual. Mendelssohn then reiterates a key distinction between the state and the church: the state addresses the relation between men, whereas the church addresses the relationship between man and God.

As many have noted, this line of argument makes it hard to account for *Jerusalem*'s second half, which presents the ancient Jewish state as an ideal instance of government. Mendelssohn distinguishes between laws and commandments: the former belongs to the sphere of the civil order, and the latter belong to the sphere governed by God.[35] Yet in ancient Israel, Mendelssohn contends, the two momentously converged. *Jerusalem*'s second part offers an apologia for Judaism as a religious tradition whose canon of holy texts establishes a national ethos. How can one claim that church and state must be separate and yet adhere to a religion that propagates communal belonging as grounded in its own national genealogy? According to Mendelssohn, the rule of separation of state and religion was suspended when God was the ruler. In that case, He dictated religious commands and laws to His citizens. This ideal situation existed only once in history, with the governing of the Jewish state. This account shows Judaism's power as an ideal political model for the purposes of the modern state.

This dynamic lies in *Jerusalem*'s twofold purpose: to illustrate contemporary Jews' ability to observe state laws and to establish Judaism as a tradition that is constitutive of modern state politics. In a sense, it is the relationship between the two—between ideal Judaism and present-day Jews—that constitutes *Jerusalem*'s contribution to Enlightenment public discourse.

Whereas Herder had presented Biblical Hebrew as representative of a particular national spirit, Mendelssohn highlights the importance of ancient Judaism not merely as a national sign but also as the universal political model. This response to Herder results from *Jerusalem*'s complex theorization of ritual and, in particular, his engagement with Baruch Spinoza's attack on Jewish exegesis.

The depictions of the Jewish state and of ritual in *Jerusalem* emerge through Mendelssohn's reply to Spinoza's critical conception of the Hebrew Bible in his *Theological-Political Treatise* (1670). The *Treatise* was a stepping-stone toward religious toleration, a position that grew out of Spinoza's focus on the power of censorship and political constraints in guiding textual interpretation. As famously demonstrated by Leo Strauss, the *Treatise* both advocates for and exemplifies transgressive reading when it analyzes the Hebrew Bible.[36] Spinoza sees the Bible, composed under political constraints, as addressing an attentive reader who is sensitive to tenets not discernible at first sight.

Mendelssohn, whose early aesthetic writings were influenced by Spinoza, had to come to terms with the critique of Judaism that dominates Spinoza's biblical exegesis.[37] Spinoza describes two main currents of traditional Jewish scriptural interpretation, both of which he finds deficient. The first is Maimonides' approach, which, according to Spinoza, privileges reason over the literal meanings of the Scriptures, as well as over the difficulties and problems that exist in the Hebrew text. Maimonides takes allegory as a way of allowing rational readings of the text while preserving its holy status. A key example of allegory is Maimonides' reading of the biblical scenes of miracles. As the rational mind is not accustomed to acknowledging the concrete presence of miracles in ancient Israel, the relevant excerpts in the Bible should be understood allegorically.

The second current of traditional Jewish scriptural interpretation privileges religious presumption over logic and contends that nothing in the Bible should be taken metaphorically. Spinoza chooses Jehuda al-Fakhar, a thirteenth-century opponent of Maimonides' rationalistic approach to the Scriptures, to represent this second, dogmatic approach. Because the Bible seems to contradict itself when it is taken literally and dogmatically, this current of exegesis creates further textual complication.[38]

Spinoza calls for a third approach that understands the Bible in its historical context. Such an approach examines the biblical text from within its own presumptions, as far as possible, without imposing external meanings on the original text. Spinoza sees the proper investigation of the text as employing the reader's reflection on the text in the activity of exegesis. Insofar as Spinoza presents the activation of human reasoning as the goal of exegesis, his approach to textual interpretation exemplifies what would become a pertinent principle of later hermeneutics: that historical and cultural contextualization of a text puts reason in motion. Since there remains "no dictionary, no grammar, no book of rhetoric" from the ancient scholars of Hebrew, the comprehension of the biblical language presents special challenges.[39] Spinoza mentions the feature of Hebrew that provoked lengthy debates in eighteenth-century philology, as we saw in Chapter 2: its partial lack of vowels.[40] The eighth-century "pointers" (the Masoretes), he asserts, were in fact interpreting the biblical text when they inserted punctuation into it, addressing both Hebrew's lack of vowels and the obscurity of its sentence structure. With this observation, Spinoza suggests that an individual reader can influence the reception of a text for generations.

The *Treatise*'s depiction of Judaism, which is Mendelssohn's major point of contestation, relies upon these hermeneutic positions. Spinoza depicts ancient Israel as a state ruled through the claim to revelation. This central theme in the Bible is meant to affirm the text's own authoritative status. According to Spinoza, the rules of the Torah are in fact political regulations that were meant to enforce a regime. Consequently, in this view, the accordance between a state's power and the content of the Scriptures occurred only once during the course of history: during the regime of the Hebrew nation. The content of the five Books of Moses is a covenant of national laws that apply to the specific and contingent Hebrew state. They do not have universal and atemporal validity or moral value; these laws apply, rather, to the Hebrew state and are means for protecting that specific and contingent country.[41] For Spinoza, the Jewish state was the only time when the contingent biblical rules perfectly adhered to the rules of the state and power. At all other times, these rules had to be manipulated to meet the state's interests.

Mendelssohn's reply to these claims can be found in his Hebrew writings, where he confronts the accusation that the Masoretes harmed the Bible. He explains that the transmission of the Hebrew Bible originates from divine revelation, and it owes its sublimity to the preference given to orality in Jewish scribal practices. Thus, in "Or la-netiva," he argues that the Masoretes were dedicated to preserving the accents of the spoken language through which the Torah was transmitted on Mount Sinai.[42] As Sorkin writes, for Mendelssohn, "spoken language is the medium for the 'vital' and 'efficacious' knowledge of practice."[43] In *Jerusalem*, Mendelssohn expands on this view that oral practices perpetuate the divine revelation at the core of true religion. There, as we shall see, he condemns textual practices and writing as harmful by nature, challenging much of his own earlier theories of aesthetics, which had held interpretive processing in high regard.

Perilous Script

Mendelssohn's complex attitude to literacy in *Jerusalem* is part and parcel of his critical views on modernity.[44] Mendelssohn argues that the focus on the written word is a problem for the religious practice of his time. Script documents the modern transformation in human beings' perception of their surroundings. In religious matters, Mendelssohn speculates, the growing use of script has also provoked shifts in believers' worldviews: "It seems to me that the change that has occurred in different periods of culture with regard to written characters has had, at all times, a very important part in the revolutions of human knowledge in general, and in the various modifications of men's opinions and ideas about religious matters, in particular; and if it did not produce them completely by itself, it at least cooperated in a remarkable way with other secondary causes."[45] The dominance of writing, particularly in the practice of theology, is a problem common to different collectives. All religions, Judaism included, involve deterioration after their initial emergence, which leads to the superfluous presence of writing in other areas of life: "We teach and instruct one another only through writings; we learn to know nature and man only from writings. We work and relax, edify and amuse ourselves through overmuch writing. The preacher does not converse with his congregation; he reads or declaims to it in a written treatise. The professor reads his written lectures from the chair. *Everything is the dead letter*; the spirit of living conversation has vanished."[46]

Along with his contemporaries, Mendelssohn recognizes the need to see religion as a vivid and dynamic engagement that occurs primarily through oral practices. He offers the discourse on Hebrew poetry as the embodiment of such a vision, while also radically shifting it to a focus on religious law. According to Mendelssohn, the importance of commandments in Judaism is that they guide believers' daily practice and adherence to their faith. He claims that Judaism thus captures the lively spirit of religion through its faithful adherence to law, which gives rise to Judaism's "living script." Through its living script, which is preserved through the bonds of tradition, Judaism is able to avoid the damaging aspects of expanded literacy in modernity..

Major Enlightenment texts, such as *Jerusalem*, relied on a long tradition of using the Bible to establish, legitimize, or elucidate new political ideas. During the early modern period, major political treatises formulated new readings of the Bible in order to advocate for the idea of tolerance. In 1689, John Locke's *A Letter Concerning Toleration* reconceptualized how the state should govern religious practices. It promoted the idea that different citizens of the modern state may adhere to different confessions and still constitute a coherent political body. In the *Letter*, the coexistence of different faiths is not seen as an obstacle to the unity of the modern state but as a characteristic of it. Religious diversity, in fact, enhances the state's political power. For Locke, the political power of the state lies in a new conception of the political actor as someone whose participation is detached from religious doctrines, concerns, and practices. Religious tolerance, now perceived as central to modern state politics, emerges in Locke's treatise as a condition of political power. Because of the *Letter*'s influence, religious diversity became a prerequisite for politics rather than a problem to which modern politics attempted to offer a solution. As part of this change, scriptural interpretation became a technique that entailed accepting, if only in the back of the reader's mind, that other readers were entitled to diverging and even contradictory interpretations of the Scriptures.

Secularism and Hermeneutics argues that, as interpretive practices were secularized and taken to be universal, they were meant to dispel religious difference—with the model example of Christian and Jewish perspectives on the Old Testament. The complexity of Mendelssohn's stance on modern hermeneutics arises from his partial endorsement of this political vision of toleration while maintaining distance from some of its major presumptions. He maintains that the Scriptures are the object of divine revelation, and he attempts to preserve both the Bible's singularity and its universal importance. This effort results in Mendelssohn's reformulation of what divine revelation is all about. He explains that the importance of God's appearance on Mount Sinai lies not in the written laws He gave to the Israelites but rather in His announcement of the unique and exemplary role Israel could play among the nations. In laying out this vision of biblical interpretation, Mendelssohn opts to present Jewish morality as eternally valid at the same time that he admits that Judaism, like all religions, undergoes the growing attraction of believers to the written word.

The greatness of Judaism as a religion derives from this adherence to law. Spinoza's characterization of the Jewish state and its religious commands as authoritarian provokes Mendelssohn to characterize Judaism as based on observance of daily rituals, which he then distinguishes from laws. This characteristic infers that Judaism does not coerce one into belief but only prescribes the command of doing: "Among all the prescriptions and ordinances of the Mosaic law, there is not a single one which says: You shall believe or not believe. They all say: You shall do or not do."[47] Judaism is founded upon the recognition that faith (*Glaube*) cannot be coerced. Its commandments concern humankind's will as expressed in action. According to this depiction of Judaism, the reading of the Bible takes place amid communal belonging and the voluntary application of the holy texts' prescriptions to one's daily actions. Mendelssohn also mentions the accordance between the regime of the Hebrew state and the inception of political law, but instead of accepting that biblical laws are contingent, he declares this former accordance between state regime and the divine commandments as a salient cultural legacy. When Mendelssohn depicts ritual as a voluntary praxis and emphasizes the oral aspects of Jewish ritual, he presents this tradition as circumventing the misunderstanding and misuse of script. Law is a means of fighting what may happen when men encounter written words and interpret them falsely.[48] The city of Jerusalem became the locus of monotheistic worship through these unchanging and atemporal Jewish practices. It is nonetheless this same presence of uninterrupted ritual that turns Jerusalem into an abstraction, a spiritual notion prevalent in all nations and confessions.

As discussed earlier in this chapter, a main topic of Mendelssohn's writing about aesthetics is poetry's ability to imitate nature. *Jerusalem* develops this theme by alerting to the iconic nature of script as illustrated by the Hebrew letters. When images function as signifiers, danger lurks in the building blocks of human language: "What wisdom builds up in one place, folly readily seeks to tear down in another, usually employing the very same means and tools. Misunderstanding, on the one hand, and misuse, on the other, transformed what should have been an improvement of man's condition into corruption and deterioration. What had been simplicity and ignorance now became seduction and error."[49] When the material aspects of script are brought to the fore, the Hebrew alphabet—which derives its forms from natural objects—exemplifies the risk of confusing letters with the world or signs with their referents. While seemingly anomalous, this warning has echoes in Mendelssohn's aesthetic writings in German as well as his writings on

Jewish liturgy largely composed in Hebrew, which highlight Judaism's faithful transmission of divine law. As we have seen, for Mendelssohn, poetry mimics but does not embody nature. Therefore, the mimetic effect that is crucial to poetry's beneficial function may be lost when the scriptural form of Judaism— or any religion—is brought to the fore. Mendelssohn sees the transformation occurring in Hebrew script as a general cultural modification. His account of Judaism should thus be understood as one aspect of his view that "images and hieroglyphics lead to superstition and idolatry, and our alphabetical script makes man too speculative."[50]

Bearing in mind the danger of idolatry that the Hebrew script entails, the flexibility that speech represents may look like a disadvantage, but it is actually its greatest advantage. Speech has a direct temporal connection to human thought. Speech entails constant changes in content but that forces speech to be truthful. By comparison, written signs constrain human thought, but they open a hazardous door to worshipping symbols themselves. This dangerous confusion obscures writing's true importance: the embodiment of the commands in their daily practice.

If Spinoza warns against the misuse of texts to promote a political agenda, Mendelssohn argues that Hebrew's most basic components already elicit misunderstanding and misuse in their inability to form absolute meanings. Mendelssohn investigates not only the miscomprehension of script but also the historical role of Hebrew script in that confusion. In this way, *Jerusalem* presents a universalist perception of the Hebrew culture that is a reply not only to Spinoza but first and foremost to Mendelssohn's more immediate, contemporary interlocutors. In stark opposition to his period's admiration of the aesthetics of Hebrew poetry, Mendelssohn portrays the Hebrew state as a model for political perfection insofar as the Hebrew state was a moment of convergence between the divine law and its enforcement, that is, between signs and their referents.

The presence of *Jerusalem* in Enlightenment discourse on religious toleration should alert the reader to the fact that political secularism was not established merely through internal Christian negotiation. Mendelssohn's presentation of Judaism as both an abstraction and a religious tradition extends political secularism and its globalization of religious practices, but it also allocates space for the continuation of material Jewish ritual. Mendelssohn's conceptualization of exegesis is a telling instance of a traditional religious minority negotiating universal values. Mendelssohn's living script mediates the view of the Scriptures as a set of godly laws with the emerging view of the Bible as an abstraction that pertains to all members of human-kind. His political interests are inextricably connected to the aesthetics and hermeneutics he formulated in his early thinking. *Jerusalem* builds on these ideological facets of his theories of interpretation in substantializing Mendelssohn's influential image of the Hebrew state.

The Foundations of Toleration

A foundation of modern Western culture is the acceptance of modern hermeneutics as a guiding principle in relation to holy texts. As theoreticians of secularism have shown, the modern state is a construct that depends upon the allocation of religious practice—and the adherence to traditional models of exegesis—to the private sphere. According to this view, the organization of modern life presumes and perpetuates the distinction between divine rule and the authority of the state. Bearing this in mind, the religious history of the regulations on religious practice has been central to reflections on secularism. Saba Mahmood has pointed out that political secularism intervenes incessantly into the practice of religion and even into the very definition of religious conduct.[51]

Mahmood has argued that hermeneutic presuppositions—which state institutions such as the media conceive as inherent to every individual—are emblematic of this enforcement of religious practices. Her 2005 article, "Secularism, Hermeneutics, and Empire: The Politics of Islamic Reformation," examines the perception that traditionalist believers threaten Western society.[52] An important aspect of their divergence from other citizens is their status as readers: "It is the traditionalists' approach to scripture, as much as their way of life, that is incompatible with Western Enlightenment values."[53] She cites testimony that sets out the dangers that these traditionalist believers pose, such as "their belief in the divinity of the Quran and a failure to regard it as a *historical* document" and "their failure to realize that Muhammad was a product of his time whose life offers little of practical value to solving the exigencies of modern existence."[54] According to their findings, these believers cannot observe the Scriptures as an object that is the contingent product of a particular historical epoch. Consequently, such readers adhere to the Bible as a true account of divine revelation and tie contemporary existence (and religious worship) to the text in its literal form. To be considered a member in the state's public sphere necessitates, as Mahmood has shown elsewhere, the ability to observe religious artifacts critically (that is, to distant oneself from their apparent presence and perceive them as objects with multiple meanings for different individuals).[55] In other words, hermeneutic principles emerge as fundamental common knowledge governing the standing of the Bible as the pillar of the modern political community—knowledge so common that it is synonymous with the apprehension of other cultural artifacts and the skills required for their interpretation.

Since their establishment, state institutions have attempted to discern and alter the presuppositions that guide believers' approaches to holy texts. Scholars have considered the role of modern Judaism and, particularly, of Jewish emancipation as eminent examples of this attempt in modernity.[56] Because of Judaism's continued existence in Europe as a minority religion, Jewish emancipation provided an opportunity to rethink the transformation of religious traditions in modernity. Religious dogmas were newly allocated to the private sphere in the late Enlightenment, where, in light of the principle of religious freedom, individuals could adhere to their religion of choice or avoid a spiritual lifestyle altogether. Moreover, the religious credo that defined where traditional law presides—whether in private or in public—also transferred to the private realm. Modern Judaism did not emerge from attempts to dispel the relevance of Jewish law for the public sphere but rather from efforts to reconcile Jewish law with the Enlightenment allocation of religious dogma to the private sphere.[57]

The tensions within Mendelssohn's theory of interpretation capture this historical process. Conceptualized as global practices, Mendelssohn's hermeneutics and aesthetics offer a case study that demonstrates how entrance into the political sphere causes major changes in religious individuals' worldview and forms a split in believers' perception of reality. Modern hermeneutics requires adaptation to new interpretive sensibilities, and the tensions I have focused on in Mendelssohn's notion of the living script articulate his attempt to preserve, within this adaptation, an attachment to holy texts that has developed in a communal context. This attachment undergirds the community's gathering around holy texts as the defining trait of a collective that informs its members' sense of faithful belonging.

On a political level, the situated universalism at the core of Mendelssohn's theory of the Scriptures is an attempt to keep religion as a private right and, at the same time, to define the right to religious self-governing as the state's common good.[58] This dual, and at times contradictory, enterprise is behind Mendelssohn's approach to textual interpretation. He believes that all individuals are capable of hermeneutics, which proves their equal skills, but that, at the same time, the circulation of the Hebrew Bible in Judaism is supreme because it transcends individual engagement in the deciphering of signs. In a sense, Mendelssohn hints at the set of sensibilities that are fostered under the auspices of Jewish liturgy and that will be kept intact.

In addition to articulating the adaptation of the religious minority to Enlightenment religion, Mendelssohn also turns the traditional attachment to Hebrew into a trope that corresponds with the process of universalizing the Old Testament and of the globalization of hermeneutic principles. His presentation of Judaism as *the* religion of toleration inscribes the traditional relation to the Scriptures within the new context of a universal community of readers. Mendelssohn's efforts show how this process occurred through an attempt to conceive of Judaism, from within its universalized status, as an uninterrupted ritual. Mendelssohn's legacy rests in his advancement of the Hebrew Bible's new status as a universal asset while reinstituting religious morality as transcendent of time. His assertion that Judaism is especially apt at facilitating believers' political participation is the apex of his situated universalism: it advances the Enlightenment ideal of toleration while grounding it in the religious tradition of a minority. This move paves the way for significant transformations in the relationship of believers to holy texts, which are continuously perceived as a communal pillar and as a universal human asset. Mendelssohn thus sharpens Judaism's dual standing in Enlightenment discourses on the Bible as a representative both of religious ritual and of reason.

Chapter 4

On Jews and Other Bad Readers

An old Christian accusation contends that Jews have failed to realize that the Old Testament prefigures the revelation embodied in the New Testament. As explicated through Christian dogma, the critique of Jewish reading centers on an incapacity for abstraction and an inability to grasp the higher importance of the teaching of their ancestors.[1] Building on this critique, Immanuel Kant claimed that the greatness of the early Christians grew out of their formulation of a universal moral religion based on some Jewish principles. Mendelssohn's influential alternative model for global hermeneutics and aesthetics thus coexisted with the long-standing claim that Jewish scriptural interpretation represented and further perpetuated a faulty perception of the world. As we saw in the previous chapter, Mendelssohn disrupted the parallels between hermeneutics and biblical exegesis with his contention that the uniqueness of faith—confessional difference—enhances human diversity.

Notwithstanding the originality of Mendelssohn's ideas and their considerable influence, attacks on Jewish ways of reading continued into the nineteenth century. As early Romanticism explored poetry as a laboratory for readerly engagement, the theological critique of Jewish reading converged with influential reflections on the medial aspects of reading. A new idea was emerging of reading per se, according to which interpretation should aim at transcending the written letter to reach a truth not immediately apparent. This trend helped to turn the New Testament into the new ideal object for hermeneutics.

This chapter focuses on Friedrich Daniel Ernst Schleiermacher's writings on exegesis. Across his writing, I trace the development of key terms in modern textual interpretation as well as their role in making the New Testament into a new model object for interpretation. Building on earlier hermeneutics,

Schleiermacher presumed that a general theory of understanding—as opposed to distinct, specialized "hermeneutics" (in the plural)—did not yet exist.[2] He sought to supply such a theory, first, through the codification of philological or linguistic hermeneutics and, second, through the description of a new approach to textual interpretation that would become known as the psychological or biographical approach. Schleiermacher presented scriptural interpretation as a dynamic process of apprehending the personal and social context of authorship. This view reflected the intellectual climate of German idealism, which placed Christianity at the beginning of abstract thinking. Kant's plea for independent rational reflection on the Bible and Schleiermacher's attempts to supply the reader with a collective and emotive Christian ethos as the point of departure for reading the Scriptures are two sides of the same coin. Both projects established theological reading as universal and dependent upon communal readership and the skills that it could cultivates. And they both endorsed a specific Christian engagement with the Scriptures— namely, individualistic scrutiny of the Bible guided by readers' capacity and moral responsibility.

This book has so far focused on the confluence of modern readership and processes of secularization. This chapter turns in a different direction to consider how literary texts might challenge or disrupt the reciprocity of these two processes. Because literary texts involve the anticipation and negotiation of norms of interpretation, they also highlight the history of interpretive paradigms and the contingency of their cultural predominance at any given time or place. From this perspective, I approach the work of Heinrich Heine, who reflected on the norms of reading in both his poetry and his writing on European literary history. I read his work as challenging the view of interpretation as an individual effort and responsibility, which took hold after Schleiermacher.

Reading Heine's novel *The Rabbi of Bacharach* (*Der Rabbi von Bacherach*, 1840), I describe how literature may construct for its reader an epistemological experience that revokes the religious neutrality presupposed by modern interpretive positions. I show that, as the novel progresses, its protagonists reveal an uncanny attachment to the Hebrew Bible because they believe their partaking in the Genesis narratives will determine their own fate. The portrayals of liturgical reading in Heine's works highlight how interpretation is grounded in religious belonging and traditional communal training. Moments of hermeneutic hindrance, which occur, for example, in view of the novel's fragmentary form, are infused with the alerts that readers' dispositions draw on the moral and social norms of the religious communities to which they belong.

Kant on Communal Exegesis

In 1793, the already-famous philosopher Immanuel Kant created a breach between his critical metaphysics and fundamental principles of traditional Christian dogma with the publication of his *Religion Within the Bounds of Reason Alone (Die Religion innerhalb der Grenzen der bloßen Vernunft)*.[3] Here, Kant seeks to establish that the natural tendency of man is toward the adherence to morality and that state institutions should govern and cultivate this tendency (but not coerce it). Claiming that committing evil acts goes against the individual's own natural tendencies, Kant provocatively discredits the notion of original sin as inherent to human existence. Sin, claims Kant, is steeped in an individual's choice and responsibility.[4] Accordingly, repentance for sin depends upon the individual and cannot be performed by another agent. This additional provocative contention invalidates the principle that Christ repented for human sin through His misery. In accordance with this presentation of individual agency as the source of morality, Kant defines a moral religion as one that reinforces ethical conduct in the individual's heart. Renouncing the ascendancy of divine miracles compels morality and positions the individual to be the supreme moral voice and the judge of his or her own acts. This view leads to a new reading of the Scriptures that diminishes the importance of historical evidence for divine revelation.[5]

Kant furthers this principle of moral autonomy when he contends that the "supreme principle of all scriptural exegesis" must lie in the moral improvement of humankind. People require, and will probably always require, the confirmation of divine revelation to guide their moral conduct. According to Kant, this requirement makes the role of scriptural interpretation crucial to the strengthening of moral faith. The purpose of scriptural scholarship should nonetheless be limited to enhancing the power of the church and never that of religion, as the latter only pertains to the individual's reflection and choice.[6]

The conduct of interpretation in a communal context, however, may harden the individual's inner inclination to morality and even jeopardize it. The reliance of religious communities on a spiritual authority is hazardous, particularly when its power is inflicted upon the group's members without any subjective reflection. In religious communities, the danger of adhering to a dubious authority is intertwined with the conduct of scriptural interpretation.

Biblical exegesis, when it forms the foundation of a spiritual group, bears the risk of a false or harmful mediation: "A holy book commands the greatest respect even among those (indeed, among these most of all) who do not read it, or are at least unable to form any coherent concept of religion from it; and no subtle argument can stand up to the knockdown pronouncement, *Thus it is written.* . . . The appointed interpreters of such scripture are themselves, by virtue of their very occupation, consecrated persons, as it were; and history proves that never could a faith based on scripture be eradicated by even the most devastating political revolutions."[7] Kant's depiction of religious communities as reading cultures is illuminating. His account highlights the social dynamics that derive from unequal access to the Scriptures. He includes nonreaders as well as readers as categories that render the religious community hierarchical and its faith ineradicable. The centrality of the Scriptures sets the tone for interactions between group members. Kant distinguishes different social strata that correspond to the believers' literacy, as assessed by other members of the community. The ability to read and to make sense of written texts forms the basic condition for gaining respect, and the entitlement to interpret the Scriptures professionally elevates the interpreters above this position of basic acceptance to high esteem.[8] Kant's account implies that undertaking an unmediated relationship with the Bible through scrutiny would free the individual from these arbitrary power relations.

Kant's assertion that text-based religions enjoy longevity may be read as a reference to Judaism. It is therefore surprising that, for Kant, Judaism does not count at all as a religion. He gives three reasons for this. First, Judaism's historical origins are to be found in the attempt to establish a secular state based on laws that aim for a political (rather than religious) constitution. The second reason is the absence from Jewish dogma of the belief in future life, which again demonstrates, according to Kant, Judaism's incompetence in cultivating faith. Kant's third argument is the most relevant to my discussion. He ponders the separatism of spiritual groups, which makes them inept at providing believers with true morality, as Judaism's defining characteristic: "Judaism rather excluded the whole human race from its communion, a people especially chosen by Jehovah for himself, hostile to all other peoples and hence treated with hostility by all of them."[9] The early Christians, who endeavored to present their faith as a continuation of Judaism, did so in order to emphasize how they had overcome Jewish materiality with their enterprise of establishing morality as universal. They wished to introduce a new moral faith without offending the believers accustomed to the old faith. Jewish exegesis remains separatist in that it excludes individuals from approaching the holy text on an egalitarian basis.

Moving away from Jewish separatism, the early Christians exercised openness to sociopolitical difference as they formulated a new kind of faith that could apply to all individuals. They believed that such principles as a belief in immortal life satisfy a fundamental human striving toward divine providence, the presence of which cannot be proven or refuted on scientific terms. The emergence of early Christianity promised a religious community that could dispute hierarchies within its membership. In a sense, this promise could be fulfilled through an inclusive model of literacy and *Bildung*, which strengthens the direct connection between an individual and Scripture. Scripture would stand, in the early Christian model, as a platform for experimenting with one's skills, rather than as a forceful instrumental for blind obedience.

Schleiermacher on Judaism

Although utterly different in its theological motivation, Schleiermacher's model of scriptural interpretation bolsters Kant's claim that reading is central to a new conceptualization of the theological community. In his historical account of scriptural interpretation, Schleiermacher attaches the position of Jews as practicing believers to their traditionalist, communal adherence to a Jewish way of reading. He presents Jewish scriptural interpretation as embedded in what he describes as Jewish characteristics that endure through the act of reading. Although these so-called Jewish traits signal just one momentary stage in the development of civilization, he sees the Jewish worldview, perpetuated through ritual, as unchanging. Schleiermacher's denigration of what he called "Jewish staleness" catalyzed the move toward nineteenth-century hermeneutics and a method of interpretation that emphasizes the reader's emotional rapport with texts.

In his *On Religion: Speeches to Its Cultured Despisers* (*Über die Religion: reden an die Gebildeten unter ihren Verächtern*, 1799), Schleiermacher describes Judaism as perpetuating stagnation, "since in effect Judaism has been a dead religion for a long time. Some people still show some allegiance to Judaism; but they are like mourners over an imperishable mummy, bewailing both its departure and its sad legacy."[10] This infamous image of Judaism as a corpse draws upon the view of the Jews as a group adhering to common ritual. Religious ritual keeps the Jewish community together and so perpetuates its macabre immortality. Yet Schleiermacher does not mention ritual or liturgy overtly; they are alluded to in the characterization of the group of Jewish mourners through their continual lamentation. In his analysis of the above passage, Jonathan Sheehan has shown that Schleiermacher sees the Jews as hindered by an inability to translate the content of the Scriptures into the pressing circumstances of everyday life.[11] Because their texts constrain them, the Jews fail to acquire a dynamic interpretive disposition and to adapt their texts to the contemporary state of affairs through translation into contemporary languages.

In his later writings on politics, Schleiermacher considers citizenship to be a universal modality that should accommodate members of different confessions. These statements seem to soften and even transgress his strict views on Judaism. He writes, "Reason demands that all [men] will become citizens, but does not condition that all must be Christian. It should be possible, in various ways, to be a citizen and a non-Christian."[12] Being a member of the Jewish confession does not necessarily entail exclusion from political engagement, but, Schleiermacher adds, Jews must renounce certain religious notions and practices as conditions for their possible political rights. One example he lists is the Jewish notion of the messianic end of days, which he sees as necessary to change in order to prioritize the well-being of the state over religious convictions.[13]

As made evident in his preference for the New Testament over the Old Testament, Schleiermacher seeks to establish a general paradigm of textual comprehension while relying on a Christian narrative to explain the conceptual origins of interpretation's universal aims. His lectures on hermeneutics, given between 1805 and 1833, embrace Lutheranism and its emphasis on individual interpretation as the leading principle of scriptural reading. He presents a historical narrative that depicts the receipt of Christ's message and its dissemination—that is, the emergence of the Christian church—as the peak of civilization. Schleiermacher's entire body of work promotes the New Testament as the text that contains the historical revelation of the Christian spirit to the church. With Schleiermacher's rendering of hermeneutics into a widely accepted cultural practice, his praise of exegesis as a revelatory process grows into an imperative of modern subjectivity.

Hermeneutics of the New Testament

If the Hebrew Bible was the epitome of hermeneutic reading for thinkers of the late Enlightenment and early Romanticism, the New Testament is that epitome for Schleiermacher and his successors. Whereas earlier thinkers sought to restore the message of the Hebrew Bible that had been lost, Schleiermacher seeks to restore an entire way of thinking. Breaking with a stale mode of religious existence, the New Testament represents a new message for humankind, and he seeks to understand the psychological conditions that compelled it to be written. Against the view that the goal of interpretation is the exposure of the original text, Schleiermacher grounds hermeneutics in speech. His theory of interpretation posits that an original utterance is intelligible only when readers grasp the context in which it was conceived. Schleiermacher's hermeneutics thus has at its center the transformation of the original text, not its discovery. For Schleiermacher, the New Testament documents a new beginning for civilization. As such, it is not only an exemplary object for hermeneutic reading, but it also shapes the subject who is exposed to its transformative, civilizing mission. As James Duke has explained, Schleiermacher approaches Christianity as the ideological framework that yielded the emergence of a new language. In this way, the new faith gave rise to new forms of thinking and perceiving reality.[14] The New Testament documents a break with the stale mode of religious existence that preceded its authorship.

The attempt to break free from the conditions that were essential for the development of this new mode of thinking typifies the transition from Judaism to Christianity. Schleiermacher's paradigm necessitates, therefore, the examination of linguistic evolution. For Schleiermacher, the transition from Hebrew to Aramaic and later to Greek demonstrates that a linguistic revolution follows a people's spiritual transformation: "For if there is a spiritual development in a people, then there is also a new development of language. In the way every new spiritual principle forms language, so did the Christian spirit."[15] But, he continues, the Christian spirit had to negotiate the continued linguistic influence of Hebrew: "In the N.T. the new Christian spirit emerges in a mixture of languages where the Hebrew is the root in which the new was first thought; the Greek was, though, grafted on."[16]

At the center of Schleiermacher's hermeneutics is the conceptualization of authorship as the work of an individual. Schleiermacher transfers Herder's cultural relativism to a new model of interpersonal relations. Herder had insisted on understanding culture contextually, through attention to its poetic conventions, historical setting, and cultural norms. Schleiermacher, on the other hand, replaces culture with the author, whom he examines in relation to another individual—the reader. Drawing an extensive parallel between hermeneutics and speech, Schleiermacher personalizes the reader and writer in a dialectical interaction. His reframing of hermeneutics in terms of communication scrutinizes speech not only as an interpersonal dynamic but also as a way for a subject to articulate ideas: "Thought is prepared by inner discourse, and to this extent discourse is only the thought itself which has come into existence. But if the thinker finds it necessary to fix the thought for himself, then the art of discourse arises as well, the transformation of the original thought, and then explication also becomes necessary."[17] Interpretation is needed when a thinker has changed his or her mind. In that case, the utterance should be interpreted in the context of an author's life, just as a linguistic utterance should be interpreted in the context of that language's overall usage and grammar.

Key to Schleiermacher's project is the view that every corpus of texts demands scrupulous attention, and as we have seen, the New Testament is the exemplary model for textual interpretation because it emerged as a new beginning for civilization. The New Testament is exemplary for the practice of such hermeneutics not only because it demands broad consideration of the conditions that accompany the emergence of a new linguistic modality but also because it enables a reconstruction of how individual authors sought to express this new modality. Authors such as Luke and John engage the Christian spirit and offer differing attempts to express Christian principles. They do so in a language that is in the making and that must overcome its antecedent. Furthermore, the New Testament's division into books exemplifies how this mode of thinking generates multiple ventures—all of which reflect an author's specific personality, life circumstances, and character.[18] When compared, the self-expression of the different New Testament authors sheds light on the thought of the other authors and on the overall infrastructure that evoked the Christian spirit in its new linguistic and textual modality.[19]

A linguistic utterance is always grasped by virtue of the underlying linguistic system, and so, by drawing an analogy between text and speech, Schleiermacher proposes that a text should be understood as an utterance in the context of the author's biography. The New Testament conveys a new message to humanity at the same time as it represents the individual personas of its authors. Consequently, the focus of his hermeneutics shifts from language per se to language as an analogy for psychological understanding. Schleiermacher's emphasis thus swerves to the psychological aspect of interpretation; this shift reduces language to the status of a metaphor. According to Richard Palmer, "Hermeneutics becomes psychological, the art of determining or reconstructing a mental process, a process which is no longer seen as essentially linguistic at all."[20] The interpretation of the New Testament parallels the historical account that it offers. Reading the New Testament puts into play one's cognitive and behavioral attributes, which have been granted to humanity with the church's acceptance of Christ's doctrine. Therefore, Schleiermacher's preference for the New Testament qualifies his account of history according to which the coming of Christian civilization brought about a new mode of thinking and a higher form of existence.

For Schleiermacher, the merit of the Scriptures lies in their unfolding of the church's history of receiving God's word. In his lectures on hermeneutics, Schleiermacher considers the religious community to be what guides the course of scriptural interpretation. It also shapes the reader's disposition to understand history as a global human history attuned to progression. Schleiermacher's historical-theological endeavor tells the story of how the human subject reaches its climactic position as a free agent and thinker through its participation in a homogenous reading culture. This view upholds his near-complete exclusion of the Hebrew Bible from his hermeneutic writings. Because he sees the transition from Hebraism to Christianity as the high point of the transformation of the subject into a free and able thinker, he depicts the reading subject in close conjunction with the Christian Bible.

In Schleiermacher's theory of interpretation, every person engages with a text in order to have a personal, subjective experience with it. Here, he builds upon two seemingly contradictory trends: attempts to establish a system of education that relies on the universal human capacity to exercise reason (as seen in the works of Kant, Johann Gottlieb Fichte, and others) and the Romantics' experimentation with the subjective and passionate expression. Schleiermacher attempts to reconcile both ideologies in a Lutheran model of a direct, individual engagement with the text that builds on the Romantic aspiration to do so through a subjective and passionate engagement of one's character. Along with this resolution, Schleiermacher develops key notions in textual interpretation, such as biographical readings, affective identification with authors, and attention to the interpersonal connection between the author and the reader.

Schleiermacher's reconciliation of both ideologies with the view of literary hermeneutics as the practice of reason is shown in his distinction between one's associations when encountering a text and one's detection of the author's intentions. Declaring the latter act as the goal of hermeneutics, Schleiermacher revokes the cultural importance of allegory, which was important for Romanticism, and relegates it to the second-degree level of interpretation, together with associations. His new hermeneutic theory marries Lutheran and Romantic efforts to equate literary texts to the Bible. Schleiermacher's interpretive paradigm informs the hermeneutic object as equivalent to the Bible; the effort to decipher an author's intentions analogizes the attempt to conceive God's message.

The Lives of the Biblical Authors

With consideration of the lineage of hermeneutic thinking, Protestant reading techniques in the early nineteenth century disseminated the idea that a reader should affectively identify with authors—an idea that was largely conceived in the late eighteenth century—and turned it into a broad cultural phenomenon. As such, Schleiermacher's contribution accelerated the shift away from philological approaches, with their demands of prior knowledge, and toward interpretation in its abstract form. Interpretation became an attempt to decipher not the literal (*buchstäblich*) meaning of a text but its spirit.[21] As noted by Robert Scott Leventhal, "The object of interpretation was . . . not so much the book or discourse itself, but the ideas behind the discourse, or material that subtends the signs, the mental content behind the semiotic realization."[22] With the writings of Herder and Schleiermacher, language as a system of referents became subject to idealization and abstraction. The Bible as a material object—with its ritual purposes and usages—was gradually replaced by the Bible as a symbolic model for the reading of all texts.

The reading of the New Testament as the representation of Christ's life from multiple perspectives became a point of origin for new interpretative approaches. Textual interpretation began to presuppose that an author's individual life circumstances should be scrutinized in order to understand the target text. Throughout the nineteenth century, such interpretative approaches to cultural artifacts came to be recognized as representative of modernity. Cultural transformations, such as a modernized notion of empathy and scientific reading, prompted new strands of interpretation theory, as hermeneutics came to be defined in terms that crossed confessional affiliations.[23]

Schleiermacher's reading of Luke is the only actual instance of him performing biblical exegesis—a surprising fact in view of the extensiveness of his theoretical writings on hermeneutics. The genre of theological commentary helps Schleiermacher to position the tracing of religious experience—the change in a believer's epistemology and being in the world—as central to hermeneutics. He makes frequent comparisons to the other synoptic Gospels and often ascribes the differences between them to the differing proximities of the authors (in time and space) to Christ during his life and the conferral of his message. In his reading of Luke, Schleiermacher writes that scriptural reading should be attuned to the affect that the text creates in its self-presentation as the documentation of the word of Christ: "It must after all be left to the reader's feelings . . . to conceive the unity which exists in this passage, and to form a lively idea of the way in which all this may have been spoken consecutively."[24]

Schleiermacher's theory of hermeneutics shaped the tools not only for textual analysis but also for the perception of reality. In a transformation built upon his conceptualization of readership as embodied in interpersonal communication, textual understanding became an asset of a universal community of readers. With feelings at the center of readership, modern hermeneutics contributed to the self-definition of the modern community of readers as inclusive. Schleiermacher's approach, as well as this sense of readership's inclusiveness, is at odds with forms of affective attachment to the Scriptures that are grounded in distinct communal belonging and that are inherently nonuniversal. As the next section will show, by bringing attention to religious doctrines as a determining factor of interpretation, literature may unearth this conception of the readers' community as universal.

In his comprehensive study of hermeneutics through Schleiermacher's biography, Wilhelm Dilthey finds the urge to go beyond Kant's philosophy—with its refusal to make claims on God's existence—to be an essential condition of nineteenth-century trends in philosophy. Introducing Schleiermacher's hermeneutics as a transformative moment of modern history facilitates, moreover, Dilthey's own innovations in hermeneutics. Throughout the first half of the nineteenth century, hermeneutics was becoming emblematic of interpersonal exchange. The hermeneutic act was viewed as a possible proof of the affinity between humans. In his effort to conceptualize hermeneutics anew as a scientific method, Dilthey famously wrote, "Understanding is the retrieving of the I in the you" (Das Verstehen ist ein Wiederfinden des Ich im Du).[25] The statement diverges from Kant's pioneering formulation of the task of hermeneutics in *Critique of Pure Reason* (*Kritik der reinen Vernunft*, 1781), according to which the interpreter should strive to understand an author better than he understands himself. Dilthey reinforces the function of reason in interpretation but shifts it from the exploration of one's higher faculties to the exploration of the self, who is an autonomous subject. Notwithstanding their differences, Dilthey and Kant both distance themselves from other approaches that look for the meaning of a text in factors other than its rapport with the reader. Such alternate approaches might attend to a text's material status or grasp its value within the insular moral systems of a specific collective.

Under the influence of Schleiermacher's view of the text as a coherent system that grants its different parts their meanings, Dilthey grants importance to readers' ability to compose a whole picture out of the "pieces" (that is, moments, scenes, or paragraphs). The conceptualization of this ability gave rise to the "hermeneutic circle": the attempt to trace the meaning of a section in a text based on its entirety, while holding that the entirety of the text can be assessed only in view of the meanings of its parts.[26] According to Dilthey, the challenge of reading lies in the fact that readers strive to understand the text by assembling its parts, and yet this process of deciphering is always done in view of a certain interpretation of the text that the reader has pieced together from his or her understanding of the world. Textual interpretation seeks a meaning that is always already in a process of consolidation. Dilthey sees readers as building on their own experiences when they strive to understand a text. Their universal experience as human beings mediates their interpretation.

At midcentury, hermeneutic thinking relied on a coherent tradition of thinkers, who shared presumptions regarding the human aptitude for interpretation: the ideal of a holistic apprehension of texts, the notion of empathy with an author, and the belief that each text contains the keys for its interpretation.[27] These presumptions underwrote the historical sense that Schleiermacher believed one should practice in the reading and translation of texts.[28] The emergence of Protestant hermeneutics as the conceptual pillar of the new textual interpretation reflects the political, social, and cultural changes in the status of the Bible. Theological shifts and interpretive tenets developed reciprocally, as the New Testament became the model object of human comprehension exercised through reading.

Bonds of Jewish Reading in Heine's Oeuvre

Heine's multifaceted oeuvre challenged in various ways the vision of the interpretive community whose major presupposition is readers' autonomy. Heine depicted traditional believers as rooted in their shared world perception. As we have seen, such thinkers as Kant and Schleiermacher depicted Jews' scriptural interpretation as flawed at its core. As German idealism progressed, the guiding principles of traditionalist exegesis were attacked as corrupting influences on basic human skills. Heine, in contrast, described Jewish epistemology as encapsulating a collective understanding of the world and as providing an alternative apparatus for textual comprehension.

When hermeneutics emerged as an interpretive paradigm, basic interpretive skills were brought to the fore. But what happens when biblical interpretation becomes the actual topic of works of literature and art? Heine presents reading as embedded in a set of common agreements about the world (e.g., about chronology, logic, or interpretation). A binding thread in his oeuvre is the presentation of religious belonging—especially in Jewish society—as both volatile and inevitable. Heine's representations of Jewish communities as a separate world converge with his reflections on the nature of writing literature in the modern age. This poetics problematizes the notion of reading as a universal human skill by bringing the very ideology of universal readership to the fore. Modern hermeneutics aims to diminish or alter some major customs of traditional religious communities; religious minorities are nonetheless an active influence on the reading and writing of literature, not least because of the inclusive political and social atmosphere that has given rise to modern hermeneutics.[29] The persistence of the Scriptures as an object of worship embodies this conundrum. The materiality of the Bible is a constant reminder that literary hermeneutics is not globally valid. As such, it serves to challenge paradigmatic attempts to solicit meaning from literary texts.

Born into an assimilated family, Heine's identification as Jewish has been considered critical to his oeuvre.[30] Heine's poetic persona functions as a cultural trope in its own right. It embodies the transitory nature of religious and national belonging. Heine's familiarity with Jewish holidays and his cursory exposure to Hebrew and Aramaic serve as tools in many of his poetic works, often contributing to the portrayal of religious communities as esoteric.[31] Heine's reflections on modernity in his poetry are of a piece with his writings on theology and the historical chronology of Jews as a political and ethnic minority. His Jewish figures are often insular in their perception of reality, which is governed by communal life.[32] Material and spiritual poverty, as well as ongoing persecution, taint their group existence, leaving the impression that continual sorrow hovers about Jewish communal life.

Heine's "Hebrew Melodies" ("Hebräische Melodien," 1851) can be seen to capture the conflict at the core of modern textual interpretation. This cycle of poems explores the emergence of modern Jewish identity in relation to national myths, primarily those evolving out of the biblical descriptions of the

Jewish Diaspora.[33] The cycle evokes how belonging to the Jewish community is bound up with ritual reading and how reading depends on religious affiliation. Liturgical texts, the cornerstone of this religious group, also perpetuate mythical narratives that are entangled with one's personal and historical life circumstances. A fragment from the cycle, which is the second part of the poem "Jehuda ben Halevy," shows how Heine's work produces an experience in the reader that counters the normative disposition cultivated in secular hermeneutics.

> "By the Babylonian waters
> There we sat and wept—our harps were
> Hung upon the weeping willow . . ."
> That old song—do you still know it?
>
> That old tune—do you still know it?—
> How it starts with old elegiac
> Whining, humming like a kettle
> That is seething on the hearth?
>
> Long has it been seething in me—
> For a thousand years. Black sorrow!
> And my wounds are licked by time
> Just like Job's dog licked his boils.
>
> Dog, I thank you for your spittle,
> But its coolness merely soothes me—
> Only death could really heal me,
> But, alas, I am immortal![34]

The poem is framed by a shift from the first-person plural voice of the Psalms at the beginning to the declarative tone of a sole lyric speaker at the end. The allusion to the Psalms evokes an exclusively Jewish perspective for the telling of history. This narration of history begins in a moment of destruction and mourning. Similar to Schleiermacher's portrayal of Jews mourning an "imperishable mummy" in a typical scene of Jewish communal life, the poem depicts biblical hermeneutics as an inherent feature of Jewish tradition from its beginnings. In both Heine's and Schleiermacher's depictions, Jewish communality depends upon a shared consideration of the Scriptures' documentation of how Judaism's greatness and centrality have passed from the world. Both take reading in general and the attachment to a corpus of texts in particular not merely to be characteristic of the Jewish community but, even more so, to be its raison d'être.

The centrality of the Hebrew Bible to Jewish self-definition constitutes Jews as a group of victims and as history's defeated nation, and we see this in Heine's scene of mourning Zion through perpetual, communal crying. Echoing Schleiermacher's tone, Heine's Jewish scriptural reading carries a macabre form throughout his oeuvre. The poem shows the Jews' eternal "whining" to be a unifying practice, and their mourning leads to a surprising vitality. Sacramental reading serves to preserve tradition, as we observe in the kettle simile, where an instrument of longevity signals its eruptive potential.

In its penultimate and final stanzas, the poem refers to the book of Job as a liturgical source for collective mourning. The references signal one community member, Job, as the subject of suffering, whose social isolation from the community of Jewish believers greatly compounds his anguish in the biblical story. On the one hand, this allusion thus strengthens the impression that attachment to the Scriptures posits a universal human experience as the center of suffering. On the other hand, the shift to the first person signals Jewish belonging as a realm of insular and individualistic self-perception. If viewed as a metapoetic comment on the reception of literature, the poem appears to invoke confessional difference—building on and at the same time ridiculing the presupposition that, as literary hermeneutics becomes a paradigmatic interpretive method, confessional difference can be overcome.

The enchanting nature of mourning resembles a poetic text. The "old tune" with which the addressee may be familiar evokes both, as do the exiles' harps. The fragment's repetitive rhythm and rhyme strengthen the parallel between poetic creation and Jewish liturgy, but they come to a halt in the fragment's very last line. This moment of rhythmic discordance transforms the phantom essence of the Jewish community into a trait of the lyric speaker in his expression of eternal suffering. The speaker's self-identification with the biblical protagonist suggests that Jewish belonging informs a unique poetic disposition. What Heine will view as the ghost of Jewish existence is also a lyrical tool for wearing a perpetual, individualistic persona. The individuality of the reader and the author, which the hermeneutic seeks, emerges as a quality deeply rooted in the worldview of a religious minority.

Jewish knowledge of Hebrew is a constant reminder of a material Bible that cannot be fully comprehended through the utilization of reason alone.

Likewise, the presence of Jews constantly signals their divergent communal belonging and, therefore, also the disparities among different readers. The presence of Jews as readers of Hebrew highlights, more specifically, the social functions of textual interpretation that have been suppressed in the process of transforming the Scriptures into a universal asset. The materiality of the Hebrew word calls to mind the Bible's juridical status operating in the context of segregated traditional communities. The biblical language thus shows the interpretive process as reliant on religious training and emphasizes the codependence of hermeneutics and religious education, as well as the moral and ethical norms specific to an insular community of biblical readers.

Jewish Fate in The Rabbi of Bacharach

Researchers often present Heine's work *The Rabbi of Bacharach* as representing the poet's views on Judaism and Jewish communal belonging.[35] Although the novel does not confirm Heine's Jewishness, its references to the Hebrew Bible are manifold. The novel tells the story of Rabbi Abraham and his wife, Sara, who live in a small town not far from the Rhine—the river at the center of many canonical texts of German literature.[36] The protagonists' names and old-age childlessness mirror the Genesis stories. Like the biblical patriarch, Rabbi Abraham leads a quiet life in his longtime home, where he is well respected and well established. This situation lasts until the moment when, on Passover evening, two visitors come to his house in order to provoke the blood libel of a ritual murder. Like the biblical Abraham, the rabbi welcomes strangers into his house with gracious hospitality, but whereas in Genesis the guests bring Abraham the tidings of the birth of his son, the rabbi's guests bring the body of a dead child. In the novel, this child's death takes the place of a child's birth that, in the biblical story, makes Rabbi Abraham a patriarch, the father of a new people. Without explaining what happened, Abraham urges his wife to flee their hometown immediately after the Passover ceremony is over. The two flee without telling their community about the blood libel. The text's final scenes insinuate that their loved ones have been killed because of that decision.

Another correspondence between the life of the protagonists and the Genesis narrative emerges as the protagonists flee along the Rhine.[37] In Heine's novel, Sara, during their flight, recalls how in their youth, shortly before departing for Spain on a business trip, Abraham married her in a zealous attempt to emulate Jacob's life with Rebecca, whose love was realized after seven years anticipating reunion. The novel ends with the reading of the Torah in a synagogue upon Sara and Abraham's integration into a new Jewish community. A new figure, Don Isaak Abarbanel, invites the couple to dine with him, and this concluding banquet demonstrates Abarbanel's preference for material enjoyments over religious practice.[38]

In what follows, I trace the correlation that *The Rabbi of Bacharach* draws between biblical reading and reading in general, specifically through the appearances of Jewish ritual in the text. The novel centrally portrays Jewish readership as inseparable from the community's connection to the Bible. The grounding of one's life in ritual reading practices appears as a fateful, cross-generational link. The task of interpreting the novel thus emerges as contradictory to the text's portrayal of reading as inseparable from a material, deterministic attachment to the Hebrew Bible.

The Scriptures as a cultural artifact have an overwhelming presence in the plot of *The Rabbi of Bacharach*. As we have seen in Chapters 1 and 2, the Hebrew Bible had gained the status of a cultural asset that every literate person should be able to recognize. However, even if *The Rabbi of Bacharach* appears to perform intertextuality, it actually subverts the very idea of it. Intertextuality presumes an audience familiar with the reference text; this presumption makes the rendering of the former text into a substantial part of the new one conceivable. A cultural background shared by readers—be it on ethnic, religious, or other grounds—is what makes intertextuality possible. Several scenes in the novel, where the Hebrew Bible is read out loud to a group, bring the disparities between confessional positions to the fore and show them to be decisive in constructing reader positions. Heine's attention to the communal context of readership and to its purported historical and sociocultural ramifications in the lives of readers is inseparable from the realist traits of the text.

In a moment of *mise en abîme*, the protagonist demonstrates his awareness of the correspondence of his life to that of the biblical Abraham when he hints that the visitors to his house may bless him with the birth of a son: "Showing how the three angels came to Abraham, announcing that he would have a son by his wife Sara, who, meanwhile, urged by feminine curiosity, is listening slyly to it all behind the tent-door."[39] The story then proceeds with Sara's eavesdropping on the strangers' words. The allusion to the biblical text leaves the difference between the modern and the biblical stories indistinct and finds the biblical Sara in the figure of the modern Sara: "This little sign caused a threefold blush to rise to the cheeks of beautiful Sara, who looked down, and then glanced pleasantly at her husband, who went on chanting the wonderful story."[40] The reaction of the biblical Sara to the tidings of Isaac's birth converges with that of the modern Sara. The acknowledgment that the paragraph deals with the modern Sara only occurs with the notification that she follows her husband as he is reading "the wonderful story." This demonstrates the text's emphasis on the circulation of the Holy Scriptures, whose continuity in modernity is what has entangled the biblical stories with the lives of modern-day Jews in the first place.

Climactic moments in the novel revolve around Jewish ritual and liturgy. Jewish communal ritual is both the catalyst for individuals' emotions and a possible tool for keeping them in order. The moment when Sara notices a dramatic transformation in her husband's behavior is indicative of this dual function. Abraham is reading the Passover Haggadah when he notices the child's body under the table. At that moment his face freezes in terror, but he soon continues reading with enhanced zeal and uncanny jolliness:

> As Beautiful Sara listened with devotion while looking at her husband, she saw that in an instant his face assumed an expression as of agony or despair, his cheeks and lips were deadly pale, and his eyes glanced like balls of ice; but almost immediately he became calm and cheerful as before, his cheeks and lips grew ruddy, he looked about him gaily nay, it seemed as if a mad and merry mood, such as was foreign to his nature, had seized him. Beautiful Sara was frightened as she had never been in all her life, and a cold shudder came over her less from the momentary manifestation of dumb despair which she had seen in her husband's face, than from the joyousness which followed and which passed into rollicking jollity.[41]

Abraham's liturgical reading is a stage upon which he projects a spectrum of emotions. But although his feelings vary dramatically, the framework of ritual enables him to return to his typical good nature. His behavior while reading the Haggadah appears startling not because of the irregular nature of the text but because of his familiarity with the situation. He regains his jolliness "almost in that very moment." Abraham is accustomed to his mood shifting rapidly between religious zeal, terror, and calmness (*Ruhe*). Ritual activity epitomizes the volatility of Jewish existence as it recalls the precariousness of Jewish life. At the same time, ritual allows for repetitiveness and circularity. Jewish liturgy provokes emotional peaks and troughs but also gives the believers tools to restrain affect.

In this regard, one scene is particularly telling. Upon their arrival in their new Jewish community, Abraham and Sara encounter a new, tragicomic character, Nosey Stern, who invites them to visit the synagogue. Stern is the sole guard of the community's gates, a surprising fact that begs an explanation. Stern attests to the community's unity as he explains that all its other members are assembling in the synagogue where the story of the Sacrifice of Isaac is being read. Stern confesses that he has heard this "wonderful story" many times already and tells the couple about his feeling that he has inherited untimely fear through his mother's blood. The reader is led to conclude, once again, that fear in the face of the possibility of fatal sacrifice is not an occasional companion of Jewish customs but an immanent component. Because it presents the lives of its protagonists as a replica of the biblical narrative, the novel suggests that reading communities are distinct, cultural monads that resist assembling under the umbrella of global readership.

Given the entanglement of Jewish identity with the purportedly mythical nature of holy texts, the binary opposition of "true" and "fictional" is unproductive. For instance, while the accusation of a child's murder was libelous, this Passover libel was so common that it has become inseparable from the cultural associations attached to this Jewish holiday. Moreover, since the Passover liturgy describes God's punishment of the Egyptians—the ten plagues—readers may recall the culmination of His punishment with the tenth plague: the death of the firstborn. The tenth plague echoes the accusation that Jews rejoice at the death of gentile children, an accusation ascribed to Jews in the modern age. Because of their common grounding in "fictional history," ritual and the historical reception of ritual converge.

Jewish ritual appears to establish a community of readers who are inextricably connected to the Hebrew Bible as the supreme and ascendant text that predetermines their lives. A historical novel, *The Rabbi of Bacharach* seems at first glance an apologia for the lives of the Jews. Yet as it unfolds, its composite relationship to the Hebrew Bible raises the question of the Bible's deterministic influence on life. Jews are fatefully tied to the Holy Scriptures, a tie that is perpetuated not only through their ritual reading and circulation of the Scriptures but also through others' identification of Jews with the Jewish liturgical texts. The biblical text therefore appears as a determining factor in one's life, not only because Jews cannot escape their communal attachment to the Scriptures but also because non-Jews perpetuate the biblical narratives regarding the Jews' persecution as a religious minority. In that sense, Jewish life circumstances are indeed predetermined by religious texts. The novel confirms the Bible's status among religious communities as a text with a true claim to amend reality, ironically, by rewriting the Bible's narratives in an original manner.

A major way in which Heine employs literary devices to evoke the Bible's ritual status is through the novel's depictions of emotions. Ritual emerges as a practice that stimulates human feelings—an effect that is achieved, first and foremost, through the communal reading of biblical texts. The detailed description of how the reading of religious texts elicits emotion parallels the reading of the novel itself. Through detailed descriptions of the fictional reader's feelings, the novel, too, provokes feelings in its reader. Manifesting the ability of texts to stimulate their readers underscores the claim of religious texts to exceed fictional or literary status. Heine detaches affect from its role in the period's interpretive paradigm, where affect was previously understood as facilitating universal empathy. This power to bring about universal empathy is achieved through the Scriptures' claims about reality, which are ingrained in the circulation of holy texts within distinct, traditionalist societies and under specific historical circumstances.

In referencing its own ability to stimulate readers' emotions, Heine's novel has the Bible transgress its role as a model for establishing universal empathy and reveals textual affect as contingent upon confessional and ethnic differences rather than as a bridge beyond them. Reading the biblical narratives emerges not as a way of identifying with the author but as a way of self-positioning within a tradition of readers who are themselves potential figures in the narrative they share. Heine's text stresses confessional difference as the critical factor in determining a reader's identification with a narrative.

One scene, once again, recognizes religious reading in two respects: the ontological claims that religious reading makes on the world and reading as embedded in sacrament. The power of liturgy perpetuates readers' inescapable belonging to the community. The novel's ending finds Sara collapsing once she hears Abraham's prayer of mourning for the dead, as she realizes that her loved ones and relatives in Bacharach have been murdered.

Beautiful Sara had swooned from a singular cause. It is a custom in the synagogue that anyone who has escaped a great danger shall, after the reading of the extracts from the Law, appear in public and return thanks for his Divine deliverance. As Rabbi Abraham rose in the multitude to make his prayer, and Beautiful Sara recognized her husband's voice, she also observed how its accents gradually subsided into the mournful murmur of the prayer for the dead. She heard the names of her dear ones and relations, accompanied by the words which convey the blessing on the departed; and the last hope vanished from her soul, for it was torn by the certainty that those dear ones had really been slain.[42]

Needing rescue from her own overflowing emotional reaction, Sara witnesses the performative power of Jewish liturgy, which retells the story of the Sacrifice of Isaac through a recurring sacrifice. The affective economy of Jewish ritual appears to build on Jews' victimized position and to strengthen it, even as they thank God for momentously saving them. *The Rabbi of Bacharach* offers a metapoetic inquiry into the conditions of the emotional rapport between texts and readers. The text's reflexivity does not preclude its own provocation of the reader's emotions. Thus, the sudden, startling ending of the novel parallels Sara's detachment from the synagogue's communal sphere and emotive surroundings through her somatic collapse as she faints: "And she too would have died from the agony of this conviction, had not a kind swoon poured forgetfulness over her soul."[43] Her last resort is to escape from reality and to detach completely from the affective confines of interpretation.

Early nineteenth-century hermeneutics located the supreme merits of the Bible in the individuals' processing of the text, an activity that arises from within one's membership in the universal community of rational readers. This new consideration of the Bible aimed to transcend confessional specificity by presenting reading as a subjective process wherein epistemic choices are the responsibility of the individual reader. At the same time, such approaches established reading as a capacity common to all human beings and, in so doing, perpetuated adherence to Christianity as a precondition for rational textual interpretation.

Heine's depiction of belonging to a religious minority alerts us to the unavoidable challenges that the presumed universality of textual interpretation poses. Belonging to a religious minority situates the reader in a specific textual culture and cultivates the reader's identification with that textual culture. One aspect of a textual culture is literacy in a specific language. Heine uses Jewish knowledge of the language of the Old Testament as testimony to the discrepancy between a minority community and a hegemonic society. In his

On the History of Religion and Philosophy in Germany (*Zur Geschichte der Religion und Philosophie in Deutschland*, 1834), Heine correlates the ghostly existence of the Jews to their material preservation of the Hebrew Bible: "The knowledge of Hebrew had completely died out in the Christian world. Only the Jews, who kept hidden here and there in a corner of this world, still preserved the traditions of this language. Like a ghost which watched over a treasure which was once entrusted to it when it was alive, so this murdered people, this ghost of a people, sat in its dark ghettos and there preserved the Hebrew Bible. German scholars were seen secretly climbing down into these disreputable hiding-places in order to unearth the treasure, in order to gain knowledge of the Hebrew language."[44] This view of the biblical language as a lost asset disrupts the notion of interpretation as a universal human skill that reaches its ultimate manifestation in the deciphering of one coherent world history. Jewish knowledge of Hebrew is a constant reminder of a material Bible that cannot be fully comprehended through the utilization of reason alone. Likewise, the perseverance of Jews signals their divergent communal belonging and also the disparity between the positions of different readers. The presence of Jews as readers of Hebrew highlights, more specifically, the social functions of textual interpretation suppressed in the process of turning the Scriptures into a universal asset. The materiality of the Hebrew word calls to mind the Bible's juridical status in the context of segregated traditional communities. The biblical language shows the interpretive process to be reliant on religious training and emphasizes the interdependence of hermeneutics and moral codes. Consequently, textual interpretation perpetuates individual decision-making, which in turn deepens the modern disjunction between epistemic choices and religious institutions. The presentation of the Hebrew letter as a startling warning of the disappearing moral ascendancy of the Scriptures in the age of individual interpretation will be the topic of the next chapter.

Chapter 5

The Return of the Repressed Bible

As with Heine's novel in Chapter 4, I will here examine instances of biblical reading in realist prose as reflections on interpretive conventions. Literary hermeneutics assumes a reader's interpretive competence, but by defining its tasks, it also creates the conditions in which interpretation comes to a halt and readers are judged as incompetent at textual interpretation. At the core of the chapter is a reading of Annette von Droste-Hülshoff's 1842 crime novella *The Jews' Beech* (*Die Judenbuche*).[1] *The Jews' Beech* provides a case study of reflective engagement with the theological history that gave rise to literary hermeneutics. The novella prominently interrogates the expectation that modern readers exercise autonomous agency and independent judgment. In so doing, the novella contemplates the religious backdrop for modern reading. The text was written after the Bible had been transformed into a universal cultural asset and separated from the hermeneutic traditions of diverging confessions. As I shall demonstrate, the novella draws attention to readers' changing dispositions, which it presents as the result of the decline in the Bible's status as a juridical authority understood in the context of a religious tradition.

As preparation for my reading of *The Jews' Beech*, I examine Georg Wilhelm Friedrich Hegel's early theological work, "The Spirit of Christianity and Its Fate" ("Der Geist des Christentums und sein Schicksal," 1798–99). This essay shows how early Romantic philosophy established some of its major tenets through its negation of Jewish scriptural interpretation by claiming that Jews' alleged literal understanding of the Bible led to their primitive understanding of religious law. Hegel presumes that this primitive understanding in turn affects Jews' capacity for interpretation. Reflecting this distinction between Jewish and Christian hermeneutic dispositions, *The*

Jews' Beech accepts the attachment of reading and religious convictions while subverting the moral hierarchy that it dictates. The novella views Christian abstract reading as a dangerous societal influence, because it may detach the reader from moral institutions. The difficulty of coming to a conclusion about the crime at the center of the novella's plot further advances its claim for the moral deficiency of its Zeitgeist: the decline of the Bible's status as a juridical authority—a transformation that reverberates in modern hermeneutics.

Eye for an Eye: The Bounds of Biblical Law

In his "Spirit of Christianity and Its Fate," Hegel defines traditional exegesis as a factor constitutive of Jewish self-perception, which, in turn, perpetuates their (mal)function as political agents.[2] Hegel contrasts this epistemology with Christian morality, which is achieved by turning away from the Jewish relation to scriptural law. Although Hegel's essay was not published until the beginning of the twentieth century, it captures a change of thinking in German idealism about the relationship between scriptural reading and the moral dispositions of the individual as subject. Similar to Friedrich Daniel Ernst Schleiermacher, his colleague on the faculty at the University of Berlin, Hegel approaches Judaism ambivalently in his early work. On the one hand, he sees the pre-Christian Jewish existence as a fundamental stage of civilization; on the other, he contends that Judaism is an insufficient expression of man's natural abilities.[3]

"The Spirit of Christianity and Its Fate" compares Jews and Christians in terms of their respective approaches to the Scriptures. In the course of history, Hegel argues, Jews have maintained their regressive worldview through ritual practices, and their adherence to the materiality of the Scriptures represents their primitive connection to scriptural law. Their treatment of the Bible as a set of rules reveals the inability of Jews to attain higher levels of religious existence, especially the abstraction of religious law that enables one to approach a higher ontological mode of reality.[4] According to Hegel, the Jews' rudimentary theological notions—such as their fearful portrayals of the divine—perpetuate their stagnant mode of thinking about the world. Jews perceive God as a vengeful being; they take Him to be a sublime, infinite object rather than an entity with whom one could hold a dynamic, relational affinity. Jews juxtapose the godly being to man, who is finite, and therefore overlook the great merit of religion, which lies precisely in the ability to connect man to the transcendental realm.

Another option excluded from Jewish theology is seeing man as an absolute subject because he can conceive of God as an object.[5] The Jews conceive of man as animate only in the sense that God—the absolute subject—created him in order to obey His laws: "The principle of the entire legislation was the spirit inherited from his forefathers, i.e., was the infinite Object, the sum of all truth and all relations, which thus is strictly the sole infinite subject, for this Object can only be called 'object' in so far as man with the life given him is presupposed and called the living or the absolute subject."[6] Whereas Kant's *Religion Within the Bounds of Reason Alone* (1793) depicts Jesus as a Kantian, in that he overcame Jewish separatism with his enterprise of establishing morality as universal, Hegel presents Abraham, the Israelite, as the archetype of a Kantian. This replacement of Jesus with Abraham serves to criticize Kant's vision of ethics, in that Kant's categorical imperative resembles Jewish morality in cultivating adherence to law that is detached from the human drives.[7]

To support his point that Jews are inept at comprehending universal morality, Hegel quotes Deuteronomy's three exemptions from military service: a man who has built a house but not yet dedicated it, one who has planted a vineyard but not yet eaten its fruits, and one who is betrothed but has not yet married. In Hegel's summary, the principle behind these exemptions is that Jews think it is immoral to coerce someone into risking the possibility of enjoying earthly goods for self-sacrifice. True sacrifice, Hegel contends, can only be done heterogeneously, meaning that it must correspond to realms that are different from one another. Material presence and property, which may be risked if not for the exemption from battle, exist in the same realm of reality. They can be given up only for concepts that are eternal and beyond this realm, such as honor, freedom, and beauty.[8] The fact that the Jews do not consider the renunciation of earthly pleasure as a means for entering a nonearthly realm shows them to be incapable of experiencing true sacrifice, and sacrifice is the gateway to the eternal.

Hegel calls upon a surprising authority to support his argument. He refers to Moses Mendelssohn's declaration in *Jerusalem* that Judaism does not dictate higher truths—or, in Hegel's words, "eternal truths" (*ewige Wahrheiten*)—to its believers.[9] As we have seen, with this declaration Mendelssohn sought to establish that Jewish ritual frees the human mind for political engagement. Hegel's reformulation, however, presents the adherence to law as an impediment to the human potential for conceiving eternal concepts. Traditional Jewish readership, he contends, separates religious practice from the realm of higher truths, which are a matter of free decision. In contrast, according to Mendelssohn, Judaism clears the way for political deliberation; even more importantly, it is a model public religion since its principles entail free choice in matters of higher truth. But in Hegel's rendering, Mendelssohn's statement that Judaism does not dictate higher truths confirms the belief in the Jewish God as a command (*Befehl*) and places Jewish spirituality within the framework of a limited notion of reality.[10] This reading of Mendelssohn allows Hegel to further his own critique of Kant. For Kant, emotions should be separate from the practice of law, and Jews lack the ability to free themselves from adherence to biblical law in favor of a regime based on reason. Hegel sees Kant's view as a Jewishness of sorts, in that Kant's rigid concept of reason is fostered through a fear of ascendancy separate from the moral agent. Hence, it disables a supreme form of an affective attachment to the law in which the adherence facilitates the agent's aspiration to take part in an eternal world order.

According to Hegel's reading of the Scriptures, the Hebrews' endorsement of talion law—the premise of "an eye for an eye"—epitomizes the Jewish faith, with its subjection to laws, commands, and restrictions. The Hebrew stage of civilization brought about a political agent who bases moral conduct on obedience to social rules and commands. This positivistic man of sorts has since become identified with the Jews. According to Hegel, the Christian practice of faith, and particularly Jesus' self-sacrifice, marks a new stage of civilization and a new morality achieved through the annulment of talion law: "An eye for an eye, a tooth for a tooth, say the laws [Matthew 5:38]. Retribution and its equivalence with crime is the sacred principle on which any political order must rest. But Jesus makes a general demand on his hearers to surrender their rights, to lift themselves above the whole sphere of justice or injustice by love, for in love there vanish not only rights but also the feeling of inequality and the hatred of enemies which this feeling's imperative demand for equality implies."[11] The all-important fault of the Jewish people, to Hegel, is their understanding that biblical law is incapable of abstraction.

Hegel builds on this purported deficiency to draw a line between the Hebrew law and modern-day Jews (ironically reiterating, for that purpose, Mendelssohn's presentation of Judaism as a perpetual tradition). By the same token, Hegel contends that the influence of Judaism on its believers is carried forward through liturgy and ritual practices. The Hebrew language is the most crucial element of this ongoing transmission because its flawed forms miseducate people: "The state of Jewish culture cannot be called the state of childhood, nor can its phraseology be called an undeveloped, childlike phraseology. There are a few deep, childlike tones retained in it, or rather reintroduced into it, but the remainder, with its forced and difficult mode of expression, is rather a consequence of the supreme miseducation of the people. A purer being has to fight against this mode of speaking, and he suffers under it when he has to reveal himself in forms of that kind; and he cannot dispense with them, since he himself belongs to this people."[12] Hegel's description of Judaism is a pointed reply to the fascination with the Hebrew Bible in Germany in earlier decades. When observing that Hebrew preserves civilization's ancient qualities, thinkers such as Herder had portrayed Hebrew as new and wild, but Hegel replaces this affirmative presentation with a teleological account that places Hebrew in a backward stage of civilization from which humanity must recover. Much in opposition to Herder's view of Hebrew, Hegel wants to show that the childish nature of Hebrew makes it inherently faulty. Hegel transforms Herder's depiction of Hebrew into one of a continual neglect that is inherent to Jews from the birth of their nation forward.

But even for Hegel, the Christian spirit remains inseparable from the history of Hebrew. The essay's major claim regarding civilization is that the human spirit ascends only in the process of surpassing the intrinsic conditions for its existence. A "purer being" (*ein reineres Wesen*) thus must struggle with Hebrew forms in order to represent itself. This is a difficult task, since the forms of the Hebrew language are constitutive of linguistic expression. This challenge is embodied in the spirit of Jesus, who departed from the Jews to advance humankind into a higher state of existence.

Hegel here conjoins two aspects of Judaism. He attaches the position of Jews as practicing believers to their traditionalist, communal adherence, emblematized by a Jewish way of reading. He connects the practice of the Jewish confession with inherent Jewish characteristics that endure through the cultural practice of reading in common. For Hegel, these Jewish characteristics are both transitory and universal. They belong to a specific past stage of civilization, but the epistemology of that epoch persists as universal. Jewish "staleness" in following the Scriptures translates into a broad way of conceiving reality and becomes ingrained in a mode of exegesis. The greatest manifestation of that exegesis is a juridical conception of the world wherein a stringent enforcement of talion law represents the inability to transcend materiality.

Morality and Reading

This conceptualization of exegesis occurred alongside the emergence of realism in literature, such that transformations in hermeneutics were intertwined with the rise of realist fiction around 1850. Realist prose features narrators who address the moral faults of the society of which they are a part.[13] In Romantic texts, the narrator or poetic speaker had been remote from society, as in the figure of the Romantic outcast. Realist fiction replaces this outsider-narrator with a narrator who is a typical member of society.[14] How might the appearance of the Bible and its ritual functions in such prose intervene into the social acceptance of exegetical principles as normative? Literary research may renew its interest in hermeneutics, I hope to show, not by adhering to it as an interpretive method in the strict sense but rather by investigating hermeneutic models of reading as widespread practices whose interdependence with political secularism resonates in literary texts and dismantles common presuppositions behind interpretation.

Droste-Hülshoff's crime novella pronounces the cultural echoes of a departure from the rhetorical tradition in textual interpretation, a departure founded upon the modern conception of the relationship between authors, readers, and literature as embedded in a gradual process of comprehending texts' original meanings. The crime that is at the center of the novella—the murder of the Jew Aaron—calls attention to an array of hidden meanings, as the mystery of the murderer's identity is never solved. Scholars have attributed the canonical status of the novella to its original representation of a criminal investigation and its subsequent influence over the crime genre in German literature.[15] While the text invites readers to speculate about its secrets, it likewise poses difficulties throughout. The narrative style of *The Jews' Beech* has long been characterized as fragmented and hard to follow. The features that contribute to this impression include shifts in narrative perspective and breaks in the plot at peak moments, particularly during scenes in which crimes are being committed.[16] The novella's structure thus impedes the hermeneutic task of untangling the murder investigation, the events of which constitute the core of the story.

The plot of *The Jews' Beech* centers on the gradual disintegration of a village that is losing its ethical codes because of its remoteness from state sovereignty. The novella establishes a parallel between the moral deterioration of the village and the ethical corrosion of its main protagonist, Friedrich Mergel. The young Friedrich lives alone with his mother, Margreth, after his alcoholic and violent father is found dead; throughout his childhood and early adulthood, he is exposed to recurrent acts of violence and the exoneration of the perpetrators. The moral chaos in the village manifests itself in a ferocious power struggle over control of the woods, which comes to a climax in two acts of lethal violence: the murder of the villager Brandis, killed by his business rivals, and the subsequent murder of the Jew Aaron, whose dead body is found underneath the beech tree that gives the novella its name. Multiple hints suggest Friedrich's involvement in these crimes, including his witnessing Brandis's murder in the woods. Not only does Friedrich allow the assassination to happen, but he also keeps silence about his knowledge of the crime—not least since his uncle, Simon, who functions as his surrogate father, is involved in the crime. Though the exact identity of Aaron's murderer remains unknown, the novella's end offers a certain degree of closure, when Friedrich, who fled the village after the crime, returns in old age and hangs himself from the beech tree, an act that the villagers interpret as a sign of his unbearable guilt for having committed the murder.

The brief appearance of biblical language is one major impediment to following the plot of *The Jews' Beech* and unearthing the identity of Aaron's murderer. Near the middle of the novella, members of the village's Jewish community engrave a Hebrew sentence on the beech tree at the scene of the crime; it remains untranslated until the novella's final lines.[17] The Hebrew sentence references Jewish liturgy and disrupts both the reading of the novella and the hermeneutic process that the deciphering of its mystery has set into motion. Taking this moment of confusion as a starting point, the following reading approaches *The Jews' Beech* as a commentary on the social and cultural stakes of modern hermeneutics.[18] The engraving takes the reader's attention to the historical consequences of the rise of literary hermeneutics as a leading interpretive paradigm: the uprooting of textual interpretation from religious practices and the spiritual and moral dispositions that they convey. The appearance of the biblical language epitomizes the failure of hermeneutics by pointing to the general reader's inability to grasp the Bible's language and, by extension, the foundations of moral law.[19] *The Jews' Beech* contains numerous allusions to the Bible, including verses, names, and motifs. The novella thematizes the protagonists' dishonest relationship to the

Scriptures and thereby illustrates their moral deterioration. The loss of the Bible as a juridical and liturgical authority occurs simultaneously in the work's plot and in the reader's attempt to interpret the text—an effort that the novella both sets into motion and ultimately challenges.

The beginning of the nineteenth century bore witness to the reframing of the Bible as a collective cultural asset. The Bible was refashioned to fit a diverse array of aesthetic, hermeneutic, and Pietistic agendas: "The Reformation made the Protestant Bible the engine of political, religious, and imaginative life, an engine defended and cherished well into the nineteenth century."[20] The personalization of the Scriptures yielded new hermeneutic practices for engaging with texts. Late Enlightenment Protestant readership in Europe brought about a major transition in the reading of the Scriptures. A new view of scriptural reading as a process driven by individual readers' sensibilities replaced attention to the Bible's spiritual tenets. This process of interpreting Scripture, which came to influence nearly all modes of reading in Germany, relied on the Lutheran view that the Bible holds the keys to its own interpretation.[21] Ingrained in the personalization of the reader's relationship to the Bible, the interpretive act no longer demanded prior training (historical, philological, or other) for the successful undertaking of the hermeneutic act (i.e., for the deciphering of a text's unapparent meanings). Dorothea von Mücke thus demonstrates how modern practices of producing and interpreting texts—which were constitutive of a public sphere populated by autonomous thinkers—built on a new valorization of religious practices of contemplation as having universal relevance to the formation of the subject, regardless of his or her confessional belonging.[22]

This new hermeneutic model turned eighteenth-century biblical reading into an egalitarian practice that reflected each individual's mental, cognitive, and affective capacities, leading to the sweeping success of Schleiermacher's interpretative theories. *The Jews' Beech* emerged in the afterlife of the Bible's transformation into an artifact separate from the long-established hermeneutic traditions of diverging confessions. This period brought about not only the abstraction of biblical texts but also the dependence of literary hermeneutics on the globalization of scriptural readership.

Moral Corrosion and the Hindrance of Investigation

From its start, the novella presents the village as the ultimate locus of crime and recklessness. Isolated from state authority in the provincial backlands, the inhabitants become accustomed to ad hoc juridical norms, abandoning the letter of the law for a volatile legal system that seems more suited to their needs. It is this geographic and societal context that defines Friedrich's formative years. To compound matters, after losing his father at a young age, he quickly learns the immediate benefits of petty crime from Simon and his other companions.

Friedrich's moral deterioration appears to reach its peak when he is implicated in the murder of his fellow villager Brandis, an incident that foreshadows the killing of Aaron. The murder of Brandis is the first decisive moment when moral chaos correlates with hermeneutic impediment. Hermeneutic impediment characterizes the protagonists as it also alludes to the trait of modern reality that conditions the reading of the novella. The scene of Brandis's murder is focalized through Friedrich, who witnesses a group of foresters closing in on Brandis. He does not seem to be fully aware of Brandis's impending murder or of his own agency in allowing it to happen.[23] As if to mimic Friedrich's misperception, the narrative becomes fragmented at this point. The murder is only alluded to without any direct description of the act, while abrupt switches to seemingly unrelated scenes—such as Margreth making tea for Friedrich when he comes home sick—create disruptive gaps. Margreth's blindness to her son's involvement in the crime compounds the ambiguity surrounding the murder. Fragmentary narration thus parallels the protagonists' epistemic choices, which lead to their inability to conform to basic ethical norms. For both the characters and the reader, moments of incomprehensibility make circumstantial evidence slip away.

Later indications clearly point to Simon's culpability in this first murder, but the hints concerning the identity of Aaron's murderer pose larger exegetical enigmas. They are larger in the sense that they raise doubts not only about the investigation's findings but also about the very notion of securing knowledge based on evidence. Interpreting the clues in Aaron's murder case is emblematic of the process of reading the novella—that is, the crime story—as a whole.

Friedrich's suicide offers one plausible solution to the mystery. This impression is enhanced when readers discover that the Hebrew engraving on the tree refers to talion law, which holds that a crime should be punished with equivalent gravity, as in the Old Testament "eye for an eye for an eye, a tooth for a tooth." But the novella also provides several indications that a different version of Aaron's murder is plausible. In a crucial moment in their investigation of the incident, the villagers receive a letter from a local judge, the contents of which provide a promising new lead. The letter states that a Jewish resident of a convent in a different region confessed to killing a fellow Jew named Aaron. The fact that the convent dweller committed suicide soon after his confession, however, makes it difficult to pursue this possibility further. The judge accompanies his message with the French expression: "The truth is not always convincing."[24] This sentence not only comments on the nature of interpretation, but it also serves to relativize the closure at the novella's end, when the mysterious Hebrew lines are revealed: "When you approach this place, I shall do to you what you have done to me."[25] The elusive letter has led to the view among scholars that Friedrich should not be regarded as the murderer precisely because he is the most obvious suspect.[26]

The villagers live in a state of paralysis caused by faulty interpretations. The investigators ignore Friedrich's clear involvement in the murder of Brandis, allowing him to evade interrogation as to what went on in the woods. The ineptitude of officials in the Brandis case is ominous. Their inability to enforce the law results in the two main suspects in Aaron's murder killing themselves before they are properly investigated. The protagonists also have faulty memories and are generally imperceptive. When Friedrich returns to the village, he manages to disguise himself as his former companion, Johannes, a man completely different from him in character. The villagers' inability to see through the disguise further establishes them as passive "readers" who cannot or do not want to see the details as they are. They opt for an interpretation geared toward grasping a text's spirit over parsing out concrete details. In a legal context, such flexible interpretation blinds the villagers to concrete evidence. The novella's confusing storyline emulates this flexible interpretation, thus translating moral deterioration into hermeneutic hindrance. This confusion makes the reader into an incompetent seeker, whose knowledge of the events rarely ever exceeds that of the lead investigators. In other words, the reader is tainted with the same interpretive incompatibility that prevents the villagers from solving the mystery and catching the murderers.

A contrast to this interpretive stance is established through the Jewish adherence to a basic notion of morality.[27] The Jewish system of morality is elucidated when, in the aftermath of Aaron's murder, the village's Jews come together to buy the beech tree underneath which his body was found and engrave it with the cryptic message. The script bluntly materializes Jewish adherence to biblical law, specifically the law of retaliation ("an eye for an eye").

The novella thus differentiates between Christian and Jewish approaches to the Scriptures in order to show how the Christians' personalized interpretation of the Bible, which detaches the Scriptures from an agreed-upon moral imperative, brings about moral deterioration. In contrast, Jews represent a primordial obedience to the Scriptures that is effective, if still primitive, in its adherence to moral law. Judaism's persistent adherence to biblical text as juridical authority is contrasted with Christian scriptural reading, which goes beyond, or abstracts, the written word. The novella suggests that Christian reading may go astray when instrumentalized for egoistic needs, and yet, at its best, Christian reading may also achieve the sublimation of the letter through an authentic spiritual quest.

Epistemic Choices

Several scenes in *The Jews' Beech* deal directly with the process of scriptural reading and the interpretation of biblical and liturgical sources. In these scenes, the characters' interactions with the Scriptures seem to fuel their cognitive and affective relation to reality. From its beginning, the novella unfolds as a reversed bildungsroman by following Friedrich as he learns to avoid rules and evident restrictions from his mother and even more so from his uncle. Friedrich's moral corrosion worsens as he learns to emulate Christian figures who tinker with biblical law for personal gain. The egoistic way in which the village community subsumes liturgical texts has been a part of Friedrich's relationship to religion since childhood. During the storm that heralds the news of his father's death, Margreth implores Friedrich to turn to faith in moments of crisis. Her request exposes the instrumentality with which she regards religion, bluntly correlating the act of asking for forgiveness for one's sins with the physical safety of the "believers":

> The wind had shifted and now hissed in his ear like a snake through the window cracks. His shoulders stiffened; he crept deep beneath his feather bed and out of fear he lay still. After a while he noticed, that his mother was not asleep either. He would hear her cry and sometimes utter, "Hail Mary full of grace," and "pray for us poor sinners." The beads of the rosary slid passed his face. An involuntary sigh escaped him.

> "Friedrich, are you awake?"
> "Yes, Mother."
> "Pray a little, Child. You can already do half of the Lord's Prayer. That God will protect us from flood and fire."[28]

Margreth's opportunistic and rapid turn to religion in the interest of Friedrich's and her own safety appears natural, yet the novella illustrates that seeking refuge in religion for fear of one's well-being may derive from an unwillingness to face social sanctions. This opportunism can be seen quite clearly in Simon's misconduct and in the (mis)education of his nephew. The uncle's disdain for law becomes apparent when he teaches Friedrich—who is about to go to confession perhaps to cleanse his conscience of guilt for Brandis's death—a "moral" lesson. Simon makes sure to instill in him not only his own interpretation of a key biblical commandment but also a more general lesson concerning the strategic forgetting of Scripture:

> "Friedrich, where are you going?" the old man whispered.
> "Uncle, is that you? I want to go to confession."
> "I thought so. Go, in God's name, but confess like a Christian."
> "I plan to," said Friedrich.
> "Remember the Ten Commandments: thou shall not bear witness against thy neighbor."
> "No false witness!"
> "No, none at all! You have been poorly taught. One who accuses another in confession is unworthy to receive the sacrament."[29]

Simon's bending of biblical law demonstrates the moral deterioration to which personalized interpretation and oral transmission of the Bible's teachings can lead: the corruption of the written word through subjective and self-serving redactions. The oral practice of law and word-of-mouth juridical education allow for the bending of the law according to one's momentary intentions and needs, setting the scene for moral disorder.

Scholars have related the rise of German realism to the collapse of religious beliefs and philosophical systems of explanation that guide an individual's worldview and epistemic choices.[30] Realism has been understood as the goal, shared by a group of autonomous authors, to formulate an ethical-social critique through literature.[31] German literary realism, more particularly, embraces its distance from metaphysical idealism. To a large extent, German realism shifts the core of the aesthetic experience from self-exploration to self-improvement, and accordingly, it shifts the prism of the hermeneutic investigation from the unearthing of the author's self to the tracing of the ethical project that he or she opts to pursue.

The Jews' Beech thematizes societal coexistence and the conditions for moral conduct within a community. It focuses on the ramifications of the "cultural Bible" in shaping communal existence in Germany in the first half of the nineteenth century.[32] Taking a reflective and at times reactionary stance on norms of hermeneutic reading, the novella contrasts the village's moral paralysis with the conduct of the Jewish villagers. The Jewish presence alerts readers to the circulation of the Bible in traditional religious contexts. The rigor with which the Jews adhere to scriptural language opens up a broader perspective on interpretation, highlighting the contingency of hermeneutic practices on religious belonging and the continual function of exegesis as a social pillar. The appearance of Hebrew script thus signals a move from the *Buche* to the *Buch*. The Hebrew writing on the beech tree emblematizes the Jews' steady connection to the Book in a world dominated by egoistic performances of subjective interpretation.

The novella draws a clear distinction between the Bible's two parts: the Old Testament of the Jews and the New Testament of Christians. Highlighting this partition, the novella generally presents the Jewish juridical system as a primitive system of cruel retribution. Following Aaron's murder, two different verses, one from the New Testament and one from the Old Testament, reflect the respective affiliations:

> The master stood at the window and looked anxiously out into the darkness across his fields. . . .
>
> "Gretchen, check once again, pour water on it to make sure it is completely out. Come let's recite the gospel of John."
>
> Everyone knelt down and the wife began. "In the beginning was the Word, and the Word was with God, and the Word was God."

> A horrible clap of thunder. Everyone flinched; then horrible screams and turmoil sounded up the stairs.

> "For God's sake, is the house on fire?" Frau von S. yelled and sank her face into the chair. The door was ripped open and the wife of the Jew Aaron bolted in. She looked as pale as death, with her hair wildly strewn around her head, and sopping wet from the rain. She threw herself on one knee in front of the lord of the manor.

> "Justice!" she cried. "Justice! My husband has been killed." She collapsed into unconsciousness.[33]

This scene depicts a transition from the New Testament, in which God is elevated and merciful (as in the Gospel of John), to the Old Testament, in which God appears, according to the novella, vengeful and wrathful. The allusion to the Christian credo is, importantly, a statement about the sublime nature of God's word and the supreme and privileged status of the Scriptures. This Christian reverence for the word is contrasted with the Jewish woman's frantic call for action. Aaron's wife represents the Jewish attitude toward the Bible in her plea for Old Testament justice. Punishment is not left up to God alone but is dictated by a bloodthirsty, and yet effective, adherence to the law—the "eye for an eye" principle: "Her massive suspense had subsided and she now seemed half bewildered or, more accurately, stunned. 'An eye for an eye, a tooth for a tooth!' These were the few words she periodically spat out."[34] This concept of justice aligns with the text's characterization of Jewish materialism, whose emblem is talion law. By and large, the Jews in the novella are merchants, and most of them make a living from the much-despised practice of moneylending. As such, they seem to have inside knowledge of exchange value and of how to scale punishment appropriately.

Although the novella depicts the Jewish juridical norm of retribution as morally inferior, it is better suited to the violent environment of the village. In a world that corrupts the word of the law, where law is subject to individual impulses, the Jews are able to sustain their communal justice system through the primitive observance of a written code. The tree motif conveys the differences between the Jewish and the Christian juridical systems. The Jews—who are hurt corporeally, the same way that trees are damaged throughout the text—avenge their assault by casting a spell on the beech tree.

Earlier representations of divine justice in Christianity help to contextualize the novella's depiction of Christian morality as going astray in an age of excessive and personalized textual interpretation. Konrad Schaum argues that Friedrich's suicide is an alleged sinner's act of self-sacrifice.[35] As such, it embodies Dante's principle of the *contrapasso*, or punishment "by a process either resembling or contrasting with the sin itself."[36] The motif of wood in the novella, associated with this idea of moral punishment, complicates the *contrapasso* principle.[37] In the seventh canto of the *Inferno*, the narrator encounters the souls of those who died by suicide, only to find that they have been turned into trees and can only utter their thoughts by breaking their branches. As dictated by *contrapasso*, these sinners have been punished in accordance with their sin of violence against the self. Because they separated the soul and the body that God had put together, their punishment deprives them of their human body and turns them into static objects. Violence toward the trees via the breaking of branches further injures the suicides' deformed bodies while granting their souls a certain relief by providing them a way to externalize their pain. This imagery has often been associated with a well-known religious figure, Judas Iscariot, whose guilt led him to commit suicide by hanging himself from a tree. The description of the suicidal souls as hanged on the tree forever appears to be the basis for such an interpretation.

The connection between trees, wood, and violence in Dante's version of hell also finds expression in *The Jews' Beech*, and the resonances of the suicide forest are particularly germane. In both works, trees embody retribution for violence while also inciting it: the breaking of twigs in Dante or the stealing of wood that leads to further murders in *The Jews' Beech*. Both texts also depict the ultimate union of human and tree through suicide, which itself has a biblical origin in Judas Iscariot. Several readers of *The Jews' Beech* describe Friedrich as Simon's metaphorical son and suggest that Friedrich resembles the son of Simon in the Bible, namely Judas.[38] These Christian connotations are juxtaposed with the Jewish relationship to justice, language, and trees. The Jewish presence—embodied in the Hebrew writing engraved on the beech tree—is a reminder of the corporealness that follows from an adherence to the Bible's word in its basic and literal sense. Theirs is a corporeal connection to law that the Christian characters have lost. Thus, the appearance of the Hebrew script in the novella echoes the symbolic function of the Bible in the constitution of literary hermeneutics. The novella's allusions to interpretation insinuate that modern hermeneutics depends on a skewed perception of the Bible. Commenting on the Bible's moral status as forgotten and on textual interpretation as inconclusive, the novella interferes with the universality of religious presumptions in the nineteenth century and destabilizes the reading practices that underlie them.

Forms of Reading

As we saw in Chapter 4, Schleiermacher's paradigm of textual interpretation advances the idea that penetrating the author's innermost intentions is a universal ability possessed by each human being. His theory of interpretation emphasizes the importance of understanding utterances in the context of their conception: "Every speech or script is to be understood only in a larger context."[39] Schleiermacher's writings thus mark the transition from philological to psychological hermeneutics. He draws a parallel between this transition and the transition from the Old Testament to the New Testament, from Hebrew to Greek, and from talion law to Christian grace.

Hegel's account in "The Spirit of Christianity and Its Fate" juxtaposes the primitive Jewish adherence to law with the Christian transcendence of legal dictates through the notion of love. In characterizing Jewish reading as a social community whose principles continue to inform civilization, Hegel reinforces the theological paradigm shift reflected in Schleiermacher's systematized hermeneutics: the transition from the Old Testament to the New Testament as the model for ethical progress. The primary concern of this shift is the move from Biblical Hebrew to ancient Greek. Presenting the former as reflecting the spirit of primitive Jewish culture, Hegel singles out the departure of Christianity from its Hebrew forms as the most urgent task facing its members, for only in doing so will Christians be able to overcome the materiality of law.

The theological turn of the late eighteenth century originated in certain prevalent Protestant reading techniques, which presented the Bible anew as a global cultural asset. This trend construed literary hermeneutics as a coherent lineage based on a set of interconnected interpretive principles: the primacy of holistic understanding, the importance of capturing the spirit of a text, and the belief that each text contains the keys to its own interpretation.

The interconnected principles of the new literary hermeneutics accelerated the shift from philological hermeneutics and the analysis of rhetoric, with their requirements of formal training, to interpretation in its abstract form, as an attempt to decipher not the literal meaning of a text but rather its spirit. Under the influence of Schleiermacher's hermeneutics, language as a system of referents becomes subject to idealization and abstraction. The Bible as a material object with its ritual purposes and usages gave way to its new abstract image that served its role as a model for the reading of all texts.

Much at odds with the view of abstraction as the ultimate tool for textual apprehension, several of the narratological features of *The Jews' Beech* contribute to the impression that the mystery at the center of the novella cannot be solved since the text is obscure and thus indecipherable. The novella is narrated throughout by an intradiegetic narrator, who appears present during the various events but whose characteristic unreliability casts a shadow of doubt over the veracity of reported events. This feeling derives from the impersonalization of the narrator, who is neither identified by name nor presented as one of the characters. Yet the act of narration does not seem to align with a major characteristic of such a storyteller: omniscience. The suspicion that the narrator's knowledge of events—or his willingness to share it—is lacking calls into question the narrator's omniscience. Events in the story only supposedly take place, as when the narrator uses expressions such as "it says" (heißt es), "it was thought" (man meinte), and "it should turn out" (es soll . . . , dass). The narration is based on rumors or half-truths, not concrete evidence. The use of the subjunctive verb form *sei* further supports this notion.

The novella thus simultaneously suggests that the riddle of the murders may be solved with multiple clues regarding the investigation, while at the same time provoking the opposite impression—that the truth may never be uncovered. When a murder is about to take place, the narration becomes fragmented and inconclusive; yet it is suggested that with both murders— that of Brandis and that of Aaron—Friedrich was somehow involved. Accordingly, the resolution of the first murder does not come about through the description of the act as it happened. Rather, the uncovering of a single significant fact—that Friedrich's uncle, Simon, was involved in the crime— unravels the mystery. Typical of the novella's structure, this style of narration highlights the fact that descriptions of reality are often flawed. *The Jews' Beech* thus dispels the expectations raised by its appearance as a realistic account and by the generic conventions of crime literature, both of which dictate that the case should be solved and social order should be reinstated.

Several readings of the novella have focused on the question of whether the interpretative enigma at its core can be resolved. Donahue categorizes two schools of thought in this regard: "One school holds that 'undecidability' is itself the point; another is bent on teaching us how to read the novella so that we recognize Friedrich as the perpetrator hanging in the beech tree at the story's conclusion."[40] Understanding the novella as a statement on the mechanics of hermeneutics as well as on the cultural backdrop for this practice highlights the indeterminacy emerging in the course of its interpretation. However, instead of enforcing the choice between seeing the reader as capable of deciphering the mystery and cautioning against the reader's hazardous "epistemological hubris," such an analysis demonstrates that the novella's "undecidability" lies in the difficulty of determining whether any given interpretation is right or wrong; readers will never see their reading confirmed or refuted.[41] The reading that I propose shows the novella to be signaling that the keys to its interpretation cannot be found within the text itself. Consequently, the unresolvable crime at its core highlights the dangers of making individual interpretation a pillar of communal law.

Already in its opening lines, the novella frames interpretation as an act with acute social ramifications. A poem functions as a preface to the main text: "Where is the hand so tender that it unerringly may separate the narrowed mind's troubles. So surely that it without trembling may cast a stone at a poor, downtrodden being? . . . Leave rest the stone for it will strike your own head!"[42] This motto restates the New Testament conviction according to which humans, as inherently sinful beings, are not entitled to render judgment on others. The poem conveys the problem of enforcing moral imperatives as inherent to the Christian system of justice. The effectiveness of moral judgment depends on individual pretensions and motivations with regards to the social order—a dependence dramatically enhanced by modernity's separation of epistemic choices from religious institutions. By pointing out how the epistemological and the moral blend together in the act of judging, the verses at the beginning of *The Jews' Beech* frame the task of punishment as unmanageable, since it requires moral flawlessness. The poem signals the novella's presentation of hermeneutic practices as grounded in ethical and spiritual dispositions and as cultivated in confessional contexts.

By linking the process of reading texts with the navigation of epistemic choices, *The Jews' Beech* portrays acts of hermeneutics as interdependent with the adherence to metaphysical and moral dispositions, which are perpetuated and pursued in the dynamic process of interpreting a text. *The Jews' Beech* thus points out how preferences and bias inflect individual conceptions of reality, making hermeneutics a volatile enterprise in an era that opted to neutralize the religious context of hermeneutics by detaching it from confessional affiliation and by basing textual interpretation on the theological principle of a personalized connection to the Scriptures.

Competing Exegesis

The presence of the beech tree draws attention to the threatening return of biblical language to a world that has forgotten the concrete relation between Scripture and written law. The moment when biblical law is revealed in its corporealness, alongside Jewish ritual, is the moment when hermeneutics comes to a halt and readers can proceed no further. The Hebrew letter subverts an approach to literary texts that privileges individual interpretation, conceives it as an all-human capacity, and uses it as a token for the construction of a global community of interpreters.

The ambiguous manner in which the novella is narrated is an illustration of the metaphysical confusion in modernity, where epistemological judgment is detached from the supervision of religious institutions and, accordingly, from the restrictions imposed by traditional training. The paradigmatic hermeneutics of early nineteenth-century German created a precedent for the detachment of spiritual practices from their grounding in a specific confession. The dominant principles of biblical interpretation based acts of reading on the capacity of all readers to engage with the Bible as a universal imperative. This view of biblical reading as a global practice elicited a new reading culture, a transformation with pressing political and social echoes. Multiple thematic allusions to the Bible in *The Jews' Beech* merge with its narrative form to question the role of interpretation in a culture faced with moral disorder and the loss of punitive conventions.

For the general contemporary German reader whom *The Jews' Beech* addresses, it may have been alarming that the novella's Jewish characters, who engrave the beech tree with Hebrew writing, have mastered the ability to use the Bible to address present-day affairs. As we have seen in previous chapters, under the influence of Kant and Schleiermacher's tenets on exegesis, readers were disciplined to adapt texts to their life circumstances. This imperative, however, was steeped in the translation of the Scriptures into a contemporary language, which entailed distancing oneself from the literal understanding of biblical language. To the general reader who does not read Hebrew, the disruptive appearance of the Hebrew letter has an uncanny effect. This effect arises from the history of hermeneutics and from the transition of this paradigm into a religiously neutral practice that, paradoxically, owns its cultural salience to the primordial holiness of Scripture.

As the Jewish villagers use scriptural passages as pieces of living language and unearth the Bible's primordial presence in traditional reading cultures, readers may be reminded of the reliance of their literacy on practices of faith. By signaling that cultural approaches to reading are dependent on the religious and ethical codes underlying them, the novella subverts the notion of interpretation as a global practice; reading cultures are exposed as depending on religious conduct and ethical codes. In a moment that recalls the materiality of the Bible, the writing on the tree exposes the reliance of modern hermeneutics on a largely abstract model of biblical reading. The moment's threatening character arises from the anomaly of the Jewish figures. Jews do not interpret biblical law, and consequently, they abstain from amending texts in accordance with individual epistemic choices and personal needs. As such, they are the last resort for biblical law in a phantasmagoric, deteriorating society of self-seeking interpreters.

Coda

Beyond Hermeneutic Thinking

A Jewish rite probably dating back as far as the Middle Ages is still used today to infuse children with a love of reading. Hebrew letters are shown to a young boy on a slate or a page that has been smeared with honey. The boy, who typically also receives his own personal copy of the Bible on the same day, is invited to lick the letters. This sensuous first encounter with script is meant to ingrain the sweetness of the Bible in his memory. The boy will enter the traditional Jewish school, the cheder, around the age of five, and while there, life centers upon a laborious study of traditional Jewish commentaries on the Hebrew Bible. This system of education builds upon the boy's recollection of the sensuous pleasure that initiated him into a long-lasting community of believers, into an unbroken chain of adherents to the Hebrew script.

Enlightenment thinkers interfered with such rituals of reading. Without demolishing the premises of traditional communal teaching altogether, their theories altered the experience of initiation into a circle of pious learners. As we have seen in Chapter 3 with the example of Mendelssohn's translation of the Hebrew Bible into German, the sensuality of the encounter with script began drawing on such ideals as *Bildung*, which implies that the collective aspiration of human beings is to achieve literacy and, with it, intellectual autonomy. For Jews, sweetness is no longer merely the taste of belonging to a chosen people, an affinity marked through the Hebrew script. The new flavor of literacy blends pride in communal distinctiveness with the promise of universal merits.

This book has concentrated on the premise that sociocultural norms of relating to the Scriptures encapsulate an entire array of cognitive and affective relationships to texts, signs, and the act of interpretation. The investigation of the interdependency of theology and textual interpretation began between the

1750s and 1780s, at a turning point for the practice of faith in Europe, when individuals' new perception of themselves as belonging to humankind became a determining factor in their religious conduct. In describing this period, I have relied on scholarship that has shown that as Enlightenment philosophy drew from scriptural interpretation, it also annulled the doctrinal separatism of some key theological ideals, narratives, and practices. I extend this work to show that this process of universalization called upon another preoccupation of Enlightenment philosophy: the art of interpretation.

The sensibilities emerging with modern hermeneutics signaled a new political era. Jürgen Habermas's *The Structural Transformation of the Public Sphere* (*Strukturwandel der Öffentlichkeit*, 1962) famously argues that the spread of intellectual practices in the Enlightenment, such as public discussion in coffeehouses, was a boon to the view that belonging to a political community can cultivate the individual's abilities.[1] In my investigation, which pertains to the roots of literary education, I have charted a few concurrent routes by which hermeneutics conditioned the political vision of the modern nation. First, I have shown that the skills manifested in the hermeneutic act (such as autonomous judgment, interpersonal empathy, and the self-cultivation of intellectualism) were at times taken to confirm one's ability to participate in a political community. Second, I have claimed that the transformation of interpreters into a universal group worked to erase the distinctiveness of religious textual cultures. The imminent rise of the modern state drew both instrumentally and symbolically upon the notion of a global community of interpreters. The idea of a community of interpreters granted societal coherence to a group composed of equal members who also adhered to different faiths. Perhaps more importantly, it provided a conceptual understanding of this vision.

Nevertheless, amid persistent confessional differences, this unifying vision for hermeneutics was at times premature and discordant. I have provided a key example of such discordance in Schleiermacher's confirmation of Jews' aptitude as political actors, which was at odds with his critique of Jews' deficient biblical exegesis and corresponding faulty perception of the world. I have also cited Mendelssohn's insistence on the particularity of Jewish ritual despite his praise of the Jews' contributions to humanity. These instances illustrate the tensions that the conceptualization of the state as a community provoked in light of the history of the separatism of religious communities.

Although I cannot present a comprehensive history of hermeneutics since 1850, I would like to explore briefly here how the issues described in this book have reverberated in subsequent thought. My goal is to propose, in closing, that a universalist conception of the interpretive community has fueled not merely hermeneutics but also its critique.

Take, for instance, Martin Heidegger's *What Is Called Thinking?* (*Was heisst Denken?*, 1954) and the polemics it has provoked. The essay is a revolutionary intervention into the understanding of language as instrumental since it urges thinkers not to try to separate themselves from the object of their inquiry but rather to examine it from the inside. The essay engages with the question of how to think about thinking in modern society; how can one define what thought is while immersed in the process of thinking? Attentiveness to the role of language plays an important role in Heidegger's philosophical inquiry, as he ponders the connotative and etiological relations between words such as *Denken, Gedanke, Gedächtnis,* and *Danke* (thinking, thought, memory, and thanks, respectively).[2] The essay advocates the reflective use of language as free and independent from preconceived intentions, ideas, or meanings enforced by the author. Heidegger's take on language and poetic creation challenges the common concepts of hermeneutic reading. Most obviously, it cancels out the objective of tracing the intentions that the author has tried to express through the text.

One of the most famous responses to Heidegger's revolutionary suggestion came from the poet Paul Celan in both his poetics and his public speaking. In his renowned Bremen Literature Prize speech, Celan referred to Heidegger's essay in contemplating how he might express his thanks to the German audience. He played on the similarity of the verbs *danken* (to thank) and *denken* (to think). Their closeness, he noted, is typical of the interconnections between words in the German language. Reading Celan's poem "Think of It" ("Denk Dir") in tandem with Heidegger's essay reveals the links between the poetic and linguistic ideologies of the two authors and between the manifestations of those ideologies in their respective writings.[3] The poem reveals that one's identification as Jewish produces a particular disposition in readers:

Think of it:
the bog soldier of Massada
teaches himself home, most
inextinguishably,
against
every barb in the wire.

Think of it:
the eyeless with no shape
lead you free through the tumult, you
grow stronger and
stronger.

Think of it: your
own hand
has held
this bit of
habitable
earth, suffered up
again
into life.

Think of it:
this came towards me,
name-awake, hand-awake
for ever,
from the unburiable.[4]

The poem uses wordplay, sound repetition, and alliteration extensively, creating the impression that language unfolds on its own terms. Celan's use of neologisms (*namenwach*, *handwach*) confirms this impression, as do the surrealist images of the return of the dead, either as a collective noun or as an abstract idea. Detachment from coherent linguistic signification serves as the precondition for allowing language to crystalize into new and provocative images, as in the formation of the *MoorSolDAt von MaSSaDa* (the bog soldier of Masada, my capitalization). Celan's poem appears to form such surreal images through experimentation with sound, as in the repeating consonants "M," "S," and "D"). The playfulness through which the image is formed seems to stand in strong opposition to its denotation of the collective suicide act at the site of Masada in Israel. The historical massacre at Masada is a *Denkmal* (memorial) that emerges from the experiment in *denken* (thinking).

Yet against the impression of free linguistic play, the poem's reference to the soldier who comes back home, only to be persecuted by the "unburiable," alerts the reader to the poetic persona of Celan as a Jewish survivor of the

Second World War, echoing the fatality attached to Masada. Indeed, Celan's poetry shows linguistic play as undetached from the poet's own identity—at the same time as it alerts to the horrors of a disorienting world. The presence of multiple languages in Celan's poetry effectively interferes with Heidegger's notion of language as representing its own inspiration.[5] The sounds and free play with language employ words evocative of theological history.[6] At the same time that Celan's linguistic experiment diverges from premises that it seems to have in common with Heidegger's philosophy—such as the critique of positivistic views of language—Celan's poetics also puts those premises into practice. His oeuvre maps comprehension and incomprehension as existing in a nonbinary relationship with each other. It does so by challenging the belief that (in)comprehension of textual utterances should be understood in the context of a universal community of readers. His poems have a texture that makes readers constantly rethink the historical, social, and biographic circumstances granting them aptitude as interpreters rather than dismissing such an aptitude altogether.

Hebrew words and proper names—such as "Massada"—appear frequently in Celan's poems. Their evocation of the Jewish liturgy and ethos provokes another level of meaning in language, one that grounds linguistic signification and its interpretation in ritual practices. Along with the references to Jewish theology, myths, and biblical language, Celan's use of both rhythmic lines and free rhyme brings to mind communal gatherings around texts, such as holiday rituals or mourning ceremonies. These rites—at whose center is the affective attachment to texts—offer an alternative to the imperative to comprehend language as part of a global collective.

This poetic alert to the seclusion of religious circles also resonates with Celan's depictions of the individual as detached from his or her surroundings, like the soldier who returns home in the poem. In Celan's theology-laden poetics, references to biography—both the author's and the reader's—offer a theological path back to the engagement with texts. This path of personalized allegorical readings had been disavowed in modern literary interpretation. Other twentieth-century philosophical projects concerned with hermeneutics and phenomenology share this return to lost sources of meaning. Paul Ricoeur was one such thinker who claimed that literary genres and their reception rely upon theological presuppositions.[7] Yet in contrast to these views, Celan's use of Hebrew words epitomizes an overall sense that (in)accessibility is contingent upon one's participation in excluded groups. His poems maintain a view of reading that recalls the reader's position as an exception to human society and not as a member of a global community. Only from that position does meaning take shape. Celan's poetry suggests the possibility of replacing the hermeneutic assumption of global inclusion with an experience of exclusion, lonesomeness, and persecution—a position that embodies estrangement from visions of collective comprehension altogether.

Celan's is nevertheless an exceptional voice. Hermeneutics has remained a defining trait of modern societies. The dominance of this practice can be thought of in terms of substitution. Hermeneutics functions, in a sense, as a replacement for confessional religions and the social functions they provide through interpretation, communal reading, and the gathering around texts. In a stark difference from such traditions, the modernization of reading insists on and perpetuates readers' independent thought. This independence manifests itself most clearly in what Ricoeur called the "hermeneutics of suspicion"—an inquiry meant to expose the presuppositions behind taken-for-granted worldviews. Critique positioned in a judgmental and autonomous stance from a distance is perhaps the strongest propagator of modern hermeneutics. Critique is steeped in its religious history even as, or especially as, it reiterates the conditions for modern subjectivity.

Notes

Introduction

1. Competing religious ideologies, however, may be put to use in defining the neutrality of public spaces that were established during the Enlightenment as impartial to religious norms. I discuss this in Chapter 3.

2. See Saba Mahmood, "Religious Reason and Secular Affect: An Incommensurable Divide?," *Critical Inquiry* 35, no. 4 (2009): 842–43.

3. I do not presume that the thinkers I discuss in this book strove for the establishment of a political community of equal citizens in the form that is known to us today. None of the figures that make up the story I tell about hermeneutics in the late Enlightenment identified himself as republican. Rather, I follow the consolidation of the hermeneutic community as an unintended consequence of the polemics among these thinkers, as well as their individual endeavors.

4. Jonathan Sheehan, *The Enlightenment Bible: Translation, Scholarship, Culture* (Princeton, N.J.: Princeton University Press, 2005).

5. Martin Gierl claims that the ways in which Lutheran orthodoxy sought to define the movement of Pietism as a sect in the early eighteenth century accelerated the view that public debates should accommodate openness, civil manners, and fairness. *Pietismus und Aufklärung: Theologische Polemik und die Kommunikationsreform der Wissenschaft am Ende des 17. Jahrhunderts* (Göttingen: Vandenhoeck & Ruprecht, 1997). Dorothea von Mücke describes the Enlightenment notion of the public sphere and the social practices that it accommodates (predominantly the creation of aesthetic artifacts and their observation) as reliant on early modern Pietistic narratives. According to von Mücke, modes of contemplation were informed by their formerly ritual or confessional content, such as Kant's aesthetic theory that places subjective observation of art at its center. *The Practices of the Enlightenment: Aesthetics, Authorship, and the Public* (New York: Columbia University Press, 2015).

6. Chronologically, my examination in Chapters 1, 2, and 3 begins with the publication of Robert Lowth's influential *Lectures on the Sacred Poetry of the Hebrews* (1753) and ends with the publication of two works that are at the center of my study: Herder's *On the Spirit of Hebrew Poetry* (1782–83) and Mendelssohn's *Jerusalem, or On Religious Power and Judaism* (1783).

7. The work of philosopher Michael N. Forster has a similar objective to my own. In a series of publications and translations about Herder and the philosophy of language in

Germany, Forster makes the case for Herder's prominent role in constituting the tradition of hermeneutics and textual interpretation up until the work of Hans-Georg Gadamer. Although he places hermeneutics in the field of philosophy of language, Forster's analysis makes some of the same claims as literary scholars who have also embraced Herder as a figure central to modern cultural production. Forster stresses Herder's concept of translation as a paradigmatic example of his innovative conception of textual understanding. Forster, *After Herder: Philosophy of Language in the German Tradition* (Oxford: Oxford University Press, 2010); and *German Philosophy of Language: From Schlegel to Hegel and Beyond* (Oxford: Oxford University Press, 2011). Also see Forster, introduction to *Herder: Philosophical Writings*, by Johann Gottfried von Herder, ed. Michael N. Forster (Cambridge: Cambridge University Press, 2002), xviii.

8. This historical dynamic has been explored in David Sorkin's *The Religious Enlightenment: Protestants, Jews, and Catholics from London to Vienna* (Princeton, N.J.: Princeton University Press, 2008), which stresses the role of Judaism in mapping the Enlightenment as a boon for religious polemics; and Leora Batnitzky's *How Judaism Became a Religion: An Introduction to Modern Jewish Thought* (Princeton, N.J.: Princeton University Press, 2011), which scrutinizes the conceptual problems of defining Judaism through the Protestant concept of "religion."

9. In her *Sprache in der Zerstreuung: Die Säkularisierung des Hebräischen im 18. Jahrhundert* (Göttingen: Vandenhoeck & Ruprecht, 2009), Andrea Schatz presents Mendelssohn's notion of liturgy as seminal to the transformation of Hebrew into a modern national language. She presents this shift as indicative of the secularization of major elements of traditional German Jewish society as it adapted itself to the cultural norms of its Christian surroundings. I further this argument with the claim that Mendelssohn took an active stance in shaping the category of secularization as it was conceptualized in the late German Enlightenment, particularly in the field of political philosophy.

10. On this transformation, see Tomoko Masuzawa, *The Invention of World Religions, or, How European Universalism Was Preserved in the Language of Pluralism* (Chicago: University of Chicago Press, 2005).

11. See Joachim Wach, *Das Verstehen Grundzüge einer Geschichte der hermeneutischen Theorie im 19. Jahrhundert* (Tübingen: J. C. B Mohr, 1929), 2:32–33.

12. Benedict Anderson, *Imagined Communities: Reflections on the Origin and Spread of Nationalism*, rev. ed. (London: Verso, 2006), 39.

13. Pascale Casanova, *The World Republic of Letters*, trans. M. B. DeBevoise (Cambridge, Mass.: Harvard University Press, 2004), 34–35. Informed by postcolonial studies, Michael Allan considers Herder's claim that "the particularities of specific literary traditions [are] reflective of distinct national characteristics." Allan argues that this view helps to constitute the tensions between the particular and the universal that characterize classical accounts of world literature. *In the Shadow of World Literature: Sites of Reading in Colonial Egypt* (Princeton, N.J.: Princeton University Press, 2016), 13.

14. Emily Apter, *Against World Literature: On the Politics of Untranslatability* (London: Verso, 2013), 41–45.

15. Apter writes that whereas the "duty to translate is rooted in Bloom's writing in the cipher of the Hebrew Bible and its secular re-inscription in the aesthetics of romanticism, one could say that in more recent philosophy and theory, the duty to *not* translate is derived from Islamic tradition." Ibid., 253.

16. See Talal Asad, *Formations of the Secular: Christianity, Islam, Modernity* (Stanford, Calif.: Stanford University Press, 2003), 21–66. For a succinct summary of Asad's claims on political secularism, see William E. Connolly, "Europe: A Minor Tradition," in *Powers of the Secular Modern: Talal Asad and His Interlocutors*, ed. David Scott and Charles Hirschkind (Stanford, Calif.: Stanford University Press, 2006), 75–92.

17. Asad, *Formations of the Secular*, 39–40; emphasis added.

18. See especially Michael Warner, "Uncritical Reading," in *Polemic: Critical or Uncritical*, ed. Jane Gallop (New York: Routledge, 2004), 13–38; Allan, *In the Shadow*; and Saba Mahmood, "*Azazeel* and the Politics of Historical Fiction in Egypt," *Comparative Literature* 65, no. 3 (2013): 265–84.

19. Asad, *Formations of the Secular*, 40–43.

20. See especially Warner, "Uncritical Reading"; and Allan, *In the Shadow*, 1–14. Mahmood reconstructs the history of "critical reading" as contingent upon the liberal notion of religious toleration in her article "Secularism, Hermeneutics, and Empire: The Politics of Islamic Reformation," *Public Culture* 18, no. 2 (2006): 323–47.

21. In their respective articles on the Danish cartoons controversy, Asad and Mahmood argue that the interpretation of cultural symbols is inseparable from the cultivation of political secularism in the West, a process that has formed the epistemological processing of cultural objects. The experience of deep spiritual injury when observing the caricatures of Muhammad is embedded in affiliation with Muslim traditions that foster a non-Western notion of "icon." Traditionalist affiliation entails a mode of a visual reception of Muhammad's figure as continuous with one's self. According to Mahmood, the "ability" to critically observe images presupposes a universal epistemological apparatus that is based on the subject's autonomy that is foreign to Muslim observation of the world. See Asad, "Free Speech, Blasphemy, and Secular Criticism," in *Is Critique Secular? Blasphemy, Injury, and Free Speech*, ed. Wendy Brown, Judith Butler, and Saba Mahmood (Berkeley: Townsend Center for the Humanities, University of California, 2009), 26–63; and Mahmood, "Religious Reason and Secular Affect: An Incommensurable Divide?" in *Is Critique Secular? Blasphemy, Injury, and Free Speech*, ed. Wendy Brown, Judith Butler, and Saba Mahmood (Berkeley: Townsend Center for the Humanities, University of California, 2009), 64–100. See also Talal Asad, "Reflections on Blasphemy and Secular Culture," in *Religion: Beyond a Concept*, ed. Hent de Vries (New York: Fordham University Press, 2008), 580–609.

22. Of course, not all late eighteenth-century readings of the Old Testament shied away from historiographical understanding of the Bible. As Hans W. Frei has cogently shown, Herder's ability to reconcile historical investigations of the biblical text with a continual view of its atemporal ascendancy widely influenced Protestant biblical hermeneutics. *The Eclipse of Biblical Narrative: A Study in Eighteenth and Nineteenth Century Hermeneutics* (New Haven, Conn.: Yale University Press, 1974), 183. As Chapter 1 will demonstrate, Herder's suggestion to examine the Hebrew Bible as a product of a specific culture dispels the view of the Scriptures as a God-given object. Presenting textual interpretation as a process of spiritual growth, Herder manages to reconcile critical and philological observations of the Bible with its atemporal theological significance.

23. Jeffrey S. Librett's *The Rhetoric of Cultural Dialogue: Jews and Germans from Moses Mendelssohn to Richard Wagner and Beyond* (Stanford, Calif.: Stanford University Press, 2000) explores the history of German-Jewish exchange as a symbolic construct that draws its cultural importance from hermeneutics because of the dialogic structure at the core of this

paradigm. Librett argues that the idea that Judaism could be integrated in German culture under the auspices of the modern state has functioned since the Enlightenment as a major symbol. He sees this notion as an amalgamation of the Jewish letter with the Protestant spirit—an aspiration of the German Enlightenment that was rejected in other German traditions. Similar to Librett, I view the German-Jewish exchange as a cultural construct, whose importance lies in its symbolic power (rather than in a concrete materialization).

24. "In considering the integration of Jews into a modern state, Germans were necessarily dealing with the legacy of Christian universalism, with Christianity's claim to a normative status in the modern world." Jonathan M. Hess, *German, Jews and the Claims of Modernity* (New Haven, Conn.: Yale University Press, 2002), 11.

25. Moses Mendelssohn to Johann Gottfried Herder, June 1780, in *Aus Herders Nachlass* by Johann Gottfried Herder, ed. H. Düntzer (Frankfurt a.M.: Meidinger, 1856), 2: 216.

26. David E. Wellbery's work on Lessing and his interlocutors was especially influential in establishing this view. See *Lessing's Laocoon: Semiotics and Aesthetics in the Age of Reason* (Cambridge: Cambridge University Press, 1984).

27. See Rüdiger Campe, *Affekt und Ausdruck: Zur Umwandlung der literarischen Rede im 17. und 18. Jahrhundert* (Tübingen: M. Niemeyer, 1990); Robert Scott Leventhal, *The Disciplines of Interpretation: Lessing, Herder, Schlegel and Hermeneutics in Germany, 1750–1800* (Berlin: W. de Gruyter, 1994); Lothar van Laak, *Hermeneutik literarischer Sinnlichkeit: Historisch-systematische Studien zur Literatur des 17. und 18. Jahrhunderts* (Tübingen: Niemeyer, 2003); and Ethel Matala de Mazza, *Der verfasste Körper: Zum Projekt einer organischen Gemeinschaft in der politischen Romantik* (Freiburg: Rombach, 1999).

28. Suzanne L. Marchand, *German Orientalism in the Age of Empire: Religion, Race, and Scholarship* (Washington, D.C.: German Historical Institute, 2009), xviii–xxi.

29. Sorkin, *Religious Enlightenment.*

30. Ibid., 140, 190.

31. The term translates as "holiness" of historical occurrences while at the same time resonating with "healing" (since the notion encompasses the German verb *heilen*). Karl Löwith, *Meaning in History: The Theological Implications of the Philosophy of History* (Chicago: University of Chicago Press, 1949), 11.

32. Hans Blumenberg, *Die Legitimität der Neuzeit* (Frankfurt a.M.: Suhrkamp, 1966), esp. 82–86.

33. Charles Taylor, *A Secular Age* (Cambridge, Mass.: Belknap Press of Harvard University Press, 2007).

34. Martin Jay, "Faith-Based History," review of *A Secular Age*, by Charles Taylor, *History and Theory* 48, no. 1 (2009): 76–84.

35. Ibid., 84.

36. Ibid. See Walter Benjamin, "Franz Kafka: On the Tenth Anniversary of his Death," in *Illuminations: Essays and Reflections*, ed. Hannah Arendt, trans. Harry Zohn (New York: Schocken, 1968), 116.

Chapter 1

1. Frei, *Eclipse of Biblical Narrative*, esp. 1–16. Frei writes, "The Bible becomes a 'witness' to a history, rather than a narrative text. Its meaning is a unitary complex consisting of the history of saving events, the history of the witness' faithful response to them and

finally the present faithful stance toward that complex history as a present and future reality" (181).

2. Peter Szondi has shown that the emergence of literary hermeneutics relied on late Enlightenment theories of understanding (*Verstehen*), which opted to explicate the experience of literary interpretation through regulative rules. Beginning in the early eighteenth century, this trend reached a climax with Schleiermacher's view that speech exists in two parallel realms: spoken language, which makes the utterance intelligible, and the author's thought, which construes the utterance through his or her life circumstances. Szondi, *Einführung in die literarische Hermeneutik* (Frankfurt a.M.: Suhrkamp, 1975), 172–91. Schleiermacher's hermeneutics will be elaborated on in Chapter 4.

3. As John Baildam writes, "Hamann saw a close relationship between nature and poetry, each being related to the other as a specific means of divine revelation. This was reflected in Herder's earlier writings, where the underlying concept was of literature and poetry as manifestations, either in a nation or an individual, of the power of God working in and through human beings." *Paradisal Love: Johann Gottfried Herder and the Song of Songs* (Sheffield, UK: Sheffield Academic Press, 1999), 61.

4. Erich Auerbach, "Philology and World Literature," trans. Maire and Edward Said, *Centennial Review* 13, no. 1 (1969): 2.

5. For example, see Heinrich Anz, *Hermeneutische Positionen: Schleiermacher, Dilthey, Heidegger, Gadamer* (Göttingen: Vandenhoeck & Ruprecht, 1982); and Richard E. Palmer, *Hermeneutics: Interpretation Theory in Schleiermacher, Dilthey, Heidegger, and Gadamer* (Evanston, Ill.: Northwestern University Press, 1969). Kristin Gjesdal has found the traces of conceptual sources for the hermeneutic movement in earlier authors commonly associated with German idealism. Gjesdal shows that Gadamer's eminent work, *Wahrheit und Methode: Grundzüge einer philosophischen Hermeneutik*, draws widely on German idealism. *Gadamer and the Legacy of German Idealism* (Cambridge: Cambridge University Press, 2009).

6. Adam Sutcliffe, *Judaism and Enlightenment* (New York: Cambridge University Press, 2003), 16–25.

7. Sheehan, *Enlightenment Bible*, 67.

8. This tendency is common in such canonical histories of the Enlightenment as Peter Gay's *The Enlightenment: An Interpretation*, vol. 1, *The Rise of Modern Paganism* (New York: W. W. Norton, 1966).

9. Sorkin, *Religious Enlightenment*, 3.

10. "For Christians, the religious Enlightenment represented a renunciation of Reformation and Counter-Reformation militance, an express alternative to two centuries of dogmatism and fanaticism, intolerance and religious warfare. For Jews, it represented an effort to overcome the uncharacteristic cultural isolation of the post-Reformation period through appropriation of neglected elements of their own heritage and engagement with the larger culture." Ibid., 4. Sorkin offers an alternative model to the dismissal of religion from accounts of the Enlightenment by expanding the role of theology in shaping the Enlightenment public sphere. Treating such figures as William Warburton, Siegmund Jakob Baumgarten, and Moses Mendelssohn, his *Religious Enlightenment* turns out to be an account of how interpretation of biblical and extrabiblical religious law builds on the notion of *sola scriptura*, according to which every individual should be allowed to engage with the Scriptures on his or her own terms.

11. On Herder's role in a lineage of theologians who reconciled philological-historical approaches to the Bible with Protestant theology and on the cultural importance of this

mediation, see Frei, *Eclipse of Biblical Narrative*, 183–201. I see Hamann as a constructive influence on Herder's efforts to implement in his exegesis notions of reasoning from the late Enlightenment and German idealism, as evident in Hamann's presentation of reading as a platform for the reader's cognitive and affective experimentation. For a similar position that depicts Hamann not merely as antagonistic to Enlightenment thought and biblical philology but as holding a constructive dialogue with them, see Jonathan Sheehan, "Enlightenment Details: Theology, Natural History, and the Letter *h*," *Representations*, no. 61 (1998): 29–56.

12. Jonathan M. Hess has claimed that Michaelis's work signified an antagonistic shift in German culture toward the Hebrew tradition, which can be identified as early hostility toward Judaism. Hess, *Germans, Jews and the Claims of Modernity*, 51–69.

13. Johann David Michaelis, *Mosaisches Recht* (Frankfurt a.M.: J. Gottlieb Garbe, 1775), 1:235. Unless otherwise noted, all translations are my own. See also Michaelis, *Beurtheilung der Mittel, welche man anwendet, die ausgestorbene hebräische Sprache zu verstehen* (Göttingen: s.n., 1757).

14. "Poesie ist die Muttersprache des menschlichen Geschlechts." Johann Georg Hamann, *Aesthetica in nuce*, Universal-Bibliothek 926/26a (Stuttgart: Reclam, 1968), 81.

15. Ibid.

16. John Betz, *After Enlightenment: The Post-secular Vision of J. G. Hamann* (Oxford: Wiley-Blackwell, 2009), 101.

17. Ibid., 51.

18. Hamann, *Aesthetica in nuce*, 79. The English translations of both biblical passages are from the New Revised Standard Version.

19. On Hamann's own writing as performative and on his original notion of textual interpretation and philology, see Eckhard Schumacher, *Die Ironie der Unverständlichkeit: Johann Georg Hamann, Friedrich Schlegel, Jacques Derrida, Paul de Man* (Frankfurt a.M.: Suhrkamp, 2000), 109–22.

20. Horace, *Carmina* 3.1.1, quoted in Hamann, *Aesthetica in nuce*, 81.

21. On Hamann's continual attacks on Michaelis's studies of the Hebrew language, see Michael C. Legaspi, *The Death of Scripture and the Rise of Biblical Studies* (Oxford: Oxford University Press, 2010), 162.

22. John Hamilton, "Poetica Obscura: Reexamining Hamann's Contribution to the Pindaric Tradition," *Eighteenth-Century Studies* 34, no. 1 (2000): 93–115, esp. 93–95.

23. Herder's *Oldest Document of Humankind* is an exception to this rule. There, Herder's analysis of Genesis establishes that the Hebrew language won its supreme status by serving God's creation of the world through speech. In this regard, Herder considers the Hebrew Bible not only as an object of study to which he will apply his interpretation theory but also as a history of the emergence of the different components upon which the theory relies. Because of the importance that Herder's theory assigns to language and aesthetics, he presents the Hebrew Bible as a self-reflective depiction of the historical eminence of poetics, such that the Old Testament retains its status as the ethos of human origin.

24. Robert Lowth, *Lectures on the Sacred Poetry of the Hebrews*, trans. G. Gregory, new ed. (Boston: Crocker & Brewster, 1829).

25. On the radical nature of this aesthetic appreciation of Hebrew, particularly given the critical accounts of Hebrew among such figures as Voltaire, see Ofri Ilany, "Between Ziona and Teutona: The Hebrew Model and the Beginning of German National Culture" [in Hebrew], *Historia*, no. 28 (2012): 81–105. Also see Ilany, *In Search of the Hebrew People:*

Bible and Nation in the German Enlightenment (Bloomington: Indiana University Press, 2018), 22–23, 72–73. According to Betz, "Hamann was arguably the first to introduce into German letters an intentionally 'sublime style,' characterized like Hebrew poetry by elevated themes, a proliferation of symbolic figures, gnomic allusions, darkness, terseness, and vehemence of expression." Betz, *After Enlightenment*, 12.

26. Johann Georg Hamann, *Londoner Schriften*, ed. Oswald Bayer and Bernd Weißenborn, new ed. (Munich: C. H. Beck, 1993), 59.

27. See Gwen Griffith Dickson, *Johann Georg Hamann's Relational Metacriticism* (Berlin: W. de Gruyter, 1995), 189.

28. As formulated by Dickson, for Hamann, "the Bible, whatever the source of its inspiration, is written by human authors and is addressed to human beings to evoke a 'human' and personal response. Perfection . . . would be inappropriate. . . . God communicates with us on *our* terms, in *our* fashion, within *our* limitations." *Hamann's Relational Metacriticism*, 132.

29. Jonathan Hess has argued that Michaelis's depictions of the ancient Hebrews strongly differ from Herder's, in that the former does not wish his readers to establish empathy for this ancient people. *German, Jews and the Claims of Modernity*, 59.

30. Frederick C. Beiser, *Enlightenment, Revolution, and Romanticism: The Genesis of Modern German Political Thought, 1790–1800* (Cambridge, Mass.: Harvard University Press, 1992), 195.

31. As Sabine Gross and Marcus Bullock argue, ascribing the term "empathy" to Herder goes far beyond his own lexical choices. For one, Herder does not use *Einfühlung* as a noun, which detaches his notion of understanding of foreign cultures from some of the modern idealized definitions of "empathy." Gross and Bullock, "Historiography, Theology, and the *Erkenntnis*: Empathy in Herder and Benjamin," in *J. G. Herder: From Cognition to Cultural Science*, ed. Beate Allert (Heidelberg: Synchron, 2016), 159–82. In what follows, I do not attempt to trace the modern notion of empathy in Herder's theory of interpretation but rather to establish this notion heuristically from Herder's references to reading as the deciphering of a national spirit different than one's own.

32. "Die Notwendigkeit uns als Leser in die Empfindung[en] des Schriftstellers, den wir vor uns haben, zu versetzen uns seiner Verfaßung so viel mögl. zu nähern." Hamann, *Londoner Schriften*, 66.

33. Johann Gottfried Herder, *Werke in zehn Bänden*, vol. 1, *Frühe Schriften, 1764–1772*, ed. Ulrich Gaier (Frankfurt a.M.: Deutscher Klassiker, 1985), 182.

34. Ibid., 195–97.

35. Herder develops a model of oral poetry as the ideal for literature in any period; in Herder's conception of orality as an abstract principle, all poetry should be given an "oral form." As David Wellbery argues, "Herder is historically such a decisive and influential critic not because of the accuracy of his observations and judgments, but because he formulated a *new imaginary of language and literature.* . . . Herder imagines the collectivity of oral culture as a single individual that, in the inwardness of its audition, hears its own voice, the originary song of its language." *The Specular Moment: Goethe's Early Lyric and the Beginnings of Romanticism* (Stanford, Calif.: Stanford University Press, 1996), 190–91.

36. As noted by Ze'ev Levy, Herder's various writings on the Hebrew language and on Judaism reveal stark contradictions in their conception of poetry as a divine gift. *Judaism in the Worldview of J. G. Hamann, J. G. Herder, and W. v. Goethe* [in Hebrew] (Jerusalem: Mosad Bialik, 1994), 117.

37. Johann Gottfried Herder, *Werke in zehn Bänden*, vol. 5, *Schriften zum Alten Testament*, ed. Rudolf Smend (Frankfurt a.M.: Deutsche Klassiker, 1993), 28.

38. Ibid.

39. "So lange wir keine Göttliche Grammatik, Logik, und Metaphysik haben; so lange wollen wir also auch Menschlich auslegen. Sprache, Zeiten, Sitten, Nation, Schriftsteller, Zusammenhang—alles, *wie in einem Menschlichen Buche.*" Ibid., 29; emphasis added.

40. Frei, *Eclipse of Biblical Narrative*, 187–90.

41. Herder, *Schriften zum Alten Testament*, 158.

42. Warburton argues that the invention of *Schrift* provoked a shift from complex to simple ways of thinking, which marked the decline of Egypt and the rise of Israel. Taking a stark opposition to this view, Herder defines Hebrew epistemology as a milestone in the evolution of human art and culture. He praises Hebrew as an Ur-language. The description of Hebrew as the ideal language of creation appears at the very beginning of *The Oldest Document of Humankind*, where Herder establishes his theory of the hieroglyphs of creation. The supremacy of script can be seen in language's importance in the creation process.

43. Herder, *Schriften zum Alten Testament*, 318–19.

44. See Daniel Weidner, "Ursprung und Wesen der ebräischen Poesie," in *Urpoesie und Morgenland: Johann Gottfried Herders "Vom Geist der ebräischen Poesie,"* edited by Daniel Weidner (Berlin: Kadmos, 2008), 134; and Weidner, *Bibel und Literatur um 1800* (Munich: Wilhelm Fink, 2011), 50–61.

45. Jeffrey Librett has claimed that the Judaism-Catholicism-Protestantism triangle has been creating, since the eighteenth century, the impression of a cultural transmission of ideologies, which propagates the "rhetoric of cultural dialogue." Librett takes the hermeneutic tradition as central to this trend because it furthers the belief in "the symmetrical exchange of expressions of intention between dyadic partners, to the end of mutual and nonviolent understanding." *Rhetoric of Cultural Dialogue*, xvii.

46. As Pheng Cheah succinctly writes, "World-literary intercourse enables the fabrication of humanity because the philological study of the unique development of specific linguistic traditions as manifested in the world's different literary cultures can help us compose a universal history of the human spirit that underlies these literatures." Cheah, "World Against Globe: Toward a Normative Conception of World Literature," *New Literary History* 45, no. 3 (2014): 305.

47. Ibid.

48. Auerbach, "Philology and World Literature," 2.

49. Casanova, *World Republic of Letters*, 75.

50. Ibid.

51. This aspect of Herder's enterprise is also missing in the scholarly response to Casanova's work. See Aamir Mufti, *Forget English! Orientalisms and World Literature* (Cambridge, Mass.: Harvard University Press, 2016), 64–67. Mufti draws upon Said's description of the history of world literature as a colonialist project. However, he does not attend to the role that diverging theological projects within the Protestant state played in the shaping of world literature. His account of the spread of world literature as emblematic of European cultural imperialism does not deal with the theological influences on the notion of world literature. Attention to the theological debates that fueled the notion demonstrates its emergence as a contingent cultural phenomenon.

52. I agree with John K. Noyes that in allocating national literatures to geographical territories, Herder's conceptualization differs from Goethe's: "'World' for Goethe is symbolic—

it reveals, uncovers, and renders visible multiplicity as a unity. And it does this without recourse to taxonomic classification or prior judgments of form. In refusing to provide a casual narrative of the world on a geopolitical level, as Herder had attempted, Goethe believed he was providing an aesthetic alternative to its instrumentalist structuring." Noyes, "Writing the Dialectical Structure of the Modern Subject: Goethe on World Literature and World Citizenship," *Seminar* 51, no. 2 (2015): 108.

53. As John H. Zammito has shown, the precritical Kant developed a largely empiricist conception of philosophy as an anthropology meant for pragmatic purposes, a vision that he later replaced with a moralistic and metaphysical focus. Adhering to his teacher's early formulation of the project of philosophy, Herder shifts the cultural undertone of philosophical anthropology, stressing the diversity of the human population. See Zammito, *Kant, Herder, and the Birth of Anthropology* (Chicago: University of Chicago Press, 2002).

54. Johann Gottfried Herder, *Werke in zehn Bänden*, vol. 6, *Ideen zur Philosophie der Geschichte der Menschheit*, ed. Martin Bollacher (Frankfurt a.M.: Deutsche Klassiker, 1989), 34.

55. Herder takes national affiliation to be a universal trait of human beings; the conscious belonging to a nationality is no less than a human right. The importance of this principle to Herder's widespread notion of national culture points to a problem in Casanova's separation of world literatures that are universal and cosmopolitan from those that remain mostly in their national loci. As Vladimir Biti writes in his overview of the dissemination of world literature by German Romantics, "Contrary to Casanova's strong opposition between nationalism and cosmopolitanism, or politics and literature for that matter, these apparent opposites turned out to be closely interrelated." Biti, *Tracing Global Democracy: Literature, Theory, and the Politics of Trauma* (Berlin/Boston: Walter de Gruyter, 2016), 59.

56. See Maurice Olender, *The Languages of Paradise: Race, Religion, and Philology in the Nineteenth Century*, trans. Arthur Goldhammer (Cambridge, Mass.: Harvard University Press, 1992), 1–50. In *Bibel und Literatur*, Weidner analyzes the engagement with the Bible during the late eighteenth and early nineteenth centuries. Weidner demonstrates that the cultural prevalence of the Bible is revealed not merely in correspondences with biblical motifs and narratives but also in the overall literary production of the period. Literary texts emulated biblical genres, and literary interpretation built on the period's new approaches to scriptural exegesis.

57. "He was still a child when he already made himself so familiar with the forms of the Hebrew language and the figurative nature of presenting things he found in it that he used them unconsciously in a general manner whenever he wanted to say something with seriousness and strength" (Er war noch in der Kindheit, als er sich die Formen, der hebräischen Sprache und die figürliche Art die Sachen vorzustellen, die er darinnen fand, schon so bekannt gemacht hatte, daß er sie, sich selbst unbewußt, in dem gemeinen Umgange gebrauchte, so oft er etwas mit Ernst und Nachdruck sagen wollte). Bodmer's biography was published in Friedrich Cramer, *Klopstock: Er, und über ihn 1724–1747* (Hamburg: Schniebes, 1780), 41–42.

58. Despite his general appreciation of Klopstock, whom he considered the greatest contemporary German poet, Herder disfavored his *Death of Adam* because, in his view, the play did not capture the complexity of the biblical patriarchs. See Dieter Lohmeier, *Herder und Klopstock: Herders Auseinandersetzung mit der Persönlichkeit und dem Werk Klopstock* (Bad Homburg: Verlag Gehlen, 1968), 118–20.

59. Robert R. Heitner, *German Tragedy in the Age of Enlightenment* (Berkeley: University of California Press, 1963), 281–83.

60. Friedrich Gottlieb Klopstock, *The Death of Adam: A Tragedy in Three Acts*, trans. Robert Lloyd (London: Dryden Leach, 1763), 57. "Ich habe keinen Segen!—*Vor sich*. Sie ist noch nicht vorüber, die namlose Angst! Sie steigt noch! Mit diesen neuen Empfindungen steigt sie! Mein Leben, das Leben meiner ersten Tage empört sich noch einmal ganz in mir! Meine erste Unsterblichkeit, sie, sie ist es, die in meinen Gebeinen bebt!—Wo werd ich hingeführt?—Auch die Dunkelheit fällt von meinen Augen! Aber, ach, sie fällt, daß ich diese todesvollen Gefilde sehe!—Kehrt eure Blicke von mir, ihr starren Augen! . . . Er war ihr einziger Sohn! Jener fortgerissene Arm!—Dieser rauchende Schädel! Flieht! flieht! Erbarmt euch meiner, meine Kinder, ihr einsamen Übrigen, und führt mich von diesem Gefilde weg!" Friedrich Gottlieb Klopstock, *Biblische Dramen*, ed. Monika Lemmel (Berlin: Walter de Gruyter, 2005), 27.

61. See John Hibberd, *Salomon Gessner: His Creative Achievement and Influence* (Cambridge: Cambridge University Press, 1976).

62. C. M. Wieland, *Gesammelte Schriften* (Berlin: Weidmann 1916), 4:702.

63. Salomon Gessner, *The Death of Abel in Five Books*, trans. Mary Mitchell Collyer, 12th ed. (London: T. Martin, 1791), 3

64. Ibid., 9.

65. Ibid.

66. Frei, *Eclipse of Biblical Narrative*, 31.

67. As Isaiah Berlin has written, "[Herder] believed that the desire to belong to a culture, something that united a group or a province or a nation, was a very basic human need, as deep as the desire for food or drink or liberty; and that this need to belong to a community where you understood what others said, where you could move freely, where you had emotional, as well as economic, social and political bonds, was the basis of developed, mature human life." Berlin, "My Intellectual Path," in *The Power of Ideas*, ed. Isaiah Berlin and Henry Hardy (Princeton, N.J.: Princeton University Press, 2002), 13.

68. Nonetheless, as Zammito rightly points out, Herder does not believe in the notion of progress of human history. Herder is cautious of praising modernity, as Zammito notes, and is careful not to "discriminate the varieties of human excellence" as they are expressed in diverging periods and phases of civilization. *Kant, Herder, and the Birth of Anthropology*, 333.

69. Walter Benjamin, "The Translator's Task," trans. Steven Rendall, *TTR: traduction, terminologie, rédaction* 10, no. 2 (1997): 151.

70. See Winfried Menninghaus, *Schwellenkunde: Walter Benjamins Passage des Mythos* (Frankfurt a.M.: Suhrkamp, 1986), 7. Menninghaus claims that Benjamin juxtaposes the language philosophy of his Romantic precursors with a self-reflective structuralism centered on his distinction between the semiotic and the mystical characteristics of language, which are equivalent to the "referential" and "poetic" functions of language (8). Benjamin recognizes this mediation (*Mittelbarkeit*) as a characteristic of human language (17). See also Menninghaus, *Walter Benjamins Theorie der Sprachmagie* (Frankfurt a.M.: Suhrkamp, 1995). For an overview of Benjamin's references to Herder in a larger context of modern Jewish thought, see Stéphane Moses, *Der Engel der Geschichte: Franz Rosenzweig, Walter Benjamin, Gershom Scholem* (Frankfurt a.M.: Jüdischer, 1994).

71. Walter Benjamin, "On Language as Such and on the Language of Man," in *Walter Benjamin: Selected Writings*, vol. 1, *1913–1926*, ed. Marcus Bullock and Michael E. Jennings

(Cambridge, Mass.: Harvard University Press, 2002), 65. Sigrid Weigel has argued that the biblical act of naming functions in Benjamin's work as an *Urszene* that dictates his conception of the theological origins of language. "Auf der Schwelle von Schöpfung und Weltgericht," in *Profanes Leben: Walter Benjamins Dialektik der Säkularisierung*, ed. Daniel Weidner (Berlin: Suhrkamp, 2010), 84.

72. "The quintessence of this intensive totality of language as the mental being of man is the name. Man is the namer; by this we recognize that through him pure language speaks. All nature, insofar as it communicates itself, communicates itself in language, and so finally in man. Hence, he is the lord of nature and can give names to things. Only through the linguistic being of things can he get beyond himself and attain knowledge of them—in the name." Benjamin, "On Language as Such," 65.

73. Ibid.

74. As Eva Kocziszky has pointed out, the creation topos in *Aesthetica in nuce* often posits God as a sculptor or a painter. Man's creation by God thus elevates the notion of flesh, thereby also praising human sensuality. "Leib und Schrift in Hamanns *Aesthetica in nuce*," in *Die Gegenwärtigkeit Johann Georg Hamanns*, ed. Bernhard Gajek, Regensburger Beiträge zur deutschen Sprach- und Literaturwissenschaft 88 (Frankfurt a.M.: Peter Lang, 2005), 145–60.

75. Benjamin, "On Language as Such," 70.

76. In "Confession on the Subject of our Language," his famous letter to Franz Rosenzweig, Benjamin's close friend Gershom Scholem borrows the terminology of Benjamin's essay in pondering the stakes of speaking Hebrew in modern Israel—of speaking a language that is removed from its biblical origins to capture reality. "What is it with the actuality of Hebrew?" (Was ist es mit der "Aktualisierung" des Hebräischen?), Scholem asks in this text, which is unique in its expression of a momentary critique of Zionism by an otherwise enthusiastic supporter of the movement. Hebrew, a constitutive part of the Zionist project, appears as a secular means to describe reality. At the same time, the language carries its old religious, biblical connotations. Zionism thus presents a realization of theological images in modern life in Israel. Scholem goes on to state that there is a parallel between the language and the use of names that results in the act of speaking "in remainders"—an act that is not aware of its precarious effects. Particularly, such speech does not take into consideration the position of God, who is ingrained in the act of speech. The letter warns against the "demonic courage" of the creators of the new Hebrew, who ignore the Day of Judgment and lead their followers on a so-called apocalyptic path. Like his close friend Benjamin, Scholem argues that the standing of names in a given language is crucial to understanding how language operates: "Language is name [Sprache ist Namen]. In the names, the power of language is enclosed; in them, its abyss is sealed. After invoking the ancient names daily, we can no longer hold off their power. Called awake, they will appear since we have invoked them with great violence." Scholem, "Confession on the Subject of Our Language," in *Acts of Religion*, by Jacques Derrida, edited by Gil Anidjar (London: Routledge, 2002), 227.

Chapter 2

1. "Die heilige Schrift auszulegen, besteht in Anwendung der Logic." Christian Wolff, "Von dem Gebrauche der demonstrativischen Lehr-Art in Erklärung der heiligen Schrift," in *Kleine Schriften* (Halle: Renger, 1755), 264.

2. See David L. Jeffrey, *People of the Book: Christian Identity and Literary Culture* (Grand Rapids, Mich.: Eerdmans, 1996); John Jarick, ed., *Sacred Conjectures: The Context*

and Legacy of Robert Lowth and Jean Astruc (New York: T & T Clark, 2007); Stephen Prickett, *Words and the Word: Language, Poetics, and Biblical Interpretation* (Cambridge: Cambridge University Press, 1986); and Daniel Weidner, *Bibel und Literatur*, esp. 23–62, 97–122.

3. To Sutcliffe, Jewish traditions of biblical scholarship were at odds with the Enlightenment attempt to institute religion as a means for establishing a universal ground for a society of equal citizens motivated by reason. Judaism was a disturbing emblem of otherness for the Enlightenment's all-encompassing effort of inclusiveness: "While the tensions between Judaism and Enlightenment were . . . uniquely intense and historically significant, they are closely related to the more general problematics of the relationship of Enlightenment rationality to whatever it cannot readily encompass." *Judaism and Enlightenment*, 6.

4. William Robertson Smith, "On the Poetry of the Old Testament," in *Lectures and Essays* (London: Adam and Charles Black, 1912), 405.

5. The Romantic emphasis on childhood as the individual's resource for creativity and imagination is important to my analysis of how the Hebrew sublime was ingrained in early Romanticism and the development of literary hermeneutics. See Linda M. Austin, "Children of Childhood: Nostalgia and the Romantic Legacy," *Studies in Romanticism* 42, no. 1 (2003): 75–98; Meike Sophia Baader, *Die romantische Idee des Kindes und der Kindheit* (Berlin: Luchterhand, 1996); and Eugene L. Stelzig, *The Romantic Subject in Autobiography: Rousseau and Goethe* (Charlottesville: University Press of Virginia, 2000).

6. Scholarly discussions about Herder have delved into his classification as a relativist. This categorization is the topic of Sonia Sikka's *Herder on Humanity and Cultural Difference: Enlightened Relativism* (Cambridge: Cambridge University Press, 2011). Sikka rejects the view that Herder was a relativist if, as a philosophical position, relativism contends that all cultural practices are equally valid. As she notes, Herder is critical of some cultural practices, particularly those of his contemporary Europeans. Sikka thus argues that Herder "endorses a weak and fallibilistic form of universalism, resting on a minimal, empirically derived conception of human nature and a few related core values" (15). I agree that Herder does take certain values as inherently superior. Sikka insists that in some areas (such as his reflections on individual happiness) Herder takes a strong relativist position. With this characterization of Herder as a weak universalist and a strong relativist, Sikka offers an alternative position to the characterization of Herder as a pluralist (primarily by Isaiah Berlin) or weak pluralist (by Vicky Spencer). For a critical book review, see Spencer, review of *Herder on Humanity and Cultural Difference: Enlightened Relativism*, by Sonia Sikka, *Mind* 121, no. 481 (2012): 229–32. Spencer elaborates her notion of Herder's pluralism in her book *Herder's Political Thought: A Study of Language, Culture, and Community* (Toronto: University of Toronto Press, 2012). An analysis of the semantics of "pluralism" versus "relativism" is beyond the scope of my study.

7. Sorkin writes, "Baumgarten was representative of the first fully articulated version of the religious Enlightenment that enjoyed state sponsorship in the German lands. While it had an enormous impact on German Lutheranism, it also exerted significant influence among other confessions. The Protestant theological Enlightenment played a decisive role as Jews and Catholics in the German states created their own versions of religious Enlightenments." *Religious Enlightenment*, 163.

8. The fuller citation is "Nulle politesse, nulle science, nul art perfectionné dans aucun temps chez cette nation atroce." *Oeuvres complètes de Voltaire*, vol. 24 (Paris: Garnier fréres, 1877–1885), 543. *Essai sur les moeurs et lésprit des Nations* (Paris: Garnier frères, 1877–1885), 344.

9. Benedict de Spinoza, *Theological-Political Treatise*, ed. Jonathan Israel, trans. Michael Silverthorne and Jonathan Israel (Cambridge: Cambridge University Press, 2007), 9.

10. Konrad Burdach, *Die nationale Aneignung der Bibel und die Anfänge der germanischen Philologie* (Halle: M. Niemeyer, 1924), 116–17. See also Joachim Dyck, *Athen und Jerusalem: Die Tradition der argumentativen Verknüpfung von Bibel und Poesie im 17. und 18. Jahrhundert* (Munich: Beck, 1977).

11. Anderson, *Imagined Communities*, 39.

12. Ibid., 37.

13. In his account of the influence of patriotism on Germany's republic of letters at the time, Gerhard Kaiser notes poets' yearning for a common folklore, on top of having a common language and culture. *Pietismus und Patriotismus im Literarischen Deutschland: Ein Beitrag zum Problem der Säkularisation* (Wiesbaden: Franz Steiner, 1961), 32.

14. Ilany, "Between Ziona and Teutona."

15. Johann Wolfgang Goethe, *Sämtliche Werke. Briefe, Tagebücher und Gespräche*, vol. 14, *Aus Meinem Leben: Dichtung und Wahrheit*, ed. Klaus-Detlef Müller (Frankfurt a.M.: Deutscher Klassiker Verlag, 1986), 287.

16. Ibid., 14:275.

17. Johann Wolfgang von Goethe, *Truth and Poetry: From My Own Life; or, The Autobiography of Goethe*, trans. and ed. Parke Godwin (New York: G. P. Putnam, 1846–47), 1:58; emphasis added. "Man hatte nämlich bisher auf Treu und Glauben angenommen, daß dieses Buch der Bücher in einem Geiste verfaßt, ja daß es *von dem göttlichen Geiste eingehaucht und gleichsam diktiert sei*. Doch waren schon längst von Gläubigen und Ungläubigen die Ungleichheiten der verschiedenen Teile desselben bald gerügt, bald verteidigt worden. Engländer, Franzosen, Deutsche hatten die Bibel mit mehr oder weniger Heftigkeit, Scharfsinn, Frechheit, Mutwillen angegriffen, und ebenso war sie wieder von ernsthaften, wohldenkenden Menschen einer jeden Nation in Schutz genommen worden. Ich für meine Person hatte sie lieb und wert: denn fast ihr allein war ich meine sittliche Bildung schuldig, und die Begebenheiten, die Lehren, die Symbole, die Gleichnisse, alles hatte sich tief bei mir eingedrückt und war auf eine oder die andere Weise wirksam gewesen." Goethe, *Aus Meinem Leben*, 14:275–76; emphasis added.

18. A pertinent influence on the perception that belief in the Bible is a precondition for equal citizenship was Locke's *A Letter Concerning Toleration* (1689). Locke's treatise promoted tolerance and the separation of church and state, albeit under the condition that each and every citizen of the state adhere to a monotheistic faith.

19. Andrew Piper's *Dreaming in Books* highlights Goethe's profound awareness of textual circulation as a nation-building set of practices, among its other roles. Piper demonstrates how this awareness shaped Goethe's publication of his own writings: "Goethe's publishing practices were ecstatically self-referential. As they promoted the increasing difficulties of isolating a work's boundaries—its excerptual qualities—Goethe's prepublications also promoted the amplification of the authorial persona that regulated and orchestrated this print performance." *Dreaming in Books: The Making of the Bibliographic Imagination in the Romantic Age* (Chicago: University of Chicago Press, 2009), 30.

20. On Goethe's study of Yiddish and Hebrew in view of his broad interest in foreign languages and cultures, see Theodore Huebener, "How Goethe Learned Languages," *Modern Language Journal* 33, no. 4 (1949): 268–73. Goethe's enchantment with and fluency in French and his difficulty with English shows that his language study was not systematic and that his interest in Yiddish and Hebrew needs to be situated in his broader, eclectic

study of foreign cultures, as well as his distaste for formal grammar. See F. H. Reinsch, "Goethe's Interpretation of Language Mastery," *German Quarterly* 11, no. 3 (1938): 115–25.

21. Goethe, *Aus Meinem Leben*, 14:125.

22. Ibid., 14:126.

23. Goethe, *Truth and Poetry*, 1:112. Auch ward gelehrt, daß die jüdische Nation, solange sie geblüht, wirklich sich mit jenen ersten Zeichen begnügt und keine andere Art zu schreiben und zu lesen gekannt habe. Ich wäre nun gar zu gern auf diesem altertümlichen, wie mir schien bequemeren Wege gegangen; allein mein Alter erklärte etwas streng: man müsse nach der Grammatik verfahren, wie sie einmal beliebt und verfaßt worden. Das Lesen ohne diese Punkte und Striche sei eine sehr schwere Aufgabe, und könne nur von Gelehrten und den Geübtesten geleistet werden. Ich mußte mich also bequemen, auch diese kleinen Merkzeichen kennen zu lernen; aber die Sache ward mir immer verworrner. Nun sollten einige der ersten größern Urzeichen an ihrer Stelle gar nichts gelten, damit ihre kleinen Nachgebornen doch ja nicht umsonst dastehen möchten. Dann sollten sie einmal wieder einen leisen Hauch, dann einen mehr oder weniger harten Kehllaut andeuten, bald gar nur als Stütze und Widerlage dienen. Zuletzt aber, wenn man sich alles wohl gemerkt zu haben glaubte, wurden einige der großen sowohl als der kleinen Personnagen in den Ruhestand versetzt, so daß das Auge immer sehr viel und die Lippe sehr wenig zu tun hatte." Goethe, *Aus Meinem Leben*, 14:126–27.

24. Kittler, *Aufschreibesysteme 1800/1900* (Munich: Fink, 1995), 86–88. Wellbery complements this account with his analysis of the lyric as emerging from the voice that originates in the maternal reading to the child. Wellbery, *Specular Moment*, 197–98.

25. Herder, *Schriften zum Alten Testament*, 669.

26. Goethe, *Truth and Poetry*, 1:56. Also see Goethe, *Aus Meinem Leben*, 14:272.

27. Herder, *Johann Gottfried Herder: Selected Early Works, 1764–1772*, trans. Ernest A. Menze and Michael Palma (University Park: Pennsylvania State University Press, 1992), 105.

28. On the impact of biblical study on the notion of "Morgenländer," see Andrea Polaschegg, *Der andere Orientalismus: Regeln deutsch-morgenländischer Imagination im 19. Jahrhundert* (Berlin/New York: Walter de Gruyter, 2005), 157–77. Polaschegg shows how the imagination of the Morgenland as the place where the Hebrew Bible was written enabled the Bible's idealization as a text from an old age. She traces this transformation in the late eighteenth century (166).

29. Sheehan, *Enlightenment Bible*, 148–81.

30. Lowth, *Lectures on the Sacred Poetry*, 48.

31. Ibid., 16–17.

32. Ibid., 22.

33. Ibid., 32–33.

34. Herder, *Schriften zum Alten Testament*, 663.

35. Ibid., 675.

36. Lowth, *Lectures on the Sacred Poetry*, 28.

37. A more elaborated criticism of Lowth appears in Herder's essay "An Essay on the History of Lyric Poetry" ("Versuch einer Geschichte der lyrischen Dichtkunst," 1766), where he challenges Lowth's ideal description of Hebrew. He uses his own declaration of the flawed nature of poetry in its primitive stages to confront Lowth's descriptions of Hebrew as an atemporal sublime: "Lately the best connoisseur of Hebrew poetry, Lowth, went so far as to write the words: 'The beginning of the other arts is imperfect, coarse, lowly, and unworthy

attempts.' But we see the poetry in its splendor already in its origin; for it was not invented by human ingenuity but lowered from heaven; not grown by small additions but appeared fully ripe in strength and beauty at birth; she did not lend her jewelry to the lie; rather, she was the negotiator between God and men." Herder, *Johann Gottfried Herder: Werke*, vol. 1, *Herder und der Sturm und Drang, 1764–1774*, ed. Wolfgang Proß (Darmstadt: Hanser, 1984), 94.

38. J. G. Herder, *On the Spirit of Hebrew Poetry*, trans. James Marsch (Burlington: Edward Smith, 1833), 1:29. "E. Also die Sprache, die viel ausdrückende, malende Verba hat, ist eine Poetische Sprache: je mehr sie auch die Nomina zu Verbis machen kann, desto poetischer ist sie. Ein Nomen stellt immer nur die Sache tot dar: das Verbum setzt sie in Handlung, diese erregt Empfindung, denn sie ist selbst gleichsam mit Geist beseelet. Erinnern Sie sich, was Leßing über Homer gezeigt hat, daß bei ihm alles Gang, Bewegung, Handlung sei, und daß darin eben sein Leben, seine Wirkung, ja das Wesen aller Poesie bestehe. Nun ist bei den Ebräern beinahe alles Verbis: d. i. alles lebt und handelt." Herder, *Schriften Zum Alten Testament*, 675.

39. Weidner, *Die Bibel und Literatur*, 44–50.

40. Gregory Moore, introduction to *Selected Writing on Aesthetics*, by Johann Gottfried Herder, ed. and trans. Gregory Moore (Princeton, N.J.: Princeton University Press), 2006, 9.

41. For an analysis of the notion of force in Herder's oeuvre see Christoph Menke, *Kraft: Ein Grundbegriff ästhetischer Anthropologie* (Frankfurt a.M.: Suhrkamp, 2008).

42. Elsewhere, Herder compares Jews to nomadic peoples whose presence in Europe is destructive: "Die Erhaltung der Juden erklärt sich eben so natürlich, als die Erhaltung der Bramanen, Parsen und Zigeuner" (The preservation of Jews clarifies itself just as naturally as the preservation of Brahmans, Parsis, and Gypsies). Herder, *Ideen zur Philosophie*, 491.

43. In his *Ideas on the Philosophy of the History of Mankind* (1784–91), Herder elaborates on ethnic groups that are not located in designated territories. Exemplary of this phenomenon are the Gypsies. Herder recommends military training as a way to stop their harmful influence on their surroundings: "Look . . . at a numerous, foreign, heathen, subterranean people in almost all the countries in Europe: the *Gypsies*. How did they get here? How did the seven to eight hundred thousand heads, that their newest historian counts, get here? A rejected Indian caste separated by birth from everything that calls itself godly and civil, and remaining faithful for centuries for this debased destiny, for what are they suited in Europe, except for military training, which can discipline everything as quickly as possible?" Quoted in Sikka, *Herder on Humanity*, 245–46. In this same essay, Herder compares Jews and Gypsies as two ethnic groups that are not set in one geographical realm. Herder, *Ideen zur Philosophie*, 491.

44. Herder, *On the Spirit of Hebrew Poetry*, 1:217–18. "Der Glaube an die Vorsehung, den Sie mir aus den Schriften und der Geschichte des Ebräischen Volks neulich entwickelten, und als eine Blüte fürs Menschengeschlecht anpriesen, hat an mir keinen Gegner; ich wünschte vielmehr, dass ihn die Schriften dieses Volks wirklich auf eine reine und fürs menschliche Geschlecht teilnehmende Art entwickelt hätten; sollte aber das letzte geschehen sein? War bei ihnen dieser Glaube nicht ein so enger, ausschließender Nationalglaube, dass man ihn eher menschenfeindlich als menschenfreundlich nennen möchte?" Herder, *Schriften zum Alten Testament*, 876.

45. Herder, *Frühe Schriften*, 701.

46. Herder, *On the Spirit of Hebrew Poetry*, 1:32. "E.: 'Nicht eben Perlen, auch leider nicht nach dem Genius ihrer uralten Bildung. Das arme Volk was in die Welt zerstreut: Die

meisten bildeten also ihren Ausdruck nach dem Genius der Sprachen, unter denen sie lebten, und es ward ein trauriges Gemisch, an das wir hier nicht denken mögen. Wir reden vom Ebräischen, da es die lebendige Sprache Kanaans war, und auch hier nur von ihren schönsten reinesten Zeiten.'" Herder, *Schriften zum Alten Testament*, 678.

47. As Kaiser has argued, Klopstock utilized forms that placed the individuality of the poetic speaker at their center. These forms were then combined with the use of ancient poetic genres, such as the epic. Such combination resonated with and addressed the period's patriotism, with which the poet corresponded. *Klopstock: Religion und Dichtung* (Gütersloh: Gerd Mohn, 1963).

48. Wellbery, *Lessing's Laocoon*, 44–55.

49. What van Laak means by "modern hermeneutics" remains partly unclear. His book portrays the transition of the late eighteenth century as a move toward semiotic approaches to texts, which rely on the perception of the text as unfolding a plot. *Hermeneutik literarischer Sinnlichkeit*, 15–18.

50. To van Laak, the focus on the affect that texts evoke has created novel criteria for their analysis. Ibid, 5–26.

51. Ibid, 3.

52. Van Laak relies on Karlheinz Stierle's essay, "Text als Handlung." Ibid., 2. Van Laak identifies three prevailing concepts behind this new *Bildhermeneutik* (the hermeneutics of the image): *Zeitkritik*, the new conception of aesthetics, and the emerging concept of anthropology. His account of the emergence of the hermeneutics of sensuality culminates in Herder's position, which embraces a "holistic conception of knowledge and sensation." Ibid., 233.

53. Leventhal, *Disciplines of Interpretation*, 259. Rejecting the classification of Herder's interpretive approach as "Romantic" hermeneutics, Leventhal emphasizes Herder's insistence on the radical historicism of the text.

54. Ibid., 7.

55. Campe, *Affekt und Ausdruck*, 74.

56. Wellbery, *Lessing's Laocoon*, 2.

57. Ernst Cassirer, *The Philosophy of the Enlightenment*, trans. Fritz C. A. Koelln and James P. Pettegrove (Boston: Beacon Press, 1966), 353.

58. Klaus Berghahn, "From Classicist to Classical Literary Criticism, 1730–1806," in *A History of German Literary Criticism, 1730–1980*, ed. Peter Uwe Hohendahl (Lincoln: University of Nebraska Press, 1988), 15–17.

59. Reinhart Koselleck, *Kritik und Krise: Ein Beitrag zur Pathogenese der bürgerlichen Welt* (Freiburg: K. Alber, 1959).

60. See Sheehan, *Enlightenment Bible*, x. My discussion aims at expanding our understanding of this process not only through a more extensive discussion of the eighteenth-century interpretive turn in aesthetics and hermeneutics but also by attending to the fact that what was translated was not the Bible as a whole but the Old Testament in particular.

61. Herder, *On the Spirit of Hebrew Poetry*, 1:19.

62. As Thomas Tillmann has argued, the Song of Songs figured prominently in the Pietistic attempt to experience faith through sensation, a persisting tradition that suffuses Goethe's translation of the text. *Hermeneutik und Bibelexegese beim jungen Goethe* (Berlin: W. de Gruyter, 2006), 196–97.

63. As von Mücke has claimed, the Pietist movement brought about what can be described as "an unintended secularizing outcome." She shows how Bible translations "no

longer merely served as the official access to a sacred text but rather turned them into 'classics' as they moved from the exclusive domain of religion to the domain of literary culture and acquired the status of national treasures." *Practices of the Enlightenment*, xxv.

64. Baildam, *Paradisal Love*, 54.

65. Ibid., 37. On the importance to Herder of bodily love in the Song, see Rudolf Haym, *Herder* (Berlin: Aufbau Verlag, 1954), 2:105–6. Haym highlights Herder's decision to rescue the Song from Michaelis's characterization of its expression of bodily love as inferior. Instead of insisting on its allegoric nature as a means for establishing the importance of the text, Herder's subtle translation stresses the text's power of sensuality ("Nachdruck der Empfindung"). Haym, *Herder*, 2:107. Baildam's and Haym's respective descriptions evince the new form of divination through poetic transmission and comprehension. Divination happens through the exploration of human faculties (of both translator and reader) in superior (or sublime) aesthetic artifacts. Through its enhanced evocation of human sensuality, the Song is such an artifact, even if its sensuality was the reason it had previously been judged an inferior part of the Scriptures.

66. Jochen Schulte-Sasse, "Aesthetic Orientation in a Decentered World," in *A New History of German Literature*, ed. David Wellbery et al. (Cambridge, Mass.: Harvard University Press, 2004), 353.

67. Moore, introduction to *Selected Writings*, 3.

68. Dilthey develops this argument in his analysis of Schleiermacher's hermeneutics as a revolutionary intervention into Protestant theology. See his "Das hermeneutische System Schleiermachers in der Auseinandersetzung mit der älteren protestantischen Hermeneutik" in *Gesammelte Schriften*, 14,2 *Lebens Schleiermacher*, 595–626.

69. Quoted in Baildam, *Paradisal Love*, 306. The English translation is my own.

70. Robert Alter, *The Art of Biblical Poetry* (New York: Basic Books, 1985), 3.

71. The Song also embodies other aesthetic models, such as the medieval vision of the *locus amorous*, the place of loving and fondling in an idealized, isolated setting in nature. The ancient Greek and medieval visions are not competing aesthetic models; both can be viewed as contained in the Song at the same time.

72. Karin Lynn Schutjer has provided ample evidence for a complex reception of Judaism and the Old Testament in Goethe's works. She argues that "behind his very mixed representations of Jews and Judaism stand crucial tensions within his own thinking and a distinct anxiety of influence." *Goethe and Judaism: The Troubled Inheritance of Modern Literature* (Evanston, Ill.: Northwestern University Press, 2015), 4. Schutjer suggests that Goethe's ambivalent references to Jews touch upon tropes that shape his perception of modernity. One cogent example is the role of wandering in nation building, which Schutjer shows to be central to Goethe's perception of modernity. With reference to Goethe's investigation of the Hebrew Bible as a national epic and thus as a model for the narration of German nationalism, the third chapter of her book makes clear that Goethe's view of the Bible as a cultural asset pertains first and foremost to the Old Testament.

73. Ze'ev Levy relates these two aspects of Goethe's writings on the Hebrew Bible to his intellectual dependence on Herder. *Judaism in the Worldview of J. G. Hamann, J. G. Herder and W. v. Goethe*, 216.

74. Johann Wolfgang von Goethe and A. Schoell, *Briefe und Aufsätze aus den Jahren 1766 bis 1786* (Weimar: Landes-Industrie-Comptoir, 1857), 155.

75. Kittler, *Aufschreibesysteme*, 90–91.

76. Quoted in Baildam, *Paradisal Love*, 328. The English translation is my own.

77. Campe defines this trend as the "homogeneity of expression" in the European republic of letters. *Affekt und Ausdruck*, 163.

78. Wellbery, *Specular Moment*, 190–91.

79. Asad, *Formations of the Secular*, 45; emphasis added.

80. Wellbery, *Specular Moment*, 13.

81. Ibid. Wellbery claims that the lyric "I," as the most prominent conceptual invention of Goethe's poetic enterprise, was conceived under the address of theological transformations in interpretive approaches.

82. Ibid., 399–401

83. Ilany, "Between Ziona and Teutona," 104.

84. Making *Mimesis* the model of world literature in contemporary discussions relies to a large extent on Edward Said's admiring presentation of Auerbach as a "liminal intellectual." Said chose Auerbach to illustrate his notion of a "critic in exile," with the ideological agenda embodied in this position. See Said, "Intellectual Exile: Expatriates and Marginal," in *Representations of the Intellectual: The 1993 Reith Lectures* (New York: Pantheon Books, 1994), 47–64.

85. Erich Auerbach, *Mimesis: The Representation of Reality in Western Literature* (Princeton, N.J.: Princeton University Press, 2003), 3–7.

Chapter 3

1. "Sie, mein Herr, haben gezeigt, daß Sie das Hebräische sehr gut verstehen. Vielleicht haben Sie auch einige Kenntniß des Rabbinischen. Wenigstens scheinen Sie es nicht ganz zu verachten. Sie besitzen auch die Gabe, sich, so oft Sie wollen, in die Lage und Denkungsart Ihres Nebenmenschen zu versetzen, um ihn zu richten." Mendelssohn to Herder, June 1780, in Herder, *Aus Herders Nachlass*, 2:216. Frederick M. Barnard considers this letter to reflect largely positively on Herder's relationship to Jews. *Herder on Nationality, Humanity and History* (Montreal: McGill-Queen's University Press, 2002), 19–21. He claims that "when Herder wrote about the Jews, he thought of them chiefly as a collectivity, indeed as a nation *par excellence*," but at the same time, recognizing the Jews as a model nation did not stop him "from sharing the sentiments of men such as Voltaire and Montesquieu in France, or Mendelssohn and Lessing in Germany, in support of Jewish emancipation" (19). Herder advocated for Jewish emancipation without assimilation, which allowed him to preserve both the view that the Jewish people are unique and the view that national character, more generally, is not easily replaceable. Barnard's account, however, does not acknowledge the shift in Herder's writing from seeing Jews as a nation to seeing them as an ethnicity. Others have described Herder's attitude toward Jews as proto-anti-Semitic. See, for example, Liliane Weissberg, "Juden oder Hebräer? Religiöse und politische Bekehrung bei Herder," in *Johann Gottfried Herder: Geschichte und Kultur*, ed. Martin Bollacher (Würzburg: Königshausen & Neumann, 1994), 191–211. Like Barnard, Weissberg notes the role of the Jews as a model nation for Herder and that, for Herder, Judaism set an example for the organic development of a national language (193). She nonetheless contrasts this model with Herder's negative presentation of Jews in his discussion of trade as a destructive practice.

2. "Fühle dich in alles hinein!" Friedrich Meinecke was instrumental in creating the image of Herder as the forefather of empathy. Meinecke argued that Herder enriched the German language and the idea of historical perception with the term. *Die Entstehung des Historismus* (Munich: R. Oldenbourg Verlag, 1959), 357. For a comprehensive account that

follows the identification of the term with Herder and some implications of this reception in intellectual history, see Gross and Bullock, "Historiography, Theology, and *Erkenntnis*."

3. Edward Said asserted that Herder offered, in his *Ideas for a Philosophy of the History of Mankind*, a "panoramic display of various cultures, each permeated by an inimical creative spirit, each accessible only to an observer who sacrificed his prejudice to *Einfühlung*." *Orientalism* (London: Penguin, 2003), 118.

4. Allan Arkush argues that Mendelssohn's identity as a traditional Jew did not, in fact, play a major role in his contributions to philosophy. Arkush presents Mendelssohn as a Deist who established ad hoc accounts of traditional Jewish thought to "construct a version of Judaism suitable for a time when Jews would take their places as citizens alongside their Gentile neighbors in a fully liberal polity." *Mendelssohn and the Enlightenment* (Albany: State University of New York Press, 1994), 291–92. In contrast, David Sorkin has long argued that Mendelssohn's faith informed his philosophical endeavors. For Sorkin, Mendelssohn represents a current in Andalusian Jewish philosophy that adheres to reason in scriptural interpretation. See *Religious Enlightenment*, esp. 168–71, 176–95.

5. Christian Wilhelm Dohm, *Über die bürgerliche Verbesserung der Juden* (Berlin: Nicolai, 1781), 3–5.

6. This view was a late development in Lessing's thought. Under the influence of his intellectual friendship with Mendelssohn, Lessing had a change of heart from his "The Education of the Human Race" ("Die Erziehung des Menschengeschlechts," 1777). In that text, Lessing had advocated for a reconciliation between the belief in revelation and the perception of reason as an innate human trait. *Nathan the Wise*, in a stark opposition to this view, endorses the concurrent existence of the monotheistic religions as separate and unique faiths.

7. Grit Schorch has claimed that Mendelssohn differs from the Wolffian rationalist framework when he finds cultural difference (particularly Jewish-Christian difference) to be constitutive of intuitive knowledge and, subsequently, of linguistic signification. *Moses Mendelssohns Sprachpolitik* (Berlin: Walter de Gruyter, 2012), 136–38.

8. See Mendelssohn, "Betrachtungen über die Quellen und die Verbindungen der schönen Künste und Wissenschaften" (1757), in Mendelssohn, *Ausgewählte Werke*, vol. 1, *Schriften zur Metaphysik und Ästhetik, 1755-1771*, ed. Christoph Schulte, Andreas Kennecke, and Grażyna Jurewicz, student ed. (Darmstadt: Wissenschaftliche Buchgesellschaft, 2009), 169–90.

9. "In meiner Seele liegt eine Neigung zur Vollkommenheit, die ich mit allen denkenden Wesen, die ich gewissermaßen mit Gott gemein habe." Mendelssohn, *Ausgewählte Werke*, 1:57.

10. "Je ausgebreitet klarer die Vorstellung des schönen Gegenstandes, desto feuriger das Vergnügen, das daraus entspringt." Ibid., 49.

11. "Our artificial language may have displaced the language of nature, our civilized manner of life and our social polite behavior have dammed, dried out, and drained off the flood and sea of passions." Herder, *Herder: Philosophical Writings*, ed. Michael N. Forster (Cambridge: Cambridge University Press, 2002), 66.

12. As Daniel Weidner has argued, Herder's *Treatise* suggests that Biblical Hebrew is the emblem of the Oriental languages that recall the roots of human language before civilization's effects. Weidner, *Bibel und Literatur*, 100.

13. Elias Sacks has argued that Mendelssohn's entire oeuvre expresses a special concern for modern historical thinking, which Mendelssohn himself takes upon to reconcile

with traditional Judaism. *Moses Mendelssohn's Living Script: Philosophy, Practice, History, Judaism* (Bloomington: Indiana University Press, 2017).

14. Wellbery, *Specular Moment*, 97.

15. "Bey welchen Erscheinungen sind aber wohl alle Triebfedern der menschlichen Seele mehr in Bewegung, als bey den Wirkungen der schönen Künste?" Mendelssohn, *Moses Mendelssohn: Gesammelte Schriften Jubiläumsausgabe* (Stuttgart: Fridrich Frommann, 1972–), 1:168.

16. Wellbery has influentially opposed the consideration of both Mendelssohn's and Baumgarten's focus on the human reception of outside expressions as merely psychological. In his reading of Mendelssohn's aesthetic writings, Wellbery shows Mendelssohn to be a link in the chain of thinkers who amend art's ontological status; he is central to modern aesthetic theories in eliciting the transition toward an "aesthetic of representation." Wellbery, *Specular Moment*, 97.

17. Mendelssohn, *Gesammelte Schriften*, 4:20.

18. Ibid., 4:24.

19. Nils Riecken, "History, Time, and Temporality in a Global Frame: Abdallah Laroui's Historical Epistemology of History," *History and Theory* 54, no. 4 (2015): 5–26.

20. Heschel argues that Abraham Geiger's descriptions of early Christianity challenged hegemonic strands in Christian theology. She sees Geiger's emphasis on Jesus' Jewishness as underscoring alternative universal narratives that posit Judaism at their center and as intervening in the universal narratives of Christianity. Susannah Heschel, *Abraham Geiger and the Jewish Jesus* (Chicago: University of Chicago Press, 1998).

21. Hess, *German, Jews and the Claims of Modernity*, especially 91–112.

22. Mendelssohn, *Gesammelte Schriften*, 4:29.

23. Mendelssohn, *Gesammelte Schriften*, 3:317. On the review as underscoring Mendelssohn and Herder's disagreements on aesthetics, see Alexander Altmann, *Moses Mendelssohn: A Biographical Study* (London: Littman Library of Jewish Civilization, 1998), 168.

24. Altmann describes this correspondence succinctly claiming that, "Mendelssohn reproached Herder for relying overmuch on his hypothesis of the 'ages' in the life of a language. In his view, Herder had been misled by abstracting his theory entirely from the Greek language. . . . Above all, he rejected Herder's interpretation of poetry as 'wild simplicity.' Poetry, he insisted, was no longer nature but the imitation of nature." Altmann, *Moses Mendelssohn*, 168.

25. "Was wollen wir mit der Poesie?" Mendelssohn, *Gesammelte Schriften*, 3:307.

26. Mendelssohn, *Moses Mendelssohn: Philosophical Writings*, ed. Daniel O. Dahlstrom (Cambridge: Cambridge University Press, 2003), 314.

27. Sorkin, *Religious Enlightenment*, 9–10. See also Sorkin, *Mendelssohn and the Religious Enlightenment* (Berkeley: University of California Press, 1996); and *The Berlin Haskalah and German Religious Thought: Orphans of Knowledge* (London: Valentine Mitchell, 2000).

28. See Schatz, *Sprache in der Zerstreuung*, esp. 197–225, 275–83.

29. Sorkin, *Religious Enlightenment*, 186.

30. "Ich übersetze die Schrift in die deutsche Sprache . . . für den Bedarf der Söhne, die mir Gott gewährte. Mein ältester Sohn starb—eine Heimsuchung Gottes—und es blieb mir nur mein Sohn Joseph (möge Gott sein Herz mit Seiner Torah stärken). Ich legte ihm die deutsche Übersetzung in den Mund, auf daß er durch sie den einfachen Sinn der Schrift verstehe, bis der Knabe aufwüchse und von selbst verstehen würde." Mendelssohn

to Avigdor Levi, May 25, 1779, quoted in Werner Weinberg, introduction to Mendelssohn, *Gesammelte Schriften*, 15,1:xiv. Mendelssohn reiterates this declaration in "Or la-netiva." There, he describes studying the Scriptures through the "tongue of Ashkenaz" as a praxis that he started with his own son and that subsequently spread to the traditional schooling of boys. He writes that Jewish pedagogues accepted his method of teaching as both legitimate and effective. Mendelssohn, *Gesammelte Schriften*, 12:243.

31. As Edward Breuer has written, "For early proponents of the Haskalah, mastery of German and basic areas of knowledge, as well as a renewed emphasis on the teaching of ethics, bespoke a certain universalism. Jews and Christians were seen as participating in a common culture that reaffirmed, with all its attendant political implications, a shared humanity. The return to Hebrew language and Scripture also offered a sense of universal relevance and an opportunity to develop literary-aesthetic sensibilities." *The Limits of Enlightenment: Jews, Germans, and the Eighteenth-Century Study of Scripture* (Cambridge, Mass.: Harvard University Press, 1996), 20. As Breuer writes, in his "Or la-netiva," Mendelssohn presents his exegesis as perpetuating traditional commentaries on the Hebrew Bible, but he is at the same time appreciative of the aesthetic merits of German translations of the Bible (156–74). On the importance of literacy to the social integration of Jews, see also Paul Lawrence Rose, *German Question/Jewish Question: Revolutionary Antisemitism from Kant to Wagner* (Princeton, N.J.: Princeton University Press, 1992). Because my focus in this book is on Mendelssohn's engagement with prominent German intellectuals, my discussion of his Hebrew writings is limited. On their importance to the understanding of Mendelssohn's scholarship, see Sorkin's introduction to *Moses Mendelssohn's Hebrew Writings*, trans. Edward Breuer (New Haven, Conn.: Yale University Press, 2018), 1–20.

32. Schatz notes that in his description of Hebrew as a holy language, Mendelssohn makes a rare reference to the same belief in the writings of the Maskilim (propagators of the Jewish Enlightenment). At the same time, as she points out, Mendelssohn's declaration of Hebrew as holy also comes to terms with Johann David Michaelis's and Herder's respective critiques of the Jewish transmission of the Hebrew language. Schatz, *Sprache in der Zerstreuung*, 244.

33. Mendelssohn, *Gesammelte Schriften*, 14:217–19.

34. I therefore find it hard to agree with accounts that take Mendelssohn's bilingual writing in Hebrew and German as expressing a rupture between his identity as a Jewish believer and as a public intellectual. Whereas these two affiliations generate tensions in his scholarship, I do not take them to be "allocated" to the publication in two different languages. For an opposite view, see Isaac Eisenstein Barzilay, "Moses Mendelssohn (1729–1786) (A Study in Ideas and Attitudes)," *Jewish Quarterly Review* 52, no. 1 (1961): 69–93.

35. See David Biale, *Not in the Heavens: The Tradition of Jewish Secular Thought* (Princeton, N.J.: Princeton University Press, 2011), 102–3.

36. See Leo Strauss, *Persecution and the Art of Writing* (Chicago: University of Chicago Press, 1988).

37. On the importance of Spinoza to Mendelssohn's aesthetics, see Arnold Eisen, "Divine Legislation as 'Ceremonial Script': Mendelssohn on the Commandments," *AJS Review* 15, no. 2 (1990): 239–67; and Willi Goetschel's *Spinoza's Modernity Mendelssohn: Lessing, and Heine,* (Madison: University of Wisconsin Press, 2003), 147–69.

38. Spinoza, *Theological-Political Treatise*, 187.

39. Ibid., 106.

40. Ibid., 106–8.

41. Ibid., 57.

42. Mendelssohn, *Gesammelte Schriften*, 14:213–18.

43. Sorkin, *Religious Enlightenment*, 186.

44. As Matt Erlin has argued, Mendelssohn's late writings can be understood "as a response to the movements of modernity, more specifically as a critique of social fragmentation and the consequent devaluation of intersubjective experience as a source of knowledge." Erlin, "Reluctant Modernism: Moses Mendelssohn's Philosophy of History," *Journal of the History of Ideas* 63, no. 1 (2002): 85.

45. Moses Mendelssohn, *Jerusalem, or On Religious Power and Judaism*, trans. Allan Arkush (Waltham, Mass.: Brandeis University Press, 1983), 104.

46. Mendelssohn, *Jerusalem*, 103; emphasis added.

47. Mendelssohn, *Jerusalem*, 100.

48. As Elizabeth Weber puts it, Mendelssohn contends that "the very medium of recording the law is also what undermines it and causes it to fall into oblivion: the script, writing. Or, conversely, if the law was instituted to prevent idolatry, its very medium constitutes the beginning of idolatry." Weber, "Fending Off Idolatry: Ceremonial Law in Mendelssohn's Jerusalem," *MLN* 122, no. 3, (2007): 528. See also Carola Hilfrich's provocative description of Mendelssohn's philosophy of language in *Jerusalem* as foretelling poststructuralism in her *Lebendige Schrift: Repräsentation und Idolatrie in Moses Mendelssohns Philosophie und Exegese des Judentums* (Munich: Wilhelm Fink, 2000).

49. Mendelssohn, *Jerusalem*, 110.

50. Ibid., 118.

51. This structural conundrum is evident, Mahmood writes, in "the modern State's sovereign power to reorganize substantive features of religious life, stipulating what religion is or ought to be, assigning its proper content, and disseminating concomitant subjectivities, ethical frameworks and quotidian practices." *Religious Difference in a Secular Age* (Princeton, N.J.: Princeton University Press, 2016), 3.

52. Mahmood, "Secularism, Hermeneutics, and Empire," 323–47.

53. Ibid., 333.

54. Ibid., 334.

55. In Asad, Brown, Butler, and Mahmood, *Is Critique Secular?*, 66.

56. Leora Batnitzky has declared the beginning of modern Jewish thought to be the moment when Judaism first met the Protestant definition of "religion." She thus traces the emergence of "Judaism as a religion" back to Mendelssohn's advocating of the political rights of the Jews: "The invention of Jewish religion cannot be separated from the emergence of the modern nation-state. The notion that Judaism is a religion suggests that Judaism is something different in kind from the supreme political authority of the sovereign state, and may in fact complement the sovereign state. The modern concept of religion also indicates that religion is one particular dimension of life among other particular and separate dimensions." *How Judaism Became a Religion*, 6.

57. The initial discrepancy between Jewish and Christian conceptions of secularism may have stemmed from the vague distinction between the secular and the religious spheres in Jewish theology. Biale offers the understanding of Jewish secularism not as a transformation of traditional values but as ingrained in Judaism's values. He claims, "[It] is a tradition that has its own unique characteristics grounded in part in its pre-modern sources. While the Christian origins of the word 'secular' are connected to the dichotomous way Christian theologians saw the 'city of God' and the 'city of man,' Judaism never

made such a sharp distinction: the profane world is not irredeemably polluted. . . . [T]raditional Jewish sources repeatedly hold that this world is not the same as the next (or the one above)." *Not in the Heavens*, 4.

58. Schatz is correct to point out the epistemological innovations in Mendelssohn's writings, such as a novel perception of time that interferes with a traditional, circular approach to the Scriptures and the Hebrew language. *Sprache in der Zerstreuung*, 24–26.

Chapter 4

1. As representative of this view in the German Enlightenment, Jonathan Hess chooses Göttingen philosophy professor Michael Hißmann, who, significantly, was one of Mendelssohn's opponents. Hess, *Germans, Jews, and the Claims of Modernity*, 106–7.

2. Friedrich Schleiermacher, *Hermeneutik und Kritik*, ed. Manfred Frank (Frankfurt a.M.: Suhrkamp, 1977), 75.

3. Willi Oelmüller argues that Kant wanted to solve an impasse that was the cause of a gap between doctrinal Christianity and modernity. *Beiträge zu einer Theorie der Moderne von Lessing, Kant und Hegel* (Frankfurt a.M.: Suhrkamp, 1969), 103–13.

4. For an account that takes Kant's treatment of sin as emancipatory, see Jens Wolff, "Die Anverwandlung der Bibel in Kants Schrift 'Die Religion innerhalb der Grenzen der bloßen Vernunft' von 1793," in *Religion und Aufklärung: Studien zur neuzeitlichen "Umformung des Christlichen*," ed. Albrecht Beutel and Volker Leppin (Leipzig: Evangelische Verlagsanstalt, 2004), 114.

5. "If a moral religion (to be cast not in dogmas and observances but in the heart's disposition to observe all human duties as divine commands) must be established, eventually all miracles which history connects with its inception must themselves render faith in miracles in general dispensable." Immanuel Kant, *Religion Within the Boundaries of Mere Reason*, trans. Allen Wood and George Di Giovanni (Cambridge: Cambridge University Press, 1998), 98.

6. For an account that takes Kant's theology as a primary factor in promoting his philosophical principles, see Karl Barth, *Die protestantische Theologie im. 19. Jahrhundert* (Berlin: Evangelische Verlagsanstalt, 1961), esp. 237–48.

7. Kant, *Religion Within the Boundaries*, 116.

8. Kant's *Conflict of the Faculties* (*Der Streit der Fakultäten*, 1798) provides a systematic distinction between the theologian who operates under the auspices of the church and he who follows rational judgment in his interpretation of the Scriptures.

9. Kant, *Religion Within the Boundaries*, 131. The fuller citation is "Drittens ist es soweit gefehlt, dass das Judentum eine zum Zustande der allgemeinen Kirche gehörige Epoche oder diese allgemeine Kirche wohl gar selbst zu seiner Zeit ausgemacht habe, dass es vielmehr das ganze menschliche Geschlecht von seiner Gemeinschaft ausschloss, als ein besonders vom Jehovah für sich auserwähltes Volk, welches alle andere Völker anfeindete, und dafür von jedem angefeindet wurde." Kant, *Immanuel Kants Werke* (Berlin: Bruno Cassirer, 1914), 6:273.

10. Friedrich Schleiermacher, *On Religion*, trans. Terrence N. Tice (Richmond, Va.: John Knox Press, 1879), 305.

11. Sheehan writes, "Because of its dependency on an immutable Bible, Judaism was condemned to contemporary irrelevance, absolutely distinct from this entity that Schleiermacher called Christianity. In contrast to Germans freed from the originals by the work of Luther, Judaism remained imprisoned by its original texts, enslaved because it could never translate the Bible for a modern world." *Enlightenment Bible*, 234.

12. "Die Vernunft fordert, daß alle Bürger sein sollen, aber sie weiß nicht davon, daß alle Christen sein müssen und es muß auf vielerei Art möglich sein, Bürger und Nichtchrist zu sein." Friedrich Schleiermacher, *Briefe bei Gelegenheit der politisch theologischen Aufgabe und des Sendschreibens jüdischer Hausväter* (Berlin: Evangelische Verlagsanstalt, 1984), 12.

13. Ibid.

14. "Schleiermacher was convinced that Christianity brought forth a distinctive language and content. Christianity was, and remains, a language-producing power. With Jesus Christ there came a new message or 'idea' to be experienced and proclaimed. In communicating this message the authors of the New Testament thought and wrote in terms of the linguistic, religious, and intellectual milieux in which they lived. Their own understandings and expressions of their faith were conditioned by their heritage and environment. Yet at the same time they reshaped or transformed, and at times even created, patterns of thought and ways of speaking in accord with their new faith." James Duke, introduction to *Hermeneutics: The Handwritten Manuscripts*, by Friedrich Schleiermacher, ed. Heinz Kimmerle, trans. James Duke and Jack Forstman (Missoula, Mont.: Scholars Press for the American Academy of Religion, 1977), 7–8.

15. Friedrich Schleiermacher, *Hermeneutics and Criticism*, ed. Andrew Bowie (Cambridge: Cambridge University Press, 1998), 20.

16. Schleiermacher, *Hermeneutics and Criticism*, 20.

17. Ibid., 7.

18. Ibid., 196–97.

19. Wilhelm Dilthey, *Wilhelm Dilthey: Gesammelte Schriften*, vol. 2, *Leben Schleiermachers* (Göttingen: Vandenhoeck & Ruprecht, 1966), 770–71.

20. Palmer, *Hermeneutics*, 94. This is not to say that Schleiermacher presents grammatical hermeneutics as inferior to psychological hermeneutics; he presents the combination of the two as essential to the interpretive act. The point is that a linguistic apprehension of a text does not seek its literal understanding but its understanding within the language as a functional system, a procedure that is then paralleled in the psychological understanding of the author.

21. On the role of Protestantism, and specifically Luther's translation of the Bible, in stimulating print culture with its new nationalistic resonances, see Anderson, *Imagined Communities*, 41.

22. Leventhal, *Disciplines of Interpretation*, 145.

23. See Julius Goebel, "William Dilthey and the Science of Literary History," *Journal of English and Germanic Philology* 25, no. 2 (1926): 145–56. Goebel shows how Dilthey's early work on aesthetics leads him to define the humanities (*Geisteswissenschaften*) through comparison to other "sciences," an enterprise that both relies on and promotes developments in the sciences. Specifically, Dilthey's discussion of poetry develops the notion of the human mind as engaging with an array of psychic experiences.

24. Friedrich Schleiermacher, *A Critical Essay on the Gospel of St. Luke*, trans. Connop Thirlwall (London: J. Taylor, 1825), 196.

25. Dilthey, *Gesammelte Schriften*, 7:191.

26. Peter Szondi finds the origins of the hermeneutic circle earlier, in the writings of Johann Martin Chladenius, whom he takes to be a main propagator of modern hermeneutics. According to Szondi, Chladenius brought attention to the tensions between the different textual passages standing for interpretation and their continual reference to the entire system of the text within which they are intelligible. See Szondi, *Einführung in*

die literarische Hermeneutik, 96. For an elaborated explanation of the term "hermeneutic circle" that sees Dilthey's understanding as reliant on Schleiermacher, see Anna Green, *Cultural History* (London: Palgrave Macmillan, 2008), 22.

27. According to Hans-Georg Gadamer, empathy is inherent to the development of hermeneutics through Pietism and to its endorsement of affect as a major stage of reading: "In thus taking cognizance of the affective modulation of all discourse (and especially preaching) lies the root of the 'psychological' interpretation founded by Schleiermacher and ultimately of all theories of empathy." Gadamer, "Rhetoric and Hermeneutics," in *Rhetoric and Hermeneutics in Our Time*, ed. Walter Jost and Michael J. Hyde (New Haven, Conn.: Yale University Press, 1997), 52.

28. Schleiermacher develops this idea of the hermeneutic circle in the prologue and introduction to his translation of Plato. See *Platons Werke* (Berlin: Akademie Verlag, 1984), 1:3–38.

29. Na'ama Rokem has argued that Heine's poetics negotiate the universalism of the world republic of letters through the conflict of literary genres in his work, culminating ultimately in his decision to write prose: "Through the dilemmas of writing prose, as opposed to poetry, Heine addressed the seemingly unrelated quandary of his place as a Jew in the German literary public sphere in an age defined on the one hand by emancipation and on the other by . . . the ever-growing limitation of the freedom and independence of the individual by the state. Heine was negotiating at the same time the opening of the German literary public sphere to his voice as a Jewish author and its closing to his voice as a social critic." *Prosaic Conditions: Heinrich Heine and the Spaces of Zionist Literature* (Evanston, Ill.: Northwestern University Press, 2013), 20–21.

30. The secondary literature on Heine's biographical identification as a Jew is abundant. I will refrain from viewing Heine's reflections on religion through the prism of his biographical background. Heine's own identification as a Jew is important to my account only to the extent that such an affiliation informed his expectations about his work's circulation.

31. On the recognition of protagonists in Heine's oeuvre as Jewish, see Max Bienenstock, *Das jüdische Element in Heines Werken: Ein krititisch-aesthetischer Beitrag zur Heine-Frage* (Leipzig: Verlag für Literatur, Kunst und Musik, 1910), 2. Max Brod has argued that Heine alludes to his legacy by at times parodying his incomplete knowledge of Hebrew. *Heinrich Heine* (Amsterdam: Verlag Allert de Lange, 1934), 9.

32. Paul Peters points out that highly negative depictions of Jews in Heine's works are intertwined with the motif of shame in his oeuvre. Portrayals of Jews that appear almost anti-Semitic in nature thus correspond with the Romantic device of self-parody of the poet. *Heinrich Heine "Dichterjude": Die Geschichte einer Schmähung* (Frankfurt a.M.: A. Hain, 1990), 15.

33. Bluma Goldstein suggests that the Orientalization of Sephardic Jews dominates national myth involving the Diaspora in the cycle of poems. She argues that Heine's collection juxtaposes this Orientalization with more self-reflective presentations of European Jewish communities as a religious minority. "Heine's 'Hebrew Melodies': A Politics and Poetics of Diaspora," in *Heinrich Heine's Contested Identities: Politics, Religion, and Nationalism in Nineteenth-Century Germany*, ed. Jost Hermand and Robert C. Holub (New York: Peter Lang, 1999), 49.

34. Heinrich Heine, *Jewish Stories and Hebrew Melodies*, trans. Hal Draper (New York: M. Wiener, 1987), 108; and *Heinrich Heine: Werke und Briefe in zehn Bänden* (Berlin: Aufbau Verlag, 1964), 2:137.

35. Heine began working on *The Rabbi of Bacharach* in 1822–23, but the text was first published in 1840. Some commentators have taken the text to represent not so much Heine's knowledge of Hebrew and Jewish custom but his lack thereof. See Ludwig Rosenthal, *Heinrich Heine als Jude* (Frankfurt a.M.: Ullstein, 1973), 93; and Jeffery L. Sammons, "Heine's *Rabbi von Bacherach*: The Unresolved Tensions," *German Quarterly* 37, no. 1 (1964): 32.

36. See Gershon Shaked, "'Der Rabbi von Bacherach' von Heine—Hier und heute," in *Heine in Jerusalem*, ed. Naomi Kaplansky, Elisheva Moatti, and Itta Shedletzky (Hamburg: Hoffman und Campe, 2006). At the same time, Jonathan Skolnik has pointed out how other aspects of the novel (such as its panoramic views) resemble such nineteenth-century literature as Walter Scott's *Ivanhoe* (1820). *Jewish Pasts, German Fictions* (Stanford, Calif.: Stanford University Press, 2014), 47. See also Manfred Windfuhr, "Der Erzähler Heines: 'Der Rabbi von Bacherach' als historischer Roman," in *Heinrich Heine: Ästhetisch-politische Profile*, ed. Gerhard Höhn (Frankfurt a.M.: Suhrkamp, 1991), 276–94.

37. This setting and plot constitute Heine's text as a historical novel. In his reading of the text, Shaked highlights the choice of juxtaposing the Rhine with biblical legends that involve water as discerning the liminal status of Jews in the German tradition. "'Der Rabbi von Bacherach,'" 61. Eliot Schreiber has similarly described the novel as a "trenchant critique" of the Grimm ideology, as the text subverts the emphasis on folklorist purity with its multiple allusions to Jewish religious sources. "Tainted Sources: The Subversion of the Grimms' Ideology of the Folktale in Heinrich Heine's 'Der Rabbi von Bacherach,'" *German Quarterly* 78, no. 1 (2005): 23.

38. Skolnik argues that this figure's sensualism enhances the Haggadah motif (the theme of the possibility of Jewish liberation at the center of the Passover liturgy), in that Abarbanel is a figure of a modern Jew who provides new paradigms for Jewish memory and historiography. *Jewish Pasts, German Fictions*, 51–58.

39. Heinrich Heine, *The Rabbi of Bacharach*, trans. Charles Godfrey Leland (London: W. Heinemann, 1891), 187. "Wie die drey Engel zu Abraham kommen, um ihm zu verkünden, daß ihm ein Sohn geboren werde von seiner Gattin Sara, welche unterdessen, weiblich pfiffig hinter der Zeltthüre steht um die Unterredung zu belauschen." Heine, *Heinrich Heine Werke* (Frankfurt a.M.: Insel Verlag, 1968), 2:619.

40. Heine, *The Rabbi of Bacharach*, 187. "Dieser leise Wink goß dreifaches Roth über die Wangen der schönen Frau, sie schlug die Augen nieder, und sah dann wieder freundlich empor nach ihrem Manne, der singend fortfuhr im Vorlesen der wunderbaren Geschichte." Heine, *Heinrich Heine Werke*, 2:619.

41. Heine, *The Rabbi of Bacharach*, 188. "Derweilen nun die schöne Sara andächtig zuhörte, und ihren Mann beständig ansah, bemerkte sie wie plötzlich sein Antlitz in grausiger Verzerrung erstarrte, das Blut aus seinen Wangen und Lippen verschwand, und seine Augen wie Eiszapfen hervorglotzten;—aber fast im selben Augenblicke sah sie, wie seine Züge wieder die vorige Ruhe und Heiterkeit annahmen, wie seine Lippen und Wangen sich wieder röteten, seine Augen munter umherkreisten, ja, wie sogar eine ihm sonst ganz fremde tolle Laune sein ganzes Wesen ergriff. Die schöne Sara erschrak wie sie noch nie in ihrem Leben erschrocken war, und ein inneres Grauen stieg kältend in ihr auf, weniger wegen der Zeichen von starrem Entsetzen, die sie einen Moment lang im Gesichte ihres Mannes erblickt hatte, als wegen seiner jetzigen Fröhlichkeit, die allmählig in jauchzende Ausgelassenheit überging." Heine, *Heinrich Heine Werke*, 619–20.

42. Heine, *The Rabbi of Bacharach*, 228–29; and Heine, *Heinrich Heine Werke*, 643–44.

43. Heine, *The Rabbi of Bacharach*, 228. "Von dem Schmerze dieses Bewusstseins wäre sie schier selber gestorben, hätte sich nicht eine wohltätige Ohnmacht über ihre Sinne ergossen." Heine, *Heinrich Heine Werke*, 644.

44. Heinrich Heine, *On the History of Religion and Philosophy in Germany*, trans. Howard Pollack-Milgate (Cambridge: Cambridge University Press, 2007), 35–36.

Chapter 5

1. For a sociocultural examination of the popularity of the genre of crime literature in the second half of the nineteenth century, see Jörg Schönert, "Literatur und Kriminalität: Probleme, Forschungsstand und die Konzeption des Kolloquiums," in *Literatur und Kriminalität: Die gesellschaftliche Erfahrung von Verbrechen und Strafverfolgung als Gegenstand des Erzählens: Deutschland, England und Frankreich, 1850–1880*, ed. Jörg Schönert (Tübingen: Niemeyer, 1983), 1–13.

2. Hegel's early writings were published in 1907, with the enthusiastic support of Wilhelm Dilthey. Dilthey published a study of Hegel's "Spirit of Christianity and Its Fate" and understood it to reveal a Hegel who had not yet confined himself to his later philosophical system—an author whose genius was expressed in his historical investigation into civilization. Dilthey, *Gesammelte Werke* (Leipzig: Teubner, 1921), 4:68.

3. In his study of Hegel's relationship to Jews and Judaism, Yirmiyahu Yovel concludes that the philosopher's relationship to Jews is unresolved, constantly shifting between loathing and appreciation of their contribution to humanity. Yovel argues that it is impossible to determine Hegel's opinion on this matter. *Dark Riddle: Hegel, Nietzsche and the Jews* [in Hebrew] (Tel Aviv: Schocken, 1996), 123. Similarly, in his description of the negotiation of Judaism as a catalyst of Enlightenment thought, Adam Sutcliffe argues that "Hegel's struggle to distil a rational kernel from the distorting irrationalities of religion repeatedly drew him back to Judaism, the unique historical significance and endurance of which powerfully resisted accommodation within his own dialectical systems of thought." *Judaism and Enlightenment*, 255.

4. The essay's importance to the history of German idealism derives from its discussion of key terms in Hegel's philosophical system, such as "thesis" and "antithesis" and his notion of servitude. Yovel contends that the early essay not only exemplifies the master-slave dialectic but also explains the ability to transgress this power relation through work and the shaping of nature. *Dark Riddle*, 59.

5. Hegel elaborates on this possibility and its importance in his *Lectures on the Philosophy of Religion* (*Vorlesungen über die Philosophie der Religion*, 1821–31). There, he suggests that the Christian notion of the divine culminates in the merging of object and subject. See Peter C. Hodgson, *Shapes of Freedom: Hegel's Philosophy of World History in Theological Perspective* (Oxford: Oxford University Press, 2012), 142–43.

6. Georg Wilhelm Friedrich Hegel, *On Christianity: Early Theological Writings*, trans. T. M. Knox (Chicago: University of Chicago Press, 1948), 191.

7. David Nirenberg includes this transition between Kant's decision "to portray Jesus as a Kantian, a rebel against Jewish materiality" and Hegel's presentation of Abraham as "the founder of Kantian idealism" in his lineage of "anti-Judaism," an ongoing discourse of authors who comment on one another's depictions of Jews as inhuman, human, and partially human. David Nirenberg, *Anti-Judaism: The Western Tradition* (New York: W. W. Norton, 2013), 394, 400–401.

8. Hegel, *Werke*, vol. 1, *Frühe Schriften* (Frankfurt a.M.: Suhrkamp, 1970), 285–97.

9. Ibid., 1:288.

10. Ibid.

11. Hegel, *On Christianity*, 218.

12. Ibid., 256.

13. In an early lexical article on realism, Max Nussberger defines realist prose as opting for unconditional depiction of reality: one detached from any specific philosophical, moral, or sociological theory in its striving to be a pure representation."Realismus, Poetischer," in *Reallexikon der deutschen Literaturgeschichte* (Berlin: Walter de Gruyter, 1928–29), 3:4.

14. Frederic Jameson has argued that under the influence of realism, providence is translated into an ontological rule perceived as the condition for the coherent perception of the events unfolded by the text. *The Antinomies of Realism* (New York: Verso, 2013), 205.

15. On the structure of the novella and its formation of the "crime narrative," see Walter Huge, "*Die Judenbuche* als Kriminalgeschichte: Das Problem von Erkenntnis und Urteil in Kriminalschema," *Zeitschrift für deutsche Philologie* 99 (1980): 49–70. For an account that views the novella's unique "employment" of the reader as its prominent feature, see Larry D. Wells, "Indeterminacy as Provocation: The Reader's Role in Annette von Droste-Hülshoff's *Die Judenbuche*," *MLN* 94, no. 3 (1979): 475–92. Wells argues that interpreting the novella requires the reader to refute both the social norms of contemporary Westphalian society and the poem at the text's outset, which, according to Wells, warns the reader against his or her own distorted moral judgment.

16. Heinrich Henel's work has been particularly significant in calling attention to the lack of evidence offered to the reader concerning the murder mystery at the novella's core. Other interpretations of the work's perplexing narratology suggest that Aaron may have been killed by somebody other than Friedrich. See Henel, "Annette von Droste-Hülshoff: Erzählstil und Wirklichkeit," *Festschrift für Bernhard Blume: Aufsätze zur deutschen und europäischen Literatur*, ed. Egon Schwarz, Hunten G. Hannum, and Edgar Lohner (Göttingen: Vandenhoek & Ruprecht, 1967), 146–72. One proponent of this view, Norbert Mecklenburg, claims that he can prove Johannes as the killer. See his *Der Fall Judenbuche: Revision eines Fehlurteils* (Bielefeld: Aisthesis, 2008).

17. Annette von Droste-Hülshoff, *Historisch-kritische Ausgabe: Werke, Briefwechsel* (Tübingen: Max Niemeyer, 1978), 5,1:34.

18. I agree with Karin Doerr's observation that the presence of Hebrew script is meant to create suspense among the novella's readers, who are assumed to not know Hebrew. "The Specter of Antisemitism in and Around Annette von Droste-Hülshoff's 'Judenbuche,'" *German Studies Review* 17, no. 3 (1994): 457. This narratological use of Hebrew demonstrates that the novella does not include observant Jews among its potential audience.

19. Andreas Kilcher interprets the Hebrew sentence as a reference to both a "black magic" that exceeds the Christian juridical order and a "natural magic" that ascribes to the Jews the ability to recuperate the world's moral order. Kilcher concludes that the appearance of the sentence incorporates both connotations: "The magical law of the Hebrew language that presides in *The Judenbuche* is a natural one. It describes a cosmological order that—beyond the conventional notions of right and wrong, beyond opinions and common law, beyond the positivistic, governmental statutes and bodies and beyond Christian-theological imperatives—prevails and transforms itself in a magical manner." Kilcher, "Das magische Gesetz der hebräischen Sprache: Drostes *Judenbuche* und der spätromantische Diskurs über die jüdische Magie," *Zeitschrift für Deutsche Philologie* 118, no. 2 (1999): 265. For

a reading that takes Jewish ritual to hold an unfulfilled promise of pregnant mystery, see Jane K. Brown, "The Real Mystery in Droste-Hülshoff's 'Die Judenbuche,'" *Modern Languages Review* 73, no. 4 (1978): 835–46.

20. Sheehan, *Enlightenment Bible*, 1.

21. Frei, *Eclipse of Biblical Narrative*, 19.

22. Von Mücke, *Practices of the Enlightenment*, esp. 87–107, 178–79.

23. Droste-Hülshoff, *Historisch-kritische Ausgabe*, 5,1:20.

24. "Le vrai n'est pas toujours vraisemblable." Ibid., 34.

25. Ibid.

26. Mecklenburg thus argues that Friedrich's suicide is the novella's foremost dramatic moment, not because it solves the enigma of Aaron's murder but because of its cryptic nature. Reading the end of the novella as a resolution presents the Jewish community as capable of avenging the death of one of its members. As Mecklenburg demonstrates, this promise is not realized. Mecklenburg, *Der Fall Judenbuche*, 8.

27. William Collins Donahue argues that the novella propagates its moral lesson by contrasting two justice systems: a Jewish system grounded in the Old Testament and a Christian one grounded in the New Testament. According to Donahue, the juxtaposition of these systems of morality is embodied in the beech tree: "This ideologically charged symbol identifying Judaism with the *lex talionis* serves to reinscribe well-worn cultural prejudices about a worldly, material, and 'exterior' Judaism superseded by a superior, inward Christianity." Donahue, "'Ist er kein Jude, so verdiente er einer zu sein': Droste-Hülshoff's *Die Judenbuche* and Religious Anti-Semitism," *German Quarterly* 72, no. 1 (1999): 57. The novella also supplies a few hints of another confessional differentiation, namely between Protestants and Catholics. This distinction, however, is not described as explicitly in the text as is the exceptionality of Jews, who are characterized in *The Jews' Beech* through their religious belonging and whose distinct presence gives the novella its title. Following Donahue, I contend that the contrast between Jews and an unmarked group of individuals construed as Christians forms the novella's thematic center. Several readers, including Jefferson S. Chase, Raymond Immerwahr and Larry D. Wells, have argued that stereotypical conceptions of Jews are joined together in the process of attempting to make sense of the convoluted narrative. See Chase, "Part of the Story: The Significance of Jews in Annette von Droste-Hülshoff's *Die Judenbuche*," *Deutsche Vierteljahrsschrift für Literaturwissenschaft und Geistesgeschichte* 71, no. 1 (1997): 127–46; Immerwahr, "The Peasant Wedding as Dramatic Climax of *Die Judenbuche*," *Momentum dramaticum: Festschrift for Eckehard Catholy*, ed. Linda Dietrick and David G. John (Waterloo: Waterloo University Press, 1990), 321–36; and Wells, "Indeterminacy as Provocation." Critics who ask in what way the novella is an expression of anti-Semitism thus ask what impressions stay with the reader upon its reading. See Aldo Palmieri, "Die Judenbuche—eine antisemitische Novelle? Gegenbilder und Vorurteil," in *Aspekte des Judentums im Werk deutschsprachiger Schriftstellerinnen*, ed. Renate Heuer and Ralph-Rainer Wuthenow (Frankfurt a.M.: Campus Verlag, 1995), 9. In their respective interpretations of the text, Doerr and Martha B. Helfer argue that anti-Semitic sentiments grow stronger as the text progresses. Focusing her examination on what she sees as the text's "latent anti-Semitism," Helfer takes the novella to associate moral fault with Jewish attributes, concluding her examination with the claim that Friedrich himself is a symbolic Jew of sorts. *The Word Unheard: Legacies of Anti-Semitism in German Literature and Culture* (Evanston, Ill.: Northwestern University Press, 2011), 81, 110–11. My analysis focuses on confessional

difference as key to the novella's religious ideology. I am nonetheless closer to Donahue in viewing the novella's juxtaposition of Jews and Christians as indicative of the ethical deterioration of the latter.

28. Annette von Droste-Hülshoff, *The Jews' Beech Tree*, trans. Jolyon Timothy Hughes (Plymouth: University Press of America, 2014), 71. "Der Wind hatte sich gewendet und zischte jezt wie eine Schlange durch die Fensterritze an seinem Ohr. Seine Schulter war erstarrt; er kroch tief unter's Deckbett und lag aus Furcht ganz still. Nach einer Weile bemerkte er, daß die Mutter auch nicht schlief. Er hörte sie weinen und mitunter: 'Gegrüßt seyst du, Maria!' und 'bitte für uns arme Sünder!' Die Kügelchen des Rosenkranzes glitten an seinem Gesicht hin.—Ein unwillkürlicher Seufzer entfuhr ihm.—'Friedrich, bist du wach?'—'Ja, Mutter.'—'Kind, bete ein wenig—du kannst ja schon das halbe Vaterunser—daß Gott uns bewahre vor Wasser- und Feuersnot.'" (7). *Historisch-kritische Ausgabe*, 5,1:7. With the mention of the rosary, the scene signals the distinctiveness of Catholic liturgy. Droste-Hülshoff's spiritual commitment as a member of the Catholic Church—and as an author who uses her writings and especially her confessional poetry as a platform for expressing her faith—is well known. For an account that endorses Droste-Hülshoff as a leading voice in making Catholic convictions present in nineteenth-century literature, see August Weldemann, *Die religiöse Lyrik des deutschen Katholizismus in der ersten Hälfte des 19. Jahrhunderts, unter besonderer Berücksichtigung Annettens von Droste* (Leipzig: Voigtländer, 1911). My analysis of the novella shies away from a biographical study; I read *The Jews' Beech* as an expression of the Zeitgeist. Modern hermeneutics emerged in Germany largely under the influence of Protestant principles, whose impact certainly also affected those who were not Protestant.

29. Droste-Hülshoff, *Jews' Beech Tree*, 119. "'Friedrich, wohin?' flüsterte der Alte.— 'Ohm, seyd Ihr's? Ich will beichten gehen.'—'Das dacht' ich mir; geh in Gottes Namen, aber beichte wie ein guter Christ.'—'Das will ich,' sagte Friedrich.—'Denk an die zehn Gebote: du sollst kein Zeugniß ablegen gegen deinen Nächsten.'—'Kein falsches!'—'Nein, gar keines; du bist schlecht unterrichtet; wer einen andern in der Beichte anklagt, der empfängt das Sakrament unwürdig.'" Droste-Hülshoff, *Historisch-kritische Ausgabe*, 5,1:25.

30. Bruno Markwardt defines the category *religiös-ethischer Realismus* as a founding principle of German literature in the 1830s. See his *Geschichte der deutschen Poetik*, vol. 4 (Berlin: Walter de Gruyter, 1959). Fritz Martini has likewise argued that "bourgeois realism" is both a literary style and world perception (*Welthaltung*) responding to the individual's situation in the nineteenth century. See his *Deutsche Literatur im bürgerlichen Realismus, 1848–1898* (Stuttgart: Metzler, 1962).

31. "The Realist hoped to entertain, but at the same time he gently pointed the moral, not with bitter satire that could wound, but with the liberating agent of humour. The result was . . . a harmony of tone which allowed the victims to laugh at their own faults, and admire the 'Vorbilder und Urbilder höheren Lebens.'" J. M. Ritchie, "The Ambivalence of 'Realism' in German Literature, 1830–1880," *Orbis Litterarum* 15, no. 3/4 (1960): 215.

32. Sheehan, *Enlightenment Bible*, 224.

33. Droste-Hülshoff, *Jews' Beech Tree*, 133–34. "Der Gutsherr stand am Fenster und sah besorgt in's Dunkle . . . 'Gretchen, sieh noch einmal nach, gieß es lieber ganz aus!— Kommt, wir wollen das Evangelium Johannis beten.' Alles kniete nieder und die Hausfrau begann: 'Im Anfang war das Wort und das Wort war bei Gott und Gott war das Wort.' Ein furchtbarer Donnerschlag. Alle fuhren zusammen; dann furchtbares Geschrei und Getümmel die Treppe heran.—'Um Gottes willen! Brennt es?' rief Frau von S. und sank

mit dem Gesichte auf den Stuhl. Die Thüre ward aufgerissen und herein stürzte die Frau des Juden Aaron, bleich wie der Tod, das Haar wild um den Kopf, von Regen triefend. Sie warf sich vor dem Gutsherrn auf die Knie. 'Gerechtigkeit!' rief sie, 'Gerechtigkeit! Mein Mann ist erschlagen!' und sank ohnmächtig zusammen." Droste-Hülshoff, *Historisch-kritische Ausgabe*, 5,1:30.

34. Droste-Hülshoff, *Jews' Beech Tree*, 136. "Ihre übergroße Spannung hatte nachgelassen und sie schien jetzt halb verwirrt oder vielmehr stumpfsinnig.—'Aug um Auge, Zahn um Zahn!' dieß waren die einzigen Worte, die sie zuweilen hervorstieß." Droste-Hülshoff, *Historisch-kritische Ausgabe*, 5,1:31.

35. Konrad Schaum, *Ironie und Ethik in Annette von Droste-Hülshoffs Judenbuche* (Heidelberg: Winter, 2004), 108.

36. Mark Musa, ed., *The Divine Comedy*, vol. 1, *Inferno*, by Dante Alighieri (New York: Penguin Classics, 2002), 94.

37. Dania Hückmann reads *The Jews' Beech* in connection with Torquato Tasso's *Jerusalem Delivered* and Virgil's *The Aeneid* in order to demonstrate the cultural history that makes the tree an especially suitable site for the performance of talion law, on account of its ability to give the dead a voice. She writes, "Trees serve as containers for the dead in a double sense: first as places where the dead retain a material form, and second as places where their voices are preserved and address us." Hückmann, "The Dead Speak: On the Legibility of Trees in *The Aeneid, Gerusalemme liberata*, and *Die Judenbuche*," *Germanic Review* 90, no. 3 (2015): 175. My own reading also shows the novella as a link in the linage of Christian representations of talion law, yet I argue that the text ultimately shows modern society as deviating from the system of justice construed in former representations of morality.

38. Richard T. Gray cites Heinz Rölleke and Hannes Fricke on this matter. See "Red Herrings and Blue Smocks: Ecological Destruction, Commercialism, and Anti-Semitism," in Annette von Droste-Hülshoff's 'Die Judenbuche,'" *German Studies Review* 26, no. 3 (2003): 531.

39. "Jede Rede oder Schrift ist nur in einem größern Zusammenhange zu verstehen." Friedrich Daniel Ernst Schleiermacher, *Vorlesungen zur Hermeneutik und Kritik* (Berlin: W. de Gruyter, 2012), 77.

40. Donahue, "'Ist er kein Jude,'" 44.

41. Ibid., 66.

42. Droste-Hülshoff, *The Jew's Beech Tree*, 59. "Wo ist die Hand so zart, daß ohne Irren / Sie sondern mag beschränkten Hirnes Wirren, / So fest, daß ohne Zittern sie den Stein / Mag schleudern auf ein arm verkümmert Seyn? . . . Laß ruhn den Stein—er trifft dein eignes Haupt!" Droste-Hülshoff, *Historisch-kritische Ausgabe*, 5,1:3.

Coda

1. See Jürgen Habermas, *Strukturwandel der Öffentlichkeit: Untersuchungen zu einer Kategorie der bürgerlichen Gesellschaft* (Neuwied: Luchterhand, 1962).

2. Martin Heidegger, *Was heisst Denken?* (Tübingen: M. Niemeyer, 1961), 8–9, 13, 90–91.

3. Shira Wolosky discusses Celan's public address as distinguishing between two registers of perceiving reality: "Thanking a German audience by reminding them who he and they are; referring in the process to Heidegger's 'What is Called Thinking?' with all the disturbance of Heidegger's own Nazi involvement and [to Heidegger's own] "return" to a

purer, poeticized German; and finally, implicitly declaring that for Celan, not only "thanking" but every German word is a call to remember." *Language Mysticism: The Negative Way of Language in Eliot, Becket, and Celan* (Stanford, Calif.: Stanford University Press, 1995), 166–67.

4. Paul Celan, *Poems of Paul Celan*, trans. Michael Hamburger (New York: Persea Books, 1972), 269. The German original is available in Paul Celan, *Gesammelte Werke*, vol. 2, *Gedichte 2*, ed. Beda Allemann and Stefan Reichert (Frankfurt a.M.: Suhrkamp, 1983), 227.

5. One prominent use of proper names in Celan's poetry is the binary opposition in his "Todesfuge" (Death Fugue) between Margarete and Sulamith. The Hebrew name seems to function in "Todesfuge" as an emblem of Jewish identity, alluding to the Song of Songs. Katrin Schutjer suggests that Celan's juxtaposition of the two female figures evokes Margarete from Goethe's *Faust*. In her reading, "Goethe's depiction of Margarete contains repeated, unmistakable allusions to the Shulamite." Schutjer, *Goethe and Judaism*, 189.

6. Some critics posit that Celan presents poetry as alluding to transcendental meaning, as when it refers to negative theology and uses Kabbalistic motifs. For an analysis that ties the ambiguity of Celan's poetry to his correspondence with negative theology, see Wolosky, *Language Mysticism*. This correspondence situates his poetry in the context of Jewish traditionalist thinking, on the one hand, and in the historiography of self-fashioning mysticism through modernist style, on the other.

7. See Paul Ricoeur, "La philosophie et la spécificité du langage religieux," *Revue d'histoire et de philosophie religieuses* 55, no. 1 (1975): 13–26. Although Ricoeur's phenomenological approach to hermeneutics largely refrains from discussing language as independent of the subject, his thought does lay the ground for this view as implied by his statement, "For us, the world is the ensemble of references opened up by the texts." Paul Ricoeur, "The Model of the Text: Meaningful Action Considered as a Text," in *Hermeneutics and the Human Sciences*, trans. John B. Thompson (Cambridge: Cambridge University Press, 2016), 202.

Bibliography

Allan, Michael. *In the Shadow of World Literature: Sites of Reading in Colonial Egypt.* Princeton, N.J.: Princeton University Press, 2016.

Alter, Robert. *The Art of Biblical Poetry.* New York: Basic Books, 1985.

Altmann, Alexander. *Moses Mendelssohn: A Biographical Study.* London: Littman Library of Jewish Civilization, 1998.

Anderson, Benedict. *Imagined Communities: Reflections on the Origin and Spread of Nationalism.* Rev. ed. London: Verso, 2006.

Anz, Heinrich. *Hermeneutische Positionen: Schleiermacher, Dilthey, Heidegger, Gadamer.* Göttingen: Vandenhoeck & Ruprecht, 1982.

Apter, Emily. *Against World Literature: On the Politics of Untranslatability.* London: Verso, 2013.

Arkush, Allan. *Mendelssohn and the Enlightenment.* Albany: State University of New York Press, 1994.

Arouet, François-Marie [Voltaire]. *Essai sur les moeurs et lésprit des Nations.* Vol. 24, *Oeuvres complètes de Voltaire.* Paris: Garnier frères, 1877–1885.

Asad, Talal. *Formations of the Secular: Christianity, Islam, Modernity.* Stanford, Calif.: Stanford University Press, 2003.

———. "Free Speech, Blasphemy, and Secular Criticism." In *Is Critique Secular? Blasphemy, Injury, and Free Speech,* edited by Wendy Brown, Judith Butler, and Saba Mahmood. Berkeley, Calif.: Townsend Center for the Humanities, University of California, 2009, 26–63.

———. "Reflections on Blasphemy and Secular Culture." In *Religion: Beyond a Concept,* edited by Hent de Vries, 580–609. New York: Fordham University Press, 2008.

Asad, Talal, Wendy Brown, Judith Butler, and Saba Mahmood, eds. *Is Critique Secular? Blasphemy, Injury, and Free Speech.* Berkeley: Townsend Center for the Humanities, University of California, 2009.

Auerbach, Erich. *Mimesis: The Representation of Reality in Western Literature.* Princeton, N.J.: Princeton University Press, 2003.

———. "Philology and World Literature." Translated by Maire and Edward Said. *Centennial Review* 13, no. 1 (1969): 1–17.

Austin, Linda M. "Children of Childhood: Nostalgia and the Romantic Legacy." *Studies in Romanticism* 42, no. 1 (2003): 75–98.

Baader, Meike Sophia. *Die romantische Idee des Kindes und der Kindheit.* Berlin: Luchterhand, 1996.

Baildam, John D. *Paradisal Love: Johann Gottfried Herder and the Song of Songs*. Sheffield, UK: Sheffield Academic Press, 1999.

Barnard, Frederick M. *Herder on Nationality, Humanity and History*. Montreal: McGill-Queen's University Press, 2002.

Barth, Karl. *Die protestantische Theologie im 19. Jahrhundert*. Berlin: Evangelische Verlagsanstalt, 1961.

Barzilay, Isaac Eisenstein. "Moses Mendelssohn (1729–1786) (A Study in Ideas and Attitudes)." *Jewish Quarterly Review* 52, no. 1 (1961): 69–93.

Batnitzky, Leora. *How Judaism Became a Religion: An Introduction to Modern Jewish Thought*. Princeton, N.J.: Princeton University Press, 2011.

Beiser, Frederick C. *Enlightenment, Revolution, and Romanticism: The Genesis of Modern German Political Thought, 1790–1800*. Cambridge, Mass.: Harvard University Press, 1992.

Benjamin, Walter. "Franz Kafka: On the Tenth Anniversary of His Death." In *Illuminations: Essays and Reflections*, edited by Hannah Arendt, translated by Harry Zohn, 111–40. New York: Schocken, 1968.

———. "On Language as Such and on the Language of Man." In *1913–1926*, edited by Marcus Bullock and Michael W. Jennings, 62–74. Vol. 1, *Walter Benjamin: Selected Writings*. Cambridge, Mass.: Harvard University Press, 2002.

———. "The Translator's Task." Translated by Steven Rendall. *TTR: traduction, terminologie, rédaction* 10, no. 2 (1997): 151–65.

Berghahn, Klaus. "From Classicist to Classical Literary Criticism, 1730–1806." In *A History of German Literary Criticism, 1730–1980*, edited by Peter Uwe Hohendahl, 13–98. Lincoln: University of Nebraska Press, 1988.

Berlin, Isaiah. "My Intellectual Path." In *The Power of Ideas*, edited by Isaiah Berlin and Henry Hardy, 1–23. Princeton, N.J.: Princeton University Press, 2002.

Betz, John. *After Enlightenment: The Post-secular Vision of J. G. Hamann*. Oxford: Wiley-Blackwell, 2009.

Biale, David. *Not in the Heavens: The Tradition of Jewish Secular Thought*. Princeton, N.J.: Princeton University Press, 2011.

Bienenstock, Max. *Das jüdische Element in Heines Werken: Ein krititisch-aesthetischer Beitrag zur Heine Frage*. Leipzig: Verlag für Literatur, Kunst und Musik, 1910.

Biti, Vladimir. *Tracing Global Democracy: Literature, Theory, and the Politics of Trauma*. Berlin/Boston: Walter de Gruyter, 2016.

Blumenberg, Hans. *Die Legitimität der Neuzeit*. Frankfurt a.M.: Suhrkamp, 1966.

Breuer, Edward. *The Limits of Enlightenment: Jews, Germans, and the Eighteenth-Century Study of Scripture*. Cambridge, Mass.: Harvard University Press, 1996.

Brod, Max. *Heinrich Heine*. Amsterdam: Verlag Allert de Lange, 1934.

Brown, Jane K. "The Real Mystery in Droste-Hülshoff's 'Die Judenbuche.'" *Modern Languages Review* 73, no. 4 (1978): 835–46.

Burdach, Konrad. *Die nationale Aneignung der Bibel und die Anfänge der germanischen Philologie*. Halle: M. Niemeyer, 1924.

Campe, Rüdiger. *Affekt und Ausdruck: Zur Umwandlung der literarischen Rede im 17. und 18. Jahrhundert*. Tübingen: M. Niemeyer, 1990.

Casanova, Pascale. *The World Republic of Letters*. Translated by M. B. DeBevoise. Cambridge, Mass.: Harvard University Press, 2004.

Cassirer, Ernst. *The Philosophy of the Enlightenment*. Translated by Fritz C. A. Koelln and James P. Pettegrove. Boston: Beacon Press, 1966.

Celan, Paul. *Gedichte 2.* Vol. 2, *Gesammelte Werke.* Edited by Beda Allemann and Stefan Reichert. Frankfurt a.M.: Suhrkamp, 1983.

———. *Poems of Paul Celan.* Translated by Michael Hamburger. New York: Persea Books, 1972.

Chase, Jefferson S. "Part of the Story: The Significance of Jews in Annette von Droste-Hülshoff's *Die Judenbuche.*" *Deutsche Vierteljahrsschrift für Literaturwissenschaft und Geistesgeschichte* 71, no. 1 (1997): 127–46.

Cheah, Pheng. "World Against Globe: Toward a Normative Conception of World Literature." *New Literary History* 45, no. 3 (2014): 303–29.

Connolly, William E. "Europe: A Minor Tradition." In *Powers of the Secular Modern: Talal Asad and His Interlocutors,* edited by David Scott and Charles Hirschkind, 75–92. Stanford, Calif.: Stanford University Press, 2006.

Cramer, Friedrich. *Klopstock: Er, und über ihn 1724–1747.* Hamburg: Schniebes, 1780.

Dickson, Gwen Griffith. *Johann Georg Hamann's Relational Metacriticism.* Berlin: W. de Gruyter, 1995.

Dilthey, Wilhelm. *Gesammelte Schriften.* 26 vols. Stuttgart/Göttingen: Teubner/Vandenhoeck & Ruprecht, 1959–2005.

Doerr, Karin. "The Specter of Antisemitism in and Around Annette von Droste-Hülshoff's 'Judenbuche.'" *German Studies Review* 17, no. 3 (1994): 447–71.

Dohm, Christian Wilhelm. *Über die bürgerliche Verbesserung der Juden.* Berlin and Stettin: Nicolai, 1781.

Donahue, William Collins. "'Ist er kein Jude, so verdiente er einer zu sein': Droste-Hülshoff's *Die Judenbuche* and Religious Anti-Semitism." *German Quarterly* 72, no. 1 (1999): 44–73.

Droste-Hülshoff, Annette von. *Historisch-kritische Ausgabe.* Vol. 5, 1 *Prose Text.* Edited by Winfried Woesler. Tübingen: Max Niemeyer, 1978.

———. *The Jews' Beech Tree.* Translated by Jolyon Timothy Hughes. Plymouth: University Press of America, 2014.

Duke, James. Introduction to *Hermeneutics: The Handwritten Manuscripts,* by Friedrich Schleiermacher, edited by Heinz Kimmerle, translated by James Duke and Jack Forstman, 1–15. Missoula, Mont.: Scholars Press for the American Academy of Religion, 1977.

Dyck, Joachim. *Athen und Jerusalem: Die Tradition der argumentativen Verknüpfung von Bibel und Poesie im 17. und 18. Jahrhundert.* Munich: Beck, 1977.

Eisen, Arnold. "Divine Legislation as 'Ceremonial Script': Mendelssohn on the Commandments." *AJS Review* 15, no. 2 (1990): 239–67.

Erlin, Matt. "Reluctant Modernism: Moses Mendelssohn's Philosophy of History." *Journal of the History of Ideas* 63, no. 1 (2002): 83–104.

Forster, Michael N. *After Herder: Philosophy of Language in the German Tradition.* Oxford: Oxford University Press, 2010.

———. *German Philosophy of Language: From Schlegel to Hegel and Beyond.* Oxford: Oxford University Press, 2011.

———. Introduction to *Herder: Philosophical Writings,* by Johann Gottfried von Herder, edited by Michael N. Forster, vii–xxxv. Cambridge: Cambridge University Press, 2002.

Frei, Hans W. *The Eclipse of Biblical Narrative: A Study in Eighteenth and Nineteenth Century Hermeneutics.* New Haven, Conn.: Yale University Press, 1974.

Gadamer, Hans-Georg. "Rhetoric and Hermeneutics." In *Rhetoric and Hermeneutics in Our Time,* edited by Walter Jost and Michael J. Hyde, 45–59. New Haven, Conn.: Yale University Press, 1997.

———. *Wahrheit und Methode: Grundzüge einer philosophischen Hermeneutik.* 2nd ed. Tübingen: Mohr, 1965.

Gay, Peter. *The Enlightenment: An Interpretation.* Vol. 1, *The Rise of Modern Paganism.* New York: W. W. Norton, 1966.

Gessner, Salomon. *The Death of Abel in Five Books.* Translated by Mary Mitchell Collyer. 12th ed. London: T. Martin, 1791.

Gierl, Martin. *Pietismus und Aufklärung: Theologische Polemik und die Kommunikationsreform der Wissenschaft am Ende des 17. Jahrhunderts.* Göttingen: Vandenhoeck & Ruprecht, 1997.

Gjesdal, Kristin. *Gadamer and the Legacy of German Idealism.* Cambridge: Cambridge University Press, 2009.

Goebel, Julius. "William Dilthey and the Science of Literary History." *Journal of English and Germanic Philology* 25, no. 2 (1926): 145–56.

Goethe, Johann Wolfgang. *Aus Meinem Leben: Dichtung und Wahrheit.* Edited by Klaus-Detlef Müller. Vol. 14, *Sämtliche Werke. Briefe, Tagebücher und Gespräche.* Frankfurt a.M.: Deutscher Klassiker Verlag, 1986.

———. *Truth and Poetry: From My Own Life; or, The Autobiography of Goethe.* 4 vols. Translated and edited by Parke Godwin. New York: G. P. Putnam, 1846–47.

Goethe, Johann Wolfgang von, and A. Schoell. *Briefe und Aufsätze aus den Jahren 1766 bis 1786.* Weimar: Landes-Industrie-Comptoir, 1857.

Goetschel, Willi. *Spinoza's Modernity: Mendelssohn, Lessing, and Heine.* Madison: University of Wisconsin Press, 2003.

Goldstein, Bluma. "Heine's 'Hebrew Melodies': A Politics and Poetics of Diaspora." In *Heinrich Heine's Contested Identities: Politics, Religion, and Nationalism in Nineteenth-Century Germany,* edited by Jost Hermand and Robert C. Holub, 49–68. New York: Peter Lang, 1999.

Gray, Richard. "Red Herrings and Blue Smocks: Ecological Destruction, Commercialism, and Anti-Semitism in Annette von Droste-Hülshoff's 'Die Judenbuche.'" *German Studies Review* 26, no. 3 (2003): 515–42.

Green, Anna. *Cultural History.* London: Palgrave Macmillan, 2008.

Gross, Sabine, and Marcus Bullock. "Historiography, Theology, and the *Erkenntnis*: Empathy in Herder and Benjamin." In *J. G. Herder: From Cognition to Cultural Science,* edited by Beate Allert, 159–82. Heidelberg: Synchron, 2016.

Habermas, Jürgen. *Strukturwandel der Öffentlichkeit: Untersuchungen zu einer Kategorie der bürgerlichen Gesellschaft.* Neuwied: Luchterhand, 1962.

Hamann, Johann Georg. *Aesthetica in nuce.* Universal-Bibliothek 926/26a. Stuttgart: Reclam, 1968.

———. *Londoner Schriften.* Edited by Oswald Bayer and Bernd Weißenborn. New ed. Munich: C. H. Beck, 1993.

Hamilton, John. "Poetica Obscura: Reexamining Hamann's Contribution to the Pindaric Tradition." *Eighteenth-Century Studies* 34, no. 1 (2000): 93–115.

Haym, Rudolf. *Herder.* 2 vols. Berlin: Aufbau Verlag, 1954.

Hegel, Georg Wilhelm Friedrich. *Frühe Schriften.* Vol. 1, *Werke.* Frankfurt a.M.: Suhrkamp, 1970.

———. *On Christianity: Early Theological Writings.* Translated by T. M. Knox. Chicago: University of Chicago Press, 1948.

Heidegger, Martin. *Was heisst Denken?* Tübingen: M. Niemeyer, 1961.

Heine, Heinrich. *Der Rabbi of Bacharach.* Translated by Charles Godfrey Leland. London: W. Heinemann, 1891.

——. *Heinrich Heine Werke.* 4 vols. Frankfurt a.M.: Insel Verlag, 1968.

——. *Heinrich Heine: Werke und Briefe in zehn Bänden.* 10 vols. Berlin: Aufbau Verlag, 1961–1964.

——. *Jewish Stories and Hebrew Melodies.* Translated by Hal Draper. New York: M. Wiener, 1987.

——. *On the History of Religion and Philosophy in Germany.* Translated by Howard Pollack-Milgate. Cambridge: Cambridge University Press, 2007.

Heitner, Robert R. *German Tragedy in the Age of Enlightenment.* Berkeley: University of California Press, 1963.

Helfer, Martha B. *The Word Unheard: Legacies of Anti-Semitism in German Literature and Culture.* Evanston, Ill.: Northwestern University Press, 2011.

Henel, Heinrich. "Annette von Droste-Hülshoff: Erzählstil und Wirklichkeit." *Festschrift für Bernhard Blume: Aufsätze zur deutschen und europäischen Literatur,* edited by Egon Schwarz, Hunten G. Hannum, and Edgar Lohner, 146–72. Göttingen: Vandenhoeck & Ruprecht, 1967.

Herder, Johann Gottfried. *Aus Herders Nachlass.* Vol. 2. Edited by H. Düntzer. Frankfurt a.M.: Meidinger, 1856.

——. *Herder: Philosophical Writings.* Edited by Michael N. Forster. Cambridge: Cambridge University Press, 2002.

——. *Johann Gottfried Herder: Frühe Schriften, 1764–1772.* Edited by Ulrich Gaier. Frankfurt a.M.: Deutscher Klassiker Verlag, 1985.

——. *Johann Gottfried Herder: Ideen zur Philosophie der Geschichte der Menschheit.* Edited by Martin Bollacher. Frankfurt a.M.: Deutscher Klassiker Verlag, 1989.

——. *Johann Gottfried Herder: Schriften zum Alten Testament.* Edited by Rudolf Smend. Frankfurt a.M.: Deutscher Klassiker Verlag, 1993.

——. *Johann Gottfried Herder: Selected Early Works, 1764–1772.* Translated by Ernest A. Menze and Michael Palma. University Park: Pennsylvania State University Press, 1992.

——. *On the Spirit of Hebrew Poetry.* 2 vols. Translated by James Marsch. Burlington, Vt.: Edward Smith, 1833.

——. *Johann Gottfried Herder: Werke.* Vol. 1, *Herder und der Sturm und Drang, 1764–1774.* Edited by Wolfgang Proß. Darmstadt: Hanser, 1984.

Heschel, Susannah. *Abraham Geiger and the Jewish Jesus.* Chicago: University of Chicago Press, 1998.

Hess, Jonathan M. *Germans, Jews and the Claims of Modernity.* New Haven, Conn.: Yale University Press, 2002.

Hibberd, John. *Salomon Gessner: His Creative Achievement and Influence.* Cambridge: Cambridge University Press, 1976.

Hilfrich, Carola. *Lebendige Schrift: Repräsentation und Idolatrie in Moses Mendelssohns Philosophie und Exegese des Judentums.* Munich: Wilhelm Fink, 2000.

Hodgson, Peter C. *Shapes of Freedom: Hegel's Philosophy of World History in Theological Perspective.* Oxford: Oxford University Press, 2012.

Hückmann, Dania. "The Dead Speak: On the Legibility of Trees in *The Aeneid, Gerusalemme liberata,* and *Die Judenbuche.*" *Germanic Review* 90, no. 3 (2015): 171–86.

Huebener, Theodore. "How Goethe Learned Languages." *Modern Language Journal* 33, no. 4 (1949): 268–73.

Huge, Walter. "*Die Judenbuche* als Kriminalgeschichte: Das Problem von Erkenntnis und Urteil im Kriminalschema." *Zeitschrift für deutsche Philologie* 99 (1980): 49–70.

Ilany, Ofri. "Between Ziona and Teutona: The Hebrew Model and the Beginning of German National Culture." [In Hebrew.] *Historia*, no. 28 (2012): 81–105.

———. *In Search of the Hebrew People: Bible and Nation in the German Enlightenment.* Bloomington: Indiana University Press, 2018.

Immerwahr, Raymond. "The Peasant Wedding as Dramatic Climax of *Die Judenbuche.*" *Momentum dramaticum: Festschrift for Eckehard Catholy,* edited by Linda Dietrick and David G. John, 321–36. Waterloo: Waterloo University Press, 1990.

Jameson, Frederic. *The Antinomies of Realism.* New York: Verso, 2013.

Jarick, John, ed. *Sacred Conjectures: The Context and Legacy of Robert Lowth and Jean Astruc.* New York: T & T Clark, 2007.

Jay, Martin. "Faith-Based History." Review of *A Secular Age,* by Charles Taylor. *History and Theory* 48, no. 1 (2009): 76–84.

Jeffrey, David L. *People of the Book: Christian Identity and Literary Culture.* Grand Rapids, Mich.: Eerdmans, 1996.

Kaiser, Gerhard. *Klopstock: Religion und Dichtung.* Gütersloh: Gerd Mohn, 1963.

———. *Pietismus und Patriotismus im Literarischen Deutschland: Ein Beitrag zum Problem der Säkularisation.* Wiesbaden: Franz Steiner, 1961.

Kant, Immanuel. *Immanuel Kants Werke.* Edited by Ernst Cassirer. 11 vols. Berlin: Bruno Cassirer, 1914–21.

———. *Religion Within the Boundaries of Mere Reason.* Translated by Allen Wood and George Di Giovanni. Cambridge: Cambridge University Press, 1998.

Kilcher, Andreas. "Das magische Gesetz der hebräischen Sprache: Drostes *Judenbuche* und der spätromantische Diskurs über die jüdische Magie." *Zeitschrift für Deutsche Philologie* 118, no. 2 (1999): 234–65.

Kittler, Friedrich. *Aufschreibesysteme 1800/1900.* Munich: Fink, 1995.

Klopstock, Friedrich Gottlieb. *Biblische Dramen.* Edited by Monika Lemmel. Berlin: Walter de Gruyter, 2005.

———. *The Death of Adam: A Tragedy in Three Acts.* Translated by Robert Lloyd. London: Dryden Leach, 1763.

Kocziszky, Eva. "Leib und Schrift in Hamanns *Aesthetica in nuce.*" *Die Gegenwärtigkeit Johann Georg Hamanns,* edited by Bernhard Gajek, 145–60. Regensburger Beiträge zur deutschen Sprach- und Literaturwissenschaft 88. Frankfurt a.M.: Peter Lang, 2005.

Koselleck, Reinhart. *Kritik und Krise: Ein Beitrag zur Pathogenese der bürgerlichen Welt.* Freiburg: K. Alber, 1959.

Laak, Lothar van. *Hermeneutik literarischer Sinnlichkeit: Historisch-systematische Studien zur Literatur des 17. und 18. Jahrhunderts.* Tübingen: Niemeyer, 2003.

Legaspi, Michael C. *The Death of Scripture and the Rise of Biblical Studies.* Oxford: Oxford University Press, 2010.

Leventhal, Robert Scott. *The Disciplines of Interpretation: Lessing, Herder, Schlegel and Hermeneutics in Germany, 1750–1800.* Berlin: W. de Gruyter, 1994.

Levy, Ze'ev. *Judaism in the Worldview of J. G. Hamann, J. G. Herder and W. v. Goethe.* [In Hebrew.] Jerusalem: Mosad Bialik, 1994.

Librett, Jeffrey S. *The Rhetoric of Cultural Dialogue: Jews and Germans from Moses Mendelssohn to Richard Wagner and Beyond.* Stanford, Calif.: Stanford University Press, 2000.

Lohmeier, Dieter. *Herder und Klopstock: Herders Auseinandersetzung mit der Persönlich-keit und dem Werk Klopstocks.* Bad Homburg: Verlag Gehlen, 1968.

Löwith, Karl. *Meaning in History: The Theological Implications of the Philosophy of History.* Chicago: University of Chicago Press, 1949.

Lowth, Robert. *Lectures on the Sacred Poetry of the Hebrews.* Translated by G. Gregory. New ed. Boston: Crocker & Brewster, 1829.

Mahmood, Saba. "*Azazeel* and the Politics of Historical Fiction in Egypt." *Comparative Literature* 65, no. 3 (2013): 265–84.

———. *Religious Difference in a Secular Age.* Princeton, N.J.: Princeton University Press, 2016.

———. "Religious Reason and Secular Affect: An Incommensurable Divide?" *Critical Inquiry* 35, no. 4 (2009): 836–62.

———. "Religious Reason and Secular Affect: An Incommensurable Divide?" In *Is Critique Secular? Blasphemy, Injury, and Free Speech*, edited by Wendy Brown, Judith Butler, and Saba Mahmood, 64–100. Berkeley, Calif.: Townsend Center for the Humanities, University of California, 2009.

———. "Secularism, Hermeneutics, and Empire: The Politics of Islamic Reformation." *Public Culture* 18, no. 2 (2006): 323–47.

Marchand, Suzanne L. *German Orientalism in the Age of Empire: Religion, Race, and Scholarship.* Washington, D.C.: German Historical Institute, 2009.

Markwardt, Bruno. *Geschichte der deutschen Poetik.* 5 vols. Berlin: Walter de Gruyter, 1959.

Martini, Fritz. *Deutsche Literatur im bürgerlichen Realismus, 1848–1898.* Stuttgart: Metzler, 1962.

Masuzawa, Tomoko. *The Invention of World Religions, or, How European Universalism Was Preserved in the Language of Pluralism.* Chicago: University of Chicago Press, 2005.

Matala de Mazza, Ethel. *Der verfasste Körper: Zum Projekt einer organischen Gemeinschaft in der politischen Romantik.* Freiburg: Rombach, 1999.

Mecklenburg, Norbert. *Der Fall Judenbuche: Revision eines Fehlurteils.* Bielefeld: Aisthesis Verlag, 2008.

Meinecke, Friedrich. *Die Entstehung des Historismus.* Munich: R. Oldenbourg Verlag, 1959

Mendelssohn, Moses. *Ausgewählte Werke.* Vol. 1, *Schriften zur Metaphysik und Ästhetik, 1755–1771.* Edited by Christoph Schulte, Andreas Kennecke und. Grażyna Jurewicz. Student ed. Darmstadt: Wissenschaftliche Buchgesellschaft, 2009.

———. *Jerusalem, or On Religious Power and Judaism.* Translated by Allan Arkush. Waltham, Mass.: Brandeis University Press, 1983.

———. *Moses Mendelssohn: Gesammelte Schriften Jubiläumsausgabe.* Stuttgart: Friedrich Frommann, 1972–.

———. *Moses Mendelssohn: Philosophical Writings.* Edited by Daniel O. Dahlstrom. Cambridge: Cambridge University Press, 2003.

Menke, Christoph. *Kraft: Ein Grundbegriff ästhetischer Anthropologie.* Frankfurt a.M.: Suhrkamp, 2008.

Menninghaus, Winfried. *Schwellenkunde: Walter Benjamins Passage des Mythos.* Frankfurt a.M.: Suhrkamp, 1986.

———. *Walter Benjamins Theorie der Sprachmagie.* Frankfurt a.M.: Suhrkamp, 1995.

Michaelis, Johann David. *Beurtheilung der Mittel, welche man anwendet, die ausgestorbene hebräische Sprache zu verstehen.* Göttingen: s.n., 1757.

———. *Mosaisches Recht*. Frankfurt a.M.: J. Gottlieb Garbe, 1775.

Moore, Gregory. Introduction to *Selected Writing on Aesthetics*, by Johann Gottfried Herder, 1–30. Edited and translated by Gregory Moore. Princeton, N.J.: Princeton University Press, 2006.

Mosès, Stéphane. *Der Engel der Geschichte: Franz Rosenzweig, Walter Benjamin, Gershom Scholem*. Frankfurt a.M.: Jüdischer Verlag, 1994.

Mufti, Aamir. *Forget English! Orientalisms and World Literature*. Cambridge, Mass.: Harvard University Press, 2016.

Musa, Mark, ed. *The Divine Comedy*. Vol. 1, *Inferno*, by Dante Alighieri. New York: Penguin Classics, 2002.

Nirenberg, David. *Anti-Judaism: The Western Tradition*. New York: W. W. Norton, 2013.

Noyes, John K. "Writing the Dialectical Structure of the Modern Subject: Goethe on World Literature and World Citizenship." *Seminar* 51, no. 2 (2015): 100–114.

Nussberger, Max. "Realismus, Poetischer." In *Reallexikon der deutschen Literaturgeschichte*, 3:4–12. Berlin: Walter de Gruyter, 1928–29.

Oelmüller, Willi. *Beiträge zu einer Theorie der Moderne von Lessing, Kant und Hegel*. Frankfurt a.M.: Suhrkamp, 1969.

Olender, Maurice. *The Languages of Paradise: Race, Religion, and Philology in the Nineteenth Century*. Translated by Arthur Goldhammer. Cambridge, Mass.: Harvard University Press, 2008.

Palmer, Richard E. *Hermeneutics: Interpretation Theory in Schleiermacher, Dilthey, Heidegger, and Gadamer*. Evanston, Ill.: Northwestern University Press, 1969.

Palmieri, Aldo. "Die Judenbuche—eine antisemitische Novelle? Gegenbilder und Vorurteil." In *Aspekte des Judentums im Werk deutschsprachiger Schriftstellerinnen*, edited by Renate Heuer and Ralph-Rainer Wuthenow, 9–38. Frankfurt a.M.: Campus Verlag, 1995.

Peters, Paul. *Heinrich Heine "Dichterjude": Die Geschichte einer Schmähung*. Frankfurt a.M.: A. Hain, 1990.

Piper, Andrew. *Dreaming in Books: The Making of the Bibliographic Imagination in the Romantic Age*. Chicago: University of Chicago Press, 2009.

Polaschegg, Andrea. *Der andere Orientalismus: Regeln deutsch-morgenländischer Imagination im 19. Jahrhundert*. Berlin: Walter de Gruyter, 2005.

Prickett, Stephen. *Words and the Word: Language, Poetics, and Biblical Interpretation*. Cambridge: Cambridge University Press, 1986.

Reinsch, F. H. "Goethe's Interpretation of Language Mastery." *German Quarterly* 11, no. 3 (1938): 115–25.

Ricoeur, Paul. "La philosophie et la spécificité du langage religieux." *Revue d'histoire et de philosophie religieuses* 55, no. 1 (1975): 13–26.

———. "The Model of the Text: Meaningful Action Considered as a Text." In *Hermeneutics and the Human Sciences*, 159–83. Translated by John B. Thompson. Cambridge: Cambridge University Press, 2016.

Riecken, Nils. "History, Time, and Temporality in a Global Frame: Abdallah Laroui's Historical Epistemology of History." *History and Theory* 54, no. 4 (2015): 5–26.

Ritchie, J. M. "The Ambivalence of 'Realism' in German Literature 1830–1880." *Orbis Litterarum* 15, no. 3/4 (1960): 200–217.

Rokem, Na'ama. *Prosaic Conditions: Heinrich Heine and the Spaces of Zionist Literature*. Evanston, Ill.: Northwestern University Press, 2013.

Rose, Paul Lawrence. *German Question/Jewish Question: Revolutionary Antisemitism from Kant to Wagner*. Princeton, N.J.: Princeton University Press, 1992.

Rosenthal, Ludwig. *Heinrich Heine als Jude*. Frankfurt a.M.: Ullstein, 1973.

Sacks, Elias. *Moses Mendelssohn's Living Script: Philosophy, Practice, History, Judaism*. Bloomington: Indiana University Press, 2017.

Said, Edward. "Intellectual Exile: Expatriates and Marginal." In *Representations of the Intellectual: The 1993 Reith Lectures*, 47–64. New York: Pantheon Books, 1994.

———. *Orientalism*. London: Penguin, 2003.

Sammons, Jeffery L. "Heine's *Rabbi von Bacherach*: The Unresolved Tensions." *German Quarterly* 37, no. 1 (1964): 26–38.

Schatz, Andrea. *Sprache in der Zerstreuung: Die Säkularisierung des Hebräischen im 18. Jahrhundert*. Göttingen: Vandenhoeck & Ruprecht, 2009.

Schaum, Konrad. *Ironie und Ethik in Annette von Droste-Hülshoffs Judenbuche*. Heidelberg: Winter Verlag, 2004.

Schleiermacher, Friedrich. *Briefe bei Gelegenheit der politisch theologischen Aufgabe und des Sendschreibens jüdischer Hausväter*. Berlin: Evangelische Verlagsanstalt, 1984.

———. *A Critical Essay on the Gospel of St. Luke*. Translated by Connop Thirlwall. London: J. Taylor, 1825.

———. *Hermeneutics and Criticism*. Edited by Andrew Bowie. Cambridge: Cambridge University Press, 1998.

———. *Hermeneutik und Kritik*. Edited by Manfred Frank. Frankfurt a.M.: Suhrkamp, 1977.

———. *On Religion*. Translated by Terrence N. Tice. Richmond, Va.: John Knox Press, 1879.

———, trans. *Platons Werke*. 3 vols. Berlin: Akademie Verlag, 1984–87.

———. *Vorlesungen zur Hermeneutik und Kritik*. Berlin: W. de Gruyter, 2012.

Scholem, Gershom. "Confession on the Subject of Our Language." In *Acts of Religion*, by Jacques Derrida, edited by Gil Anidjar, 226–27. London: Routledge, 2002.

Schönert, Jörg. "Literatur und Kriminalität: Probleme, Forschungsstand und die Konzeption des Kolloquiums." In *Literatur und Kriminalität: Die gesellschaftliche Erfahrung von Verbrechen und Strafverfolgung als Gegenstand des Erzählens: Deutschland, England und Frankreich, 1850–1880*, edited by Jörg Schönert, 1–13. Tübingen: Niemeyer, 1983.

Schorch, Grit. *Moses Mendelssohns Sprachpolitik*. Berlin: Walter de Gruyter, 2012.

Schreiber, Eliot. "Tainted Sources: The Subversion of the Grimms' Ideology of the Folktale in Heinrich Heine's 'Der Rabbi von Bacherach.'" *German Quarterly* 78, no. 1 (2005): 23–44.

Schulte-Sasse, Jochen. "Aesthetic Orientation in a Decentered World." In *A New History of German Literature*, edited by David Wellbery et al., 350–55. Cambridge, Mass.: Harvard University Press, 2004.

Schumacher, Eckhard. *Die Ironie der Unverständlichkeit: Johann Georg Hamann, Friedrich Schlegel, Jacques Derrida, Paul de Man*. Frankfurt a.M.: Suhrkamp, 2000.

Schutjer, Karin Lynn. *Goethe and Judaism: The Troubled Inheritance of Modern Literature*. Evanston, Ill.: Northwestern University Press, 2015.

Shaked, Gershon. "'Der Rabbi von Bacherach' von Heine—Hier und heute." In *Heine in Jerusalem*, edited by Naomi Kaplansky, Elisheva Moatti, and Itta Shedletzky, 53–74. Hamburg: Hoffman und Campe, 2006.

Sheehan, Jonathan. *The Enlightenment Bible: Translation, Scholarship, Culture*. Princeton, N.J.: Princeton University Press, 2005.

———. "Enlightenment Details: Theology, Natural History, and the Letter *h*." *Representations*, no. 61 (1998): 29–56.

Sikka, Sonia. *Herder on Humanity and Cultural Difference: Enlightened Relativism*. Cambridge: Cambridge University Press, 2011.

Skolnik, Jonathan. *Jewish Pasts, German Fictions*. Stanford, Calif.: Stanford University Press, 2014.

Smith, William Robertson. "Poetry of the Old Testament." In *Lectures and Essays*, 400–451. London: Adam and Charles Black, 1912.

Sorkin, David Jan. *The Berlin Haskalah and German Religious Thought: Orphans of Knowledge*. London: Vallentine Mitchell, 2000.

———. "Introduction: The Mendelssohn Myth and the Asymmetrical Reception of the Hebrew Writings." In *Moses Mendelssohn's Hebrew Writings*, translated by Edward Breuer, 1–20. New Haven, Conn.: Yale University Press, 2018.

———. *Mendelssohn and the Religious Enlightenment*. Berkeley: University of California Press, 1996.

———. *The Religious Enlightenment: Protestants, Jews, and Catholics from London to Vienna*. Princeton, N.J.: Princeton University Press, 2008.

Spencer, Vicky A. *Herder's Political Thought: A Study of Language, Culture, and Community*. Toronto: University of Toronto Press, 2012.

———. Review of *Herder on Humanity and Cultural Difference: Enlightened Relativism*, by Sonia Sikka. *Mind* 121, no. 481 (2012): 229–32.

Spinoza, Benedict de. *Theological-Political Treatise*. Edited by Jonathan Israel. Translated by Michael Silverthorne and Jonathan Israel. Cambridge: Cambridge University Press, 2007.

Stelzig, Eugene L. *The Romantic Subject in Autobiography: Rousseau and Goethe*. Charlottesville: University Press of Virginia, 2000.

Strauss, Leo. *Persecution and the Art of Writing*. Chicago: University of Chicago Press, 1988.

Sutcliffe, Adam. *Judaism and Enlightenment*. New York: Cambridge University Press, 2003.

Szondi, Peter. *Einführung in die literarische Hermeneutik*. Frankfurt a.M.: Suhrkamp, 1975.

Taylor, Charles. *A Secular Age*. Cambridge, Mass.: Belknap Press of Harvard University Press, 2007.

Tillmann, Thomas. *Hermeneutik und Bibelexegese beim jungen Goethe*. Berlin: W. de Gruyter, 2006.

Von Mücke, Dorothea. *The Practices of the Enlightenment: Aesthetics, Authorship, and the Public*. New York: Columbia University Press, 2015.

Wach, Joachim. *Das Verstehen: Grundzüge einer Geschichte der hermeneutischen Theorie im 19. Jahrhundert*. 3 vols. Tübingen: J. C. B. Mohr, 1929.

Warner, Michael. "Uncritical Reading." In *Polemic: Critical or Uncritical*, edited by Jane Gallop, 13–38. New York: Routledge, 2004.

Weber, Elizabeth. "Fending Off Idolatry: Ceremonial Law in Mendelssohn's *Jerusalem*." *MLN* 122, no. 3 (2007): 522–43.

Weidner, Daniel. *Bibel und Literatur um 1800*. Munich: Wilhelm Fink, 2011.

———. "Ursprung und Wesen der ebräischen Poesie." In *Urpoesie und Morgenland: Johann Gottfried Herders "Vom Geist der ebräischen Poesie,"* edited by Daniel Weidner, 113–51. Berlin: Kadmos, 2008.

Weigel, Sigrid. "Auf der Schwelle von Schöpfung und Weltgericht." In *Profanes Leben: Walter Benjamins Dialektik der Säkularisierung*, edited by Daniel Weidner, 66–94. Berlin: Suhrkamp, 2010.

Weissberg, Liliane. "Juden oder Hebräer? Religiöse und politische Bekehrung bei Herder." In *Johann Gottfried Herder: Geschichte und Kultur*, edited by Martin Bollacher, 191–211. Würzburg: Königshausen & Neumann, 1994.

Weldemann, August. *Die religiöse Lyrik des deutschen Katholizismus in der ersten Hälfte des 19. Jahrhunderts, unter besonderer Berücksichtigung Annettens von Droste*. Leipzig: Voigtländer, 1911.

Wellbery, David E. *Lessing's Laocoon: Semiotics and Aesthetics in the Age of Reason*. Cambridge: Cambridge University Press, 1984.

———. *The Specular Moment: Goethe's Early Lyric and the Beginnings of Romanticism*. Stanford, Calif.: Stanford University Press, 1996.

Wells, Larry D. "Indeterminacy as Provocation: The Reader's Role in Annette von Droste-Hülshoff's *Die Judenbuche*." *MLN* 94, no. 3 (1979): 475–92.

Wieland, C. M. *Gesammelte Schriften*. Edited by Fritz Homeyer. 4 vols. Berlin: Weidmann, 1916.

Windfuhr, Manfred. "Der Erzähler Heines: 'Der Rabbi von Bacherach' als historischer Roman." In *Heinrich Heine: Ästhetisch-politische Profile*, edited by Gerhard Höhn, 276–94. Frankfurt a.M.: Suhrkamp, 1991.

Wolosky, Shira. *Language Mysticism: The Negative Way of Language in Eliot, Beckett, and Celan*. Stanford, Calif.: Stanford University Press, 1995.

Wolff, Christian. *Kleine Schriften*. Halle: Renger, 1755.

Wolff, Jens. "Die Anverwandlung der Bibel in Kants Schrift 'Die Religion innerhalb der Grenzen der bloßen Vernunft' von 1793." In *Religion und Aufklärung: Studien zur neuzeitlichen "Umformung des Christlichen,"* edited by Albrecht Beutel and Volker Leppin, 107–22. Leipzig: Evangelische Verlagsanstalt, 2004.

Yovel, Yirmiyahu. *Dark Riddle: Hegel, Nietzsche and the Jews*. [In Hebrew.] Tel Aviv: Schocken, 1996.

Zammito, John H. *Kant, Herder, and the Birth of Anthropology*. Chicago: University of Chicago Press, 2002.

Index

Acknowledgments

This book first took shape in the University of California, Berkeley's German Department, where I greatly benefited from the support of an open and intellectually challenging scholarly community. I am extremely grateful to Winfried Kudszus for his encouragement, support, and confidence in my work. I hope his modesty remains my model. Niklaus Largier's striving for excellence and creativity fueled this book as much as it continues to guide my scholarly ambitions. Chenxi Tang's dedication has been invaluable to this book from its start, and his rigor, erudition, and generosity immensely improved its quality. It was a privilege to engage with Jonathan Sheehan's original thinking about the Enlightenment and about current debates on secularism, to which he introduced me for the first time.

I am in debt to Berkeley's German Department as a whole. Anton Kaes's generous support of my scholarship grants him a copy of any book I will ever author, and I hope this will be a matter of pleasure for him. I am thankful to Karen Feldman for working with me through the various complexities of academic writing. This book benefited much from Elaine Tennant's demand for clarity and rigor. In Berkeley, Victoria Kahn provoked my interest in early modern political thought. Michael Lucey introduced me to textual circulation as a theoretical problem and drew my attention to literature's relationship to its anticipated reception. Saba Mahmood's intellectual rigor granted me the privilege of discussing with an author her own theories, which have become central to my own intellectual ventures. My conversations with Daniel Boyarin and Martin Jay significantly enriched the theoretical conceptualization of the project.

I was fortunate enough to continue working on this project as a member of the Center for Literary and Cultural Research in Berlin (ZfL) and as a fellow at the Lichtenberg-Kolleg of the Georg-August-Universität Göttingen. At the ZfL, I enjoyed Daniel Weidner's good advice, which accompanied this book from its early stages and contributed greatly to its development. Caroline Sauter was a model colleague. She read many pages of this book and gave me an array of helpful advice on how to improve it. My pleasant stay in Göttingen gave this book the final push it needed thanks to a dialogue with terrific scholars of intellectual history and the Enlightenment, including Martin van Gelderen, Martin Gierl, Dominik Hünniger, and Tony La Vopa. In Göttingen, Hans Erich Bödeker kindly agreed to read the entire manuscript and corrected several faults in its previous versions. Zsófia Lóránd's good humor made the final stages of editing manageable.

This project also enjoyed the support of the Minerva Foundation of the Max Planck Gesellschaft, the Leo Baeck Fellowship Programme, the Max Kade Foundation, the Diller Family Research Grant, the Simon-Dubnow Institute for Jewish History and Culture, the University of California, Berkeley, and the German Academic Exchange Service.

Some parts of this book have previously been published in scholarly journals. A preliminary formulation of excerpts from Chapters 1 and 2 appeared as "Sublime Readings: The Emergence of the Aesthetic Bible in Herder's Writings on Hebrew Poetry," *Simon Dubnow Institute Yearbook* 12 (2013): 337–52. A part of Chapter 1 was published in Spanish as "Estéticas de la Biblia: El imaginario del hebreo en las teorías de la interpretación de Hamann y Herder," *El Boletín de Estética es publicado* 31 (2015): 7–36. Finally, a previous version of a part of Chapter 5 was published as "*Die Judenbuche* and 'das Judens-buch': Hermeneutic Hindrance and Scriptural Reading in Droste-Hülshoff's Crime Novella," *German Quarterly* 89 (2016): 328–42. I am grateful to the journals for allowing me to republish these materials.

When I began this project, I was living abroad, and the generosity of the faculty at the Humboldt University enabled me to make Berlin my home. I am grateful to Rolf-Peter Horstmann, Karin Krauthausen, Ethel Matala de Mazza, and Joseph Vogel for their engagement with my arguments. My dear friends in Berlin, particularly David Hadar, Dani Issler, Sophia Könemann, Andrew Patten, Tanvi Solanki, and Erica Weitzman, have been wonderful intellectual companions. I am very grateful to Irit Dekel and Michael Weinman for asking me about the relevance of this book to the lives of Berliner Israelis. I am still figuring out an answer.

Several scholars maintained a connection to this project via transatlantic conversations. Adam Stern made many insightful comments on this book's various versions, and he continues to make me think hard about its arguments. The book benefited from Ruth Ginsberg's rigorous and thoughtful reading. Jane Newman opened my eyes to how to delineate this book's goals while maintaining its broad scope. With his typical gentleness, Sven-Erik Rose encouraged me to rethink the pertinence of German Jewish literature to continental philosophy. Matt Erlin, Joe O'Neil, and Jonathan Skolnik commented on portions of the manuscript and significantly improved their quality. Michael Allan, Dan Diner, Amir Eshel, Mark Gelber, Kata Gellen, Natasha Gordinsky, Dana Hollander, May Mergenthaler, Yosefa Raz, Na'ama Rokem, Sigrid Weigel, Liliane Weissberg, and Susanne Zepp supported this book and its author enduringly. I thank the team at the University of Pennsylvania Press for their prompt, careful, and professional work, especially Damon Linker for believing in my book and Erica Ginsburg for her attentive work on the manuscript.

I once told Erik Born that he deserves a whole separate acknowledgments section. I am very grateful to him for his abundant helpful advice and precious encouragement. I thank the psychoanalyst who accompanied me through writing for her sensitivity in showing me how silence matures into trust. Yoav Rinon has been my mentor, supporter, and friend virtually since I decided to become a scholar. His love for foreign literatures, which he has set for me as a model, led by extension to the writing of this book, and his support has made it possible. I am fortunate that my family in Israel has shown me time and again how proud they are of my scholarly pursuits.

Through their invaluable support, my colleagues at Berkeley have made my frequent moves between Germany and the United States not only tolerable but also fruitful. I am grateful beyond words to Nicholas Baer, Erik Born, Kfir Cohen, Lisa Eberle, Kevin Gordon, Tara Hottman, Noah Kaye, Zachary Manfredi, Annika Orich, Suzanne Scala, and Jeffrey Weiner for their friendship.